Prejudice and tolerance in Ulster

Studies in sociology/general editor Max Gluckman/1

Rosemary Harris

Prejudice and tolerance in Ulster

A study of neighbours and 'strangers' in a border community

Manchester University Press

Rowman and Littlefield, Totowa, N.J.

© 1972 Rosemary Harris

All rights reserved

Published by
MANCHESTER UNIVERSITY PRESS
316–324 Oxford Road
Manchester M13 9NR

ISBN 0 7190 0509 4

U.S.A.
ROWMAN AND LITTLEFIELD
81 Adams Drive
Totowa, N.J. 07512

ISBN 0 81471 126 6

Printed in Great Britain by
Butler & Tanner Ltd
Frome and London

Contents

Acknowledgements

My thanks are due to many people with whom, over the years, I have discussed the material here presented. In particular, however, I must single out the following: Professor Daryll Forde, of University College, London, who initially encouraged me to undertake this study and guided me through it; Professor Estyn Evans, of Queen's University, Belfast, who first gave me a love of Ulster and introduced me to Ballybeg; Professor Gluckman, who has steadily insisted that I must publish an account of Ballybeg; and finally my colleagues and students in the University College seminar on Complex Societies; and above all Professor M. G. Smith, who offered stimulating criticism of my initial discussion of the relationship between Ballybeg and the structure of Northern Irish society.

Introduction

In this book I shall be concerned with the nature of prejudice in a Northern Irish community. What I shall have to say relates to attitudes and behaviour which I found in an area in the rural west of the Province near the border with Eire. It is important to make this clear at the outset because this location undoubtedly influenced the attitudes I found. In general the west of Ulster is poorer than the east because the economy is almost entirely based on agriculture; moreover in general the nearer they are to the border the more anxious the Protestant population tends to be. It would be quite wrong, therefore, to suggest that what is true of this community necessarily applies to other areas. Indeed, it will, I think, be clear from what I have to say that behaviour and attitudes are so sensitive to variations in the general pattern of social relationships that in detail many of the features of the relationships between Catholics and Protestants are bound to be different in communities with different economic and social backgrounds. This does not, I think, detract from the value of this study because what I hope it will show, by demonstrating the complexity of the situation in Ballybeg,[1] is that attitudes and behaviour are moulded by very complex factors, and that it is absurd to stick a simple label, 'Bigots', on to people even when they seem most prejudiced. Such labels explain nothing; it is more difficult but much more rewarding to try with patience to understand their motives.

I approach the problem of understanding relationships between Catholics and Protestants by analysing in detail the relationships

[1] The name 'Ballybeg' is a pseudonym used to disguise the real identity of the place which is the subject of this study. Likewise the people mentioned are not referred to by their real names.

of particular members of these faiths in this particular community of Ballybeg, in which I spent ten consecutive months in 1952–53, and with which I was able to maintain periodic contact until I left Ulster in 1965. Because it seems abundantly clear that one of the main factors influencing behaviour and opinion is the general economic and social environment within which an individual finds himself, I begin with a description of the area, starting with the small town of Ballybeg itself and following this with an account of the immediately surrounding countryside. No mere topographical description would be adequate. It is essential to describe the pattern of farming life in the area, and even sketch the recent changes in farming organisation. Both together show that there is a very clear division of the surrounding district into two distinct geographical and social regions, and I argue that insights into relationships between Catholics and Protestants can be gained by comparing the types of contacts between them in these two regions.

It is, nevertheless, very easy to over-generalise on the subject of relationships between the religious groups; indeed I think that the hazards of doing this and of overlooking the complexity of the factors influencing any given relationship are extreme. For this reason I back the general analysis of religious relationships by giving detailed examples of the relationships maintained by a number of individual households. Even such examples could, however, consciously or unconsciously be used to give a distorted picture were they selected to illustrate particular generalisations that I later make. I seek to avoid bias by choosing as illustrative material all the households maintaining particularly close neighbourly ties with three others selected initially for a different purpose. In my introductory description of a small area selected for intensive study I give a general account of three types of living standards found within it and follow this account with a detailed description of the living conditions of three households which are to some extent representative of these three types. In the next chapter, 'Relationships within the Household', I look at these three families again, this time examining the kinds of relationship existing between the members; further I similarly describe the closest neighbours and associates of these households. On this basis I make certain generalisations about some family relationships and the factors influencing them. The most crucial relationship, that between husband and wife, cannot be analysed at this stage because it is significantly influenced by a man's relationships with his neighbours. I therefore go on, in the next chapter, to examine these households once more, this time considering the kinds of relationship they maintained with close kin and neighbours. At this point the relevance of this background material becomes evident. In tracing relationships between neighbours I necessarily describe relationships between Catholic and Protestant households: but these are not set artificially in isolation from other kinds of relationships. Rather the material from these, in a sense randomly selected, households provides material which allows us to see relationships between Protestants and Catholics set against the background of the same households' relationships with kin and with neighbours of the same religious faith.

There is a particular reason for examining the relationships of these households in such detail. In dealing with contacts between Protestants and Catholics we are dealing with that type of situation, found in certain racially and ethnically divided societies, in which members of different groups have close relationships whilst remaining essentially separate. It is a situation that poses problems of such theoretical interest that it is worthwhile looking carefully at the details concerning any of its manifestations. It seems to me that to understand this apparent paradox of intermingled yet separate populations it is essential to look closely at the patterns of interaction of individuals. This reveals how easy it is for certain people to live cheek by jowl with members of 'the other side' and yet, without necessarily intending this, be socially quite isolated from them.

Once we have examined individual cases in detail it becomes possible with some confidence to go on to talk in more general terms about the relationships between Catholics and Protestants. It is possible to base arguments on particular instances occurring in the cases described without fear of distortion, since it is open to the reader to go back to examine the examples in their context and to judge whether they will bear the weight put upon them.

In this subsequent analysis the first aspect of inter-religious relationships that I seek to stress is the extent to which the people share a common culture. Despite their differences it is apparent that there is, by and large, a vast amount in common between households at the same economic level whatever their religious affiliation. This similarity extends not merely to their standards of living, to family relationships, ideas about the roles of the sexes, and attitudes to kin in general, but to ideas about the duties neighbours owe each other, more general values regarding good and bad conduct, what commands and what loses respect, and even, somewhat surprisingly, to very similar attitudes to the external world of officialdom.

Nevertheless, having said all this, I go on to stress how separate are the social fields of members of the two religious groups. In general the social network of any individual is based overwhelmingly in most fields on ties with his co-religionists. This is partly because most formal organisations are connected in one way or another with groups that have a religious basis and most individuals have strong ties with such organisations. Their ties with co-religionists are thus constantly reinforced, whilst their links across the religious divide are, at this level, extremely tenuous. Economic relationships also, though to a lesser extent, show an in-built religious bias. Other things being more or less equal, most recognised a duty to support 'their own' even in many business transactions. Moreover, even when people did not do this from a sense of moral obligation, they often did so in practice because there was an automatic tendency where possible to support kin and close acquaintances, who were almost invariably co-religionists. Of greatest importance is the fact that kin, almost by definition, must be co-religionists. Protestants and Catholics form two endogamous groups probably more separated from each other in sexual matters than most white and negro groups in societies which supposedly abhor miscegenation. For example, in the southern United States although kinship is not recognised between members of the two racial groups sexual liaisons between white males and negro females have been, at least in the past, extremely common. By comparison such affairs have been minimal between Catholics and Protestants in Ulster and mixed marriages have been relatively unusual. The significance of this is readily apparent since the case studies show quite clearly that for many people, especially women, kin ties are of great social importance. Thus the pattern of endogamy by itself is enough to ensure that for most individuals their most significant social ties are with co-religionists. When we add all these facts together we can see how overwhelming is the part such people play in the social networks of most individuals and why Catholics and Protestants should be so separated.

Moreover the tendency for the society to be divided in this way is made even more marked by the fact that the cleavage between Protestant and Catholic is so strong that as a consequence an awareness of religious roles exists whenever they meet. Just as the behaviour and speech of individuals is influenced automatically by the sex and age of others with whom they are interacting, so here they are just as influenced by a consciousness of religious affiliation. The cleavage between the religious groups is such that on almost every issue, local or national, there is a Catholic viewpoint and a different, Protestant, viewpoint. It scarcely matters whether an individual boldly expresses a partisan opinion, or more likely, is constrained to refrain from doing so in order to avoid giving offence to his companions. Whatever alternative he chooses, the fundamental significance of the religious roles played by himself and others is necessarily reiterated whenever his behaviour is influenced by his awareness of the differing opinions of others— in other words whenever Protestant and Catholic meet. Thus all social relationships are pervaded by a consciousness of the religious dichotomy.

Because of the separation of the social fields of Protestant and Catholic, even neighbours belonging to the different sides remain in some senses strangers. This is a major factor leading the people to think about each other in terms of stereotypes. Some stereotypes are the result of simple over-generalisation. For example a majority of the poorer members of the community are Catholic and a majority of the more prosperous are Protestant, and thus the characteristics of the poor and the prosperous are assumed to be typical of Catholics and Protestants respectively. There is, however, more to the understanding of religious prejudice in Ulster than this, as must be obvious to anyone who has followed recent events there. Most outsiders feel that it is Protestant prejudice against Catholics that is particularly difficult to understand. As a Protestant myself I found it also much more easy to get frank information on prejudice from Protestants rather than from Catholics, who in talking to me on this subject were inhibited by everything they had ever learned. For both these reasons I therefore concentrate particularly on an attempt to understand all the facets of Protestant prejudice.

In order to comprehend Protestant anti-Catholic attitudes it is necessary first of all to set them in the context of Protestant attitudes to Protestants of other denominations. That Protestants should have an explicitly anti-Catholic organisation, the Orange Order, is understandable when we realise that Protestants in Ulster are riven by particularly strong denominational antagonisms and

can unite only in opposition to Catholicism. It is inevitable, therefore, than an organisation designed to unite Protestants will have
an explicitly anti-Catholic bias.

I then go on to examine the significance of economic factors that
might lead to prejudice. It is a commonly accepted view that just
as poor whites are those most opposed to negroes so it is the poor
Protestant who is most antagonistic to the Catholics. This is the
general opinion both in Ulster as a whole and in Ballybeg itself.
If it is correct it can scarcely be explained by the same kind of
arguments that explain poor white attitudes, for in Ballybeg it
is not the poor Protestant but the middle-class Protestant who
seems to be in economic competition with Catholics. Moreover
the self-esteem of the poorer Protestants does not apparently
demand that Catholics should be regarded as in any way socially
inferior to themselves. In fact an examination shows that there is
less difference in the views expressed by the different classes of
Protestants than is sometimes supposed and that much of the anti-
Catholic bias of all Protestants is made up of anti-clerical and
anti-authoritarian sentiments which make them hostile to the
Roman Catholic Church. Nevertheless a difference can be detected,
especially between the views of the Protestants of the richer valley
land and those in the upland area, who in some ways do express
stronger anti-Catholic prejudices.

At one level the explanation for the stronger bias of the Protestant hill farmers is relatively simple, for they constitute a
relatively small minority in an area in which, in all sorts of contexts, violence is not uncommon; the hill Protestant has more
reason to feel nervous than has the lowland Protestant. If the
situation is examined more carefully, however, it appears far from
simple; it is particularly the hill Protestant whose day-to-day
relationships with his Catholic neighbours are characterised by
friendship and respect, and in fact the opinions he expresses betray
a profound ambivalence. To understand why, in certain contexts,
he does express particularly strong forms of prejudice, it is necessary to look as carefully at relationships between Protestants of
different classes as it was earlier to look at relationships between
Protestants of different denominations. Examination shows that
the poorer Protestant is profoundly distrustful of his own leaders,
both at the national and at the local level. His anxieties on this
score relate especially to a cynical belief that Belfast Unionists,
and those from the east of Ulster in general, would willingly

sacrifice the political and economic interests of a community like Ballybeg if it suited them. Some of this distrust is felt even for the local, more sophisticated Protestants. Significantly Protestants of different classes show very different attitudes towards the Orange Order, and in general the poorer Protestants are more in favour of it than the more prosperous. There are a number of reasons for this, but a major factor in the loyalty to it of the uninfluential is that its meetings have an explicitly egalitarian ethos that makes it easier for them to talk bluntly to their leaders. The Orange Lodge provides the ordinary man with a setting in which it is accepted that he can oppose the middle class. In the same way the question of attitudes to Catholics provides him with an issue on which he can legitimately stand up to anyone. Loyalty to Protestantism is the ultimate value, and any failure of loyalty merits criticism. All kinds of dissatisfaction with leaders can be expressed in accusations that they are insufficiently loyal to Protestantism. It is a practice which earns for the poor a reputation for particular bigotry which in many respects they do not deserve.

Moreover, even although there is no denying the fact that within the community of Ballybeg there do exist deep antagonisms between the two main religious groups it is unrealistic to ignore certain social compensations brought about by this very cleavage. The division induces the intensification of social life, and brings about a situation in which each individual is of significance to his neighbours.

In closing I consider more generally the question of the place of Ulster society in relation to others in which there is strong ethnic or racial cleavage. In fact Ulster society poses some problems for those who are interested in the question of what constitutes a 'plural society' and why. Moreover, the problem of the conditions under which a society may become divided into two basic categories of people is also a matter to which new dimensions are added by this Northern Irish material. Ulster is both very similar to, yet extremely different from, societies divided on the basis of race; it is this fact that gives the study of any community in the Province its main theoretical interest.

Whilst social patterns had begun to change in the rural west of Ulster before the outbreak of the present troubles, the situation here described provided the formative social environment of most of those from the area now actively participating in the present struggle. These people, as I saw, prefer peaceful conditions and want above all to live at peace with all their neighbours. This is why, although I go on to show the sources of conflict, I begin by showing Ballybeg as a community in which there was a vast amount of tolerance and good will. Perhaps at this time this is the best way I can repay its people for all their kindness and hospitality to me.

Key to genealogical codes used in the text
(See genealogical charts attached to the back cover)

The initial letter refers to religious affiliation:
- C   Roman Catholic.
- P   Protestant.

The following letter refers to approximate age and generation:
- A   The generation above that of the oldest living inhabitants.
- B   Approximately 70 and over.
- C   Between 50 and 70 years of age.
- D   Between 20 and 50 years of age.
- E   Under 20. Children omitted normally.

Figures occur in sequence, from left to right of the genealogical charts.

Basically there was, within the area studied, a Protestant genealogy and a Catholic genealogy. Not everyone however could be fitted in onto one or other of these charts. Such unconnected individuals are given their relevant letter prefixes and are numbered in the test from 100 up.

List of individuals not on the genealogical charts

Andy Stuart (PC100), a 'mountainy farmer'.

Nelly Stuart (PC101), his sister.

Graham Stuart (PC102), their brother in Ballybeg, married to a Catholic.

Jim Thompson (PC103), labourer to Paul Jamison (PD10).

David Thompson (PD100), his son, labourer to John Jamison (PD25).

Arthur Little (PB100), Presbyterian elder, retired infield farmer.

Harold Heath (PD102), nephew of Arthur Little and a bachelor.

Martin Wright (PC104), infield farmer who had moved down from the hill district (in fact distantly related to Archy Wright (PD1)).

Patrick McCurdy (CB100), neighbour of Paul Jamison (PD10).

Paddy Sullivan (CC100), infield farmer, and neighbour of Pat Devine (CC10).

Owen Sullivan (CE100), son of Paddy Sullivan.

Barney James (CD100), quarry worker and newcomer to the area.

Liam McDermott (CC101), infield farmer and neighbour of Betty Laird (PD32).

Owen McConnell (CD101), infield farmer bachelor.

I Ballybeg 'town'

No one can pretend that Ballybeg is an important or imposing place, or that it is picturesque. It had a total population of only 324 in 1951 and, after the manner of many Irish country towns, its buildings varied from condemned cottages which were little more than hovels, to plain, unostentatious, but sometimes quite large houses dating from the eighteenth and nineteenth century and fronting directly on to the street. Now there is a new area of council housing, but in the early fifties there was only a tiny handful of 'suburban' houses fringing the old settlement.

Ballybeg, like most places in Ireland, has dwindled in size over the last 120 years. Before the famine of 1848 as many as 800 people lived here and, whilst it was not a hive of industry, at least there was a fair amount of local employment in the town. Still today it is possible to see the remains of a distillery and two breweries which were in operation in the nineteenth century, and one of the condemned houses started life in the early years of the last century as a workshop for the manufacture of hand-made gloves. It was backed by a local landlord who, it is said, helped to arrange for the gloves to be sold as far away as Paris. In addition people in the town carried on domestic industries. Merchants in towns not far distant organised the home-weaving of linen which died out only in the 1840's, and other crafts were also practised. A row of completely derelict cottages was said to have been occupied formerly by sieve-makers, and old marriage registers speak of white-smiths and coopers as well as the more common carpenters and blacksmiths.

In the nineteenth century, and indeed in the first years of this century too, there were big houses in the neighbourhood of Bally-beg which offered a fair amount of domestic employment. But the big houses have gone. The most important was gutted by fire in the Troubles (although there were those who maintained this was not the work of the I.R.A., but that of the owners who wanted to collect their insurance money) and a local farmer now lived in the converted stable block. The dower house stood empty and nearly derelict. Another farmer had bought it cheaply and occupied it for a time, virtually camping in one or two of the deserted rooms, but he had given up the struggle and he and his family had moved to a cottage where they felt more comfortable.

The last family which Ballybeg reckoned aristocratic had lived in reduced circumstances in the town itself, but they had left just before the war, when they were forced to sell up and move. In any case the people concerned, two elderly Catholic ladies, had for some time been of significance to other people not so much for their economic importance as for the amusement their idiosyncracies afforded. By all accounts their departure was splendidly characteristic of them, for it is said that they held a party the night before the sale of their home and invited what local gentry remained in the area. The elder sister, however, suddenly encountered an embarrassing situation, since a ring at the door announced not another friend but the auctioneer who wanted to discuss the next day's proceedings. With great presence of mind she showed him upstairs and locked him in her bedroom while she went down to continue entertaining her guests. When he eventually escaped, by hailing a passing cattle truck and climbing down its sides, he again presented himself at the door and she came out her usual, charming self: they discussed their business without once mentioning the previous little incident, but this time the auctioneer insisted on staying in the hall.

Today Ballybeg's importance in many ways is much less than it was. There are now no small industries here to provide employment for the dwindling population. It is true that it is a small-route junction and this still gives the place some significance. Long ago stage-coach routes met here. Then a branch railway line was built and for a while commercial travellers used to stop here and often stay the night before visiting the neighbouring areas in hired traps. This line too has disappeared, but it was replaced by a bus station and the long-distance bus to Belfast still links up here with local services. Nevertheless the surprising thing is that everyone talks of Ballybeg as 'the town' and not as 'the village'. At first sight 'town' seems a ridiculously inflated term for such a tiny settlement. In fact, the use of the term is not merely a quaint tradition preserved by the locals, for if we look at Ballybeg's significance to the surrounding countryside it serves, tiny as it is, more as a town than as a village. Indeed, of the 258 adults in the place only two worked full time in agriculture; Ballybeg was not a settlement of farmers and farm labourers but was important to the surrounding district for the services its shops and garages supplied to farmers, and for its monthly market, 'the Fair' as it was always known.

Ballybeg Fair is busiest in the Autumn when many of the local cattle are sold here, either for slaughter or for fattening on more sheltered farms than those on the neighbouring hills. Today the Fair is held discreetly in proper stockyards away from the centre, but when I was there it was held, as it always had been, in the main street itself, without the benefit of sheep or cattle pens. The arguments about the removal of the Fair was one of the few important discussions in which sides were taken on an entirely non-sectarian basis. Those who wanted to keep the Fair as it always had been were the shopkeepers who feared a loss of trade if it were removed, and the farmers themselves who liked to have the shops, and above all the pubs, handy. Those who hoped devoutly that the Fair would be put tidily out of sight somewhere were most of those who lived in Ballybeg and had no direct interest in all the buying and selling that went on, all those bus drivers and motorists who had to try to get through the place on a Fair day (hooting was useless since men and animals alike had a touching faith that no-one would run them down deliberately), and the County Council who in this modern, sanitary age had taken upon themselves the duty of cleansing the Augean Stables into which the streets were transformed by the end of each Fair day.

In the early fifties, the first activity of each Fair day began not in the true Fair, itself, but at the so-called Grader, for officials of the Ministry of Agriculture still helped to organise the despatch of cattle for slaughter to England, and most fat cattle were sent here. In the station yard of the old, disused, narrow-gauge railway there was a permanent weighbridge and from half-past eight on a Fair morning the Ministry vet was hard at work grading the cattle according to their age, fatness and 'emptiness' on a scale from 'A' downwards. Usually he accepted only those with at least a 'B' grading—those he failed were returned to their owners who could keep them or sell them in the Fair as they wished. Those beasts which were accepted then started the long journey ahead of them.

They were driven on to the weighbridge where the man in charge called out their colour, sex and weight to a tally clerk, who put the information down under the owner's name. Then the animals were put in lorries to be taken to the nearest station to catch the 2.30 train to Belfast and, if possible, that night's cross-channel boat for England. It was this tight time-table which led to the early start at the Grader.

The proper Fair began considerably later. Even on a September morning when a lot of cattle were brought in there were only about twenty on the street by 9.30 a.m. and the Fair was not in full swing until nearer 11 o'clock. By mid-morning the street was a mass of animals, farmers bargaining, and hucksters crying their wares. At first sight it looked like disorderly confusion but in fact by custom there was a certain regularity which determined where the people took up their places. At the top of the town were the stalls of clothes and shoes, new and secondhand, hardware, retreaded car and tractor tyres, plants and patent medicines. Then came the small area for sheep. These were brought in by cart, without dogs to help, and each farmer tied up his own bunch into a circle by roping them round their necks and making them stand either round one of their own number in the centre, or round a tub. The lambs went loose as they always stayed close to their mothers. Next were the pigs: only young ones, about eight weeks old, were brought to the Fair and these were kept in the farm carts in which they were transported, sheltered under tarpaulins. Round the corner was the place for the horses—rather a sad lot these since everyone knew these old friends were mostly destined for dog meat and their sales were concluded with little of the jovial encouragement of bystanders which characterised the sale of cattle. Interestingly the side of the street almost opposite the horse line was formerly the site of another outmoded feature of the great fairs at Michaelmas and Easter. Until the beginning of the last war farm servants, mainly men but with a few girls among them, who wanted work for the next six months used to gather outside a pub there hoping to be hired.

It was, however, the cattle which dominated the Fair, 400 to 500 being brought in for sale on an Autumn day, and changing hands not as the result of any formal auction but through a multitude of individual bargains between farmer and farmer or farmer and dealer. Almost every inch of the kerb side seemed taken up with the young stock and their owners, or the owners' sons, while groups of cattle arriving or leaving surged down the middle of the street ahead of their drivers and were surreptitiously prodded by on-lookers trying to judge their quality. On all sides bargaining was in progress—little groups of five or six centred on the two of their number who were trying, or fiercely refusing, to clinch a deal; fierce arguments everywhere about the price to be paid, and about the size of the 'luck penny' the buyer wanted back: everywhere dramatic climaxes, for final agreement was always shown by buyer and dealer literally striking hands, and a man's friends would seem either to hold his hand back to stop him making too easy a bargain, or to force him physically into symbolic acceptance.

It was essentially a man's world. Indeed, there were practically no women in the street at all when the Fair was at its height. Perhaps it would be more accurate to say it was a man and boy's world, for many of the farmers kept their sons away from school to help them in the Fair, and they came in, small imitations of their fathers, with sticks in their hands and serious expressions, their minds on cattle and not on larking about. Even the sellers at the stalls were more commonly men than women. Some girls were kept away from school on Fair day, but only those who came from the 'town' and whose mothers served tea and wanted help with the chores; they did not show themselves amongst the men outside. It was not so much that it was thought improper for women to appear but that the women themselves preferred to keep out of the throng and the noise and the dirt. Even the farmers and dealers, in their second-best suits, had their trousers hitched as high as possible to keep their turn-ups out of the cattle dung. By mid-afternoon, most of the buying and selling was done, and although the stalls and the 'spielers' continued to do a brisk trade and the pubs would be busy again in the evening the crowd had largely dispersed back to the countryside, and many more women were to be seen on the streets of Ballybeg itself.

More quietly, throughout the year, Ballybeg provided services for the surrounding countryside, for it had a surprising number and range of shops: nine grocers (four having a large delivery round); five clothing stores; four public houses; two sweetshops; one sweetshop and newsagent; two butchers; two chemists (one a pharmacist, one selling only patent medicines); three miscellaneous hardware shops selling bicycles, wirelesses, spades, etc.; and one feed merchant. In addition other services were provided. There were: three bank sub-branches, open two days a week; three cafés (apart from houses selling teas on Fair days); three hairdressers (one for men, two for women); three garages (one tiny, the others employing four and six men respectively); two petrol stations (additional to the garages); a Police barracks; a Court House where petty sessions were held; two schools; three churches; and a garage of the Ulster Transport Board.

Nothing could show more clearly than does this list that Ballybeg was in its economic functions not a village, however minute its population, for a list of businesses as long as this would not have disgraced a reasonably sized English market-town. Moreover, the significance of Ballybeg to farmers in the neighbourhood is rather under-emphasised in this list because although there was only one 'feed' merchant who was that exclusively, all the grocers with large delivery rounds also sold feeding stuffs and collected the eggs which meant so much to the finances of the farmers' wives. What seems surprising is that so many businesses were to be found in Ballybeg when we realise that there were two other similar, but rather larger, market-towns within five miles of Ballybeg to the south and the west, and that although the nearest such settlement to the north was eight miles distant the countryside in that direction was, by English standards, poverty stricken, with an agriculture characterised by small hill-farms. The inevitable question was how such a district could support so many businesses.

A little closer examination showed that the answer involved an understanding both of the standard of living on the farms, which tended to make the life of even a poor shopkeeper seem preferable, and of the pattern of sectarian loyalties, which ensured that there was a limit to the competition each shop faced. The advantages offered by one shop over its rivals had to be very considerable before a Protestant owner could attract Catholic customers, or vice versa. One shop, no matter how good, could never monopolise the trade, and no matter how poor it could normally expect a number of faithful clients. The result was to be seen not merely in the large number of businesses in Ballybeg but in their comparative poverty and in the rapidity with which they changed hands; and it must be noted in passing that when a shop or business changed hands it invariably passed to a co-religionist of the previous owner. This continues to the present day.

It was a striking fact that although, as might be expected, the number of retail businesses in Ballybeg was not expanding, so that there were no new founder-owners amongst the shopkeepers, and although all shops were locally owned and not operated by outside companies, only a fifth were owned by sons of former owners. These eight businesses—two grocery stores, two clothing shops, two public houses and two garages—were significantly the most prosperous and the general tendency against inheritance seemed to be a clear index of the lack of prosperity amongst the others. It was rare for a shopkeeper to become so unsuccessful that he actually went bankrupt but there were clearly pressures on the less successful men, who had gained a first foothold in the retail business in Ballybeg, to move out elsewhere. From what I was told it was clear that several former Ballybeg shopkeepers had bought themselves small businesses in other towns partly because they hoped for better trade there and partly because they hoped for better employment possibilities for their children. Others had stayed in Ballybeg until they had died or retired, but had been unable to persuade any of their own children to stay and carry on the business, and had therefore transferred it to someone else.

If we look a little more carefully at the reasons for this pattern we begin to understand why the population of Ballybeg was in general unusually transient. The shopkeepers moved out, or failed to transmit their property to their own children not merely because their businesses were in themselves not very prosperous, but because opportunities for employment in Ballybeg were minimal. The only jobs available were for labourers (a local quarry employed about twenty-five men), lorry and van drivers and shop assistants. Since, however, shopkeepers for a variety of reasons preferred to employ farmers' children as apprentices, and in fact every shop assistant who was not the child of the owner of the business lived outside Ballybeg on a farm, there were no suitable opportunities for employment for the children of small business-men in the town. Only one son could usefully be found work in the father's business; the others, if they were to achieve a status equivalent to, or better than, that of their father had either to be apprenticed to shopkeepers in some other town (and have their expenses paid whilst they were earning very little), or be trained for some post in the civil service or the professions. A man with several children had to have an unusually prosperous business in Ballybeg to be able to afford this, and one who could not do so was under some pressure to move out. Men unable or unwilling to pay their own children eventually more than the small wage which was paid to apprentices found that neither sons or daughters were willing to work indefinitely for a pittance, which was not easily supplemented by the private dealing that could give farmers' sons some measure of independence. This problem of the lack of employment open to the young people was a major factor influencing the relatively rapid turnover of Ballybeg businesses.

This lack of employment also explains the general lack of stability of the population of Ballybeg as a whole. At the time this study was made there were only 258 people over 18 living there, yet although this figure is in line with the general decline of population throughout the area, and in Ballybeg itself in particular, it disguises the full extent of the movement of people from the 'town' because only 138 of these adults had in fact been born in Ballybeg—120 people had been born in the countryside surrounding it and had moved in. Those who had moved in were farmers' sons who had become shopkeepers, and their wives were invariably from the country and not from Ballybeg; there were those too who were attracted here by the cheap, though sometimes dilapidated, housing: these were retired farmers and labourers, labourers content to remain more or less unemployed, and widows or the few women, four in all, deserted by their husbands and trying to bring up young families on their own. Significantly, too, although this was a very rare form of marriage, there were five couples living here who had moved in after contracting a mixed Catholic and Protestant union, marriages which made them unacceptable to their former neighbours. Those who grew up in Ballybeg were, for the most part, faced with the alternatives of taking poor-type jobs locally, commuting expensively to larger towns fifteen to twenty miles away (in fact only seven did so), or reconciling themselves to being for the most part officially unemployed (some managed to combine part-time jobs and unemployment benefit). It is not surprising that local advancement was minimal. The sons of two former Ballybeg labourers had, after some travelling outside the area, raised their status locally, one becoming a teacher and two becoming shop owners, but these were exceptions that seemed to prove the rule.

If anything were needed to indicate further the rapid turnover of the population it would be provided by an examination of the pattern of kinship connectedness of the households in Ballybeg. In many villages it is possible to trace out a network of close ties of kinship embracing the majority of the inhabitants. In Ballybeg, however, if we look at kinship ties regarded locally as being really significant—i.e. ties with kin up to, and including, first cousins—we find that of the ninety-two separate households: two were related to four households in Ballybeg, eleven to three, fifteen to two, and twenty-four to one, leaving forty not related to any other household. That almost half the households should be thus isolated from others in Ballybeg is a very remarkable fact accounted for by the 'town's' role as a kind of social staging-post and country service-centre rather than as a settlement offering any permanent niche to a substantial number of its inhabitants.

Ties other than kinship also seemed weak. There were very few occasions when events occurred about which the inhabitants seemed to share a common opinion. One example during the course of my stay in the area was the announcement by the County Health Department that the local water supply was contaminated, and that Ballybeg would have to be supplied from elsewhere. The slur this cast on the town and the prospect of increased rates produced an indignant reaction against the report from almost everyone. But this occasion was unique in the unanimity it aroused. Apart from this I could discover no situation in which it could be said that a majority of the inhabitants shared a common viewpoint, still less that they acted together for a common end, no matter how trifling. Apart from the Fair there were no formal or informal gatherings involving a large cross-section of the inhabitants. There was in fact no hall in which such a cross-section could have assembled since there was no non-sectarian meeting place, not even a cinema. Further there were no informal gatherings of, say, the most influential residents, or the majority of young men. Little groups gathered to play cards or to drink, or to watch the first television set, but these were essentially private affairs and did not serve to establish any general public opinion about particular matters. There were no sports clubs that were thought of as uniting Ballybeg even on the occasion of their matches with outsiders; indeed there was not a single organisation of any kind that was thought of as even intended to link all the men or the women or the children or young people of the 'town'.

To understand why this should be so it is essential to look more generally at the pattern of social relations in this society in which sectarian affiliation is so strong. The lack of unity in Ballybeg itself merely reflected the lack of unity in the larger society round about. To understand the divisions in Ballybeg we have to look outside the 'town' itself.

2 Ballybeg rural area

In order to understand the economic life and the pattern of relationships in the countryside we have to examine the physical
background and the recent social history of the area.

Ballybeg lies at the edge of comparatively fertile lowlands, which
are 300 to 400 feet above sea-level, but immediately to the north,
and running from the south-west to the north-east, is the line of
a steep, scarp-like slope usually about 250 feet high. Beyond lie
uplands, rising in places to over 1,000 feet, covered with a poor,
thin soil, or in places with peat bogs. This steep slope, 'the brae
face', forms a sharp dividing line between two different types of
country, 'the mountain' and 'the infield'. These local terms
originated centuries ago when 'the infield' was the land immediately round a settlement arable land kept continually in cultivation
through the use of manure; while by contrast 'the mountain' was
the area, whatever its height, more distant from the settlement,
from which crops could be taken periodically but which was not
carefully and continuously farmed. The terms 'mountain' and
'infield' for the hills and the lowlands respectively carry, therefore,
implications about their relative richness and poverty as well as
about their relative heights.

The existence of such implications is understandable. In this
northern area even the difference in height and exposure alone
would have had agricultural significance, but other factors serve
to increase the contrast between the two areas. In the first place
the uplands are formed of a sandstone that is rather less fertile
than the carboniferous limestone of the lowlands. In addition the
distinction between the areas had been increased by the effects of
the ice age, for the ice had removed a lot of the soil from the hills
and had dumped it wherever the land flattened out. This, sur-

prising as it may seem, is still agriculturally significant, for as a result the uplands are areas where the slopes have only thin soils and the flatter areas are covered with bogs, whilst the lowlands, though tending to be poorly drained, nevertheless, have a thick, rather fertile soil of mixed sand and lime.

These conditions have had agricultural consequences and ultimately social consequences. The upland farms, exposed to strong winds and heavy rainfall with lower temperatures, also face problems of soil acidity, waterlogging and the rapid deterioration of pasture that put them at a disadvantage as compared with the lowlands. The lowland farm also suffers from drainage troubles; and, in the days before myxomatosis, rabbits, which found ideal burrowing sites in mounds of glacial drift, were a considerable nuisance. Nevertheless conditions in the lowlands are much kinder and this had been particularly significant in recent years since it was easier to lay land here down to permanent pasture—an important consideration when the costs of labouring land had risen sharply.

An indication of the difference in the prosperity of the two regions was the fact that over the previous century, when emigration caused a dramatic fall in population throughout the Ballybeg district, the population of the hills had fallen even more heavily than had the lowland population. In 1953 the lowland population was only 20 per cent of what it had been in 1841, but the hill population was a mere 16 per cent of the 1841 figure. Moreover, the relative loss of population from the hills had been particularly marked in recent years. The lowland population in 1953 was 64 per cent of the 1901 figure, whereas the hills had lost almost exactly half their inhabitants in that time, the 1953 total being only 51 per cent of the 1901 figure.

Very obviously such a tremendous exodus of people had involved great social changes in the area even if only because farmhouses once surrounded by neighbours had become isolated. I knew one hill farm, for instance, quite on its own, where a middle-aged brother and sister, both unmarried, lived in a house they had inherited from an elderly aunt. They had no near neighbours, yet in their aunt's childhood in the 1870's the house had stood in the middle of a busy little hamlet where there had been thirteen other inhabited houses, including a shop and a pub, and a fair had been held there at least twice a year. But changes had been brought about not merely by the drop in population but by increases in the size of farms, by changes in farming techniques, and by the much greater involvement of farmers with production for the market instead of farming for subsistence.

Even if we go back only to the 1900's, within the lifetime of many of the people still living in the area, conditions both economic and social were very different from the post-war world. From the valuation lists it is evident that at the beginning of the century about 55 per cent of farms in the lowlands were under twenty acres, whilst in the poor hill district, where a higher acreage is necessary to achieve the same production levels, over 66 per cent of the farms were under twenty acres in extent, and in some areas there were many cottiers with holdings of five acres or less. Not surprisingly oral tradition suggests that farm equipment at that time was for the most part suited to the cultivation of small-holdings only. In the 'infield', the larger, more prosperous farmers possessed horse-drawn iron ploughs, but these were uncommon in the hill districts where the commonest implement was often the wooden plough or the spade. On many farms virtually everything was done by hand work, with little reliance on horses, for not only were total acreages small but fields were tiny; and, moreover, the fields of several farmers were sometimes intermingled so that even where horse-drawn machinery could be afforded its use presented real problems. The land was prepared by hand, potatoes were planted individually, oats and flax were broadcast by hand, the crops were weeded by hand, and finally they were harvested by hand. Threshing on the smaller farms was mostly done with flails.

Even the smallest farmers were, of course, to some degree involved in production for the market, but to a considerable extent they relied for their needs on what they produced themselves. Potatoes provided the staple diet for human beings and none but the relatively prosperous could afford to buy animal feeding-stuffs in any quantity, so that potatoes were also the staple diet of poultry and pigs and some were given to calves. Significantly a great emphasis seems to have been put on planting potatoes as early in the year as possible. Today none are put in before the end of March, but traditionally they were the first crop of the year to be planted and it is said that they were normally finished by St. Patrick's day, 17 March. (This may be an exaggeration of earlier prowess, but as there are technical reasons why this would have been practicable when they were planted by hand, and as the incentive to aim at an early potato harvest must then have been considerable, traditions concerning the early planting of potatoes may be well founded.) One factor helping to make most farms relatively self-sufficient was the ready availability of fuel. At the cost of a good many days' labour in the summer, winning turf from the bogs, most farmers could supply their total annual fuel requirements; by long-standing arrangements even the 'infield' farmers had access to turf bogs in the hills.

Cash incomes came principally from the sale of livestock and their products. The men sold calves and young cattle, a few lambs and pigs; their wives marketed a little butter and eggs; their production of all these animals was limited by the general inability to afford to buy feeding-stuffs for them. With the poor communications of the time there was little market for fresh milk although it played an important part in supplying home needs. Every farmer tried to market some of his crops of oats, beans and potatoes but the only purely cash crop was flax. This could not be grown in the hills, but was an important crop on some of the best of the infield land.

The importance of flax is significant because it is a labour intensive crop, for not only does it require careful planting but it has to be meticulously weeded while it is growing, and it is a laborious crop to harvest. It must be carefully pulled by hand, not cut, and then it has to be retted, that is steeped in ponds to rot some of the tissues and loosen the fibres. Labour was readily available and cheap and it was this that made flax important to the economy of the infield farmers. Farms there of forty or fifty acres usually employed several men semi-permanently, but in addition there was a reservoir of labour in the upland districts and in the busy harvest season it was usual for gangs of men and women from the hill farms to go together to the more prosperous infield farms to work as 'boon' labourers for a few days at a time. As many as twenty people might work together on one man's land. On the hill farms labourers were less commonly employed. It was, however, very common for neighbours to join together to help one another with work, partly because a task could sometimes be done more quickly this way, but partly the reason seems to have been simply to relieve boredom. Men preferred to be in one another's company rather than to work on their own.

By the 1950's the situation had radically altered. General depopulation, greater involvement in the market, and post-war wage-levels had produced really significant differences. An examination of the yearly round on the farms will make clear the way in which alterations had taken place.

The agricultural year ran from December to November when the potatoes were harvested. There was no autumn ploughing or planting of corn but December and the first half of January were a time for relaxation. Interestingly throughout the area, farmers, Catholic and Protestant, observed the Twelve Days of Christmas as an almost complete holiday from all field tasks (a practice formerly widespread in England, but which appears to have died out there before the beginning of the nineteenth century[1]). The first task of the year was one of general maintenance, the cleaning out of ditches, 'redding sheughs' in the local phrase. During the busy harvest season these became choked with vegetation that there was no time to cut back, and the ditches had to be cleared to allow the heavy winter rains to drain away. The next task was that of carting manure on to the fields. Every farm had its big midden and it was a task of several days to cut the dung out, load it on to carts and spread it on the land. It was a job done between the middle of January and the end of February. The more land the farmer intended to plough and the slower the method he employed the earlier he had to begin to cart the manure.

Ploughing began in March and marked the beginning of the first rushed season of the year. There were still two ways of plough- ing, with tractors or with horses, but tractors were gaining rapidly. In 1938 there had been only one tractor in the district, but there were many now owned locally, and men who did not own one could often hire a man who did to do their ploughing for them— it was a regular way in which farmers' sons could earn some money. According to the method used ploughing took either ten days to a fortnight or a mere three to four days. The time taken for sowing grain was still much the same as it had been earlier, for no-one in the district possessed a seed-drill. Once the ploughed land had been harrowed, a fairly quick process, oats were still sown broad- cast, by hand. Many a man in fact still used an old sheet slung over his shoulder and across his arm to hold the grain. Others used a 'fiddle', a canvas bag, slung from the shoulder. The bag was fitted at the bottom with a small wheel like a water-wheel, which was worked by a 'bow' that, moving backwards and forwards, sent out a steady stream of seeds. It was quicker and more efficient than the sheet, but this was true only if a second man was at hand ready to

[1] See Tusser (1812), p. 270, n. 3.

fill the bag regularly as required. For this reason the 'fiddle' was not very commonly used.

Flax was no longer grown because the necessary labour was no longer available at a price the farmer was prepared to pay; beans also had disappeared now that the demand for horse-fodder had declined. In consequence potatoes were the only really significant crop grown on many farms. Some hand labour was still needed for their preparation. Each man normally saved his own seed, and for the sake of economy each eye was cut out and used separately. Still the pieces were for the most part planted by hand: first went a man with a mould plough opening a drill, then came a helper who 'dropped' the potatoes, then artificial manures were scattered on the land, and finally the drills were closed again with the mould plough. Only a few of the larger farmers owned drill ploughs that could do these jobs mechanically.

From the end of April to the time that the harvest began there was a pause in field operations except for the occasional harrowing of the land to keep down the weeds. There were, however, other jobs to be done. In May grass was still scarce and the fences had to be strengthened to prevent the stock breaking out in search of food. Again, rabbits were a particular pest at this time and odd days were spent in trying to gas them.

At this period, too, the bogs became dry enough for cutting to begin, and as in the old days, each family still needed the cutting of one week to keep them in fuel for the year. Cutting turf took a lot of labour, for each man cutting with a spade needed three others to help. Moreover, the cutting was only part of the process of obtaining turf. When cut the turves had still to be turned frequently to enable them to dry out, and this entailed a trip to the bogs about once a week until August. These operations still took the same amount of time as formerly. The only way in which any part of this task had been shortened was in the bringing home of the loads in the summer. Here the use of tractors to draw them had speeded the operation.

In July and early August the hay was cut, by mower now, not by hand, and was spread out to dry. As soon as it was in a fit state it was built into fairly large cocks in the fields, making it comparatively safe from the weather. In September, oats were harvested. They were still bound into sheaves by hand after the reaping and this was therefore a task that called for as many helpers as possible. By the end of September the crop was normally in the farmyard and the stacks had been built and thatched. After this the hay cocks were lifted bodily on to trailers with the help of winches and were drawn up to the 'haggard', the farmyard, where they were built into ricks.

Flails had become things of the past, although they were still to be found lying about many farms. For the threshing of the crop all relied on big machines which quickly did the job. They visited the farms twice in the season. They came first when the crop was just harvested and the farmer was anxious to get some of it, at least, into a usable condition. To save space in the barns, however, threshing was not all done at the same time and half-way through the winter the farms were again visited and the rest of the corn was threshed. The farmer had to pay for this machine by the hour and consequently an attempt was made to do the work as quickly as possible and, as throughout most of the British Isles, threshing was the task for which it was most common to rely on the help of neighbours.

The last task of the harvest was to lift and store the potatoes. This again still made fairly heavy demands on the labour force, but it was a job that could be done much more swiftly than formerly since a mechanical digger, drawn by a horse or a tractor, was now used instead of a spade to lift the crop. As the digger passed down the rows in a cloud of dirt and flying potatoes, helpers were still needed to go forward in pairs with a basket between them to gather potatoes. While rather a laborious job, it was not hurried as the only difference that the weather made was to the comfort of the pickers. If necessary the work could be spread over two or three weeks, although usually it was done more quickly.

From this account of farming practice in the 1950's the most important fact to be noticed is the decline in the amount of time spent in working in the fields. Formerly for many men work in the fields, either their own or someone else's, was a more continuous process and the only really slack period was around Christmas. By the 1950's, however, there were fairly long periods when field work was far from pressing. Moreover, at all times the average man spent a larger proportion of his day not in the fields but around the yard, caring for his stock, for in the previous fifty years the emphasis of farming life had changed from subsistence to cash, and the change had come mainly with an increase in the value of the livestock on the farm. Compared with the beginning of this century new opportunities for sales had appeared through the setting up of marketing arrangements for fresh milk, the demand for eggs and the better arrangements for the handling of fat cattle and pigs. The result was that the importance of the dairy herd and of pigs and poultry had increased enormously. On some infield farms the numbers of beef cattle had been reduced as the farmers now paid more attention to other animals. On most farms, however, the numbers of beef had increased, and although their importance as providers of cash may have declined relatively they were still of considerable significance.

The consequence of all these changes was that the farmer spent a bigger proportion of his time looking after his animals than he had at the beginning of the century. In the slack winter season when dusk came soon after four o'clock almost all the daylight hours were spent in cleaning out houses, and in feeding and watering the stock. Even in the busy spring season a man who had little help would not normally expect to be out in his fields before ten o'clock in the morning.

These farmers then, although they might seem to be old-fashioned, had certainly been prepared to move with the times. There was no belief that what was good enough for their fathers was, in farming practice, good enough for them. On the contrary, financial gains and easier working conditions were the acknowledged goals for farmers and their families. Indeed, if they looked at the implements, or talked over the methods used by their fathers, they often remarked: 'Those fellows had strong backs and weak minds!' At times it was possible to detect a certain conflict of values arising out of the changed conditions of farming. Thus while all men took a pride in the appearance of their animals, to some, especially the older men and the hill farmers, 'good farming' still meant good crop husbandry, and they judged a man's skill mainly by the state of his fields. On the other hand, the younger men tended to laugh at this, saying that they could find better ways to spend their time than in 'redding sheughs'. Yet while they differed in what they considered to be the most profitable method of farming, in the long run all the farmers were prepared to be judged by their cash returns and to adopt, so far as possible, any new methods whose profitability they thought had been proved.

The sensitivity of farmers to market prices was shown by their behaviour when, in the early fifties, milk prices fell in comparison with those for beef. Many farmers sold off some of their cows to buy young cattle; it had, apparently, been hoped that farmers in

c

general, not just the Northern Irish ones, would have reacted by raising more of their young stock instead of killing them for veal. In Ulster few calves were in any case sold for veal, and the reaction of the local farmers was caused by their desire to cash in quickly on a good market, and by their distrust of government agencies which made them fear that beef prices might be lowered again before they had time to rear their own home-bred calves into beef animals. Local agricultural officers advised the farmers against selling their cows, but since most farmers believed that the Ministry of Agriculture was not merely occasionally unwise or genuinely mistaken but had no real desire to help them no notice was taken of this advice.

This brings us to one of the most significant differences between the organisation of farming between the 1900's and the 1950's. In the earlier period many of the farmers had been little more than semi-subsistence cultivators on whom the outside world had impinged only indirectly. By the 1950's the outside world was exerting an enormous influence on everyone in the area. This difference could be demonstrated even if we consider only the number and variety of outsiders in the district. Even in the 1900's, of course, it had not been completely isolated. Even then many of the positions in the society had been filled by those born and educated outside it; the professional men such as the doctors, clergymen and teachers, and the policemen had often come from other parts of Ireland. Now, however, there were proportionately more of these people and they had been joined by agricultural officers, poultry instructresses and officials of the Ministry of Food. At the same time, because the area was being drawn ever more closely into the wider economic system, even those jobs such as nursing posts that usually in the end went to local people, were advertised in the general press; and notices of the sale of shops and farms were given in the same way, and in a mobile age complete outsiders might enter the district in response to such advertisements.

In the 1950's it was most strikingly government agencies, especially the Ministry of Agriculture, that influenced the whole area through their implementation of the Government's economic policies towards agriculture. By fixing prices and subsidies these agencies determined the relative attractiveness of different courses of action on the farms, and to a more limited extent, through the introduction of regulations concerning such things as the building of byres, the officials governed the activities of farmers in other ways also. Of crucial importance to the district was the post-war establishment of the Welfare State, with levels of unemployment pay and National Assistance that were very high relative to the local standard of living. Equally significant was the establishment of a much increased minimum wage for farm workers. Locally farmers' incomes were often, in cash terms, low enough to make it genuinely difficult for them to pay this wage. Further, many labourers had previously had a standard of living so low that if they chose to remain idly on National Assistance their families experienced little drop in income. At the same time the post-war labour shortage in other parts of Britain attracted the more ambitious labourers to leave the district in search of relatively high wages paid to even unskilled men elsewhere. All these factors combined meant that an entirely new labour situation had been created to which the farmers had to adjust; and this adjustment essentially consisted in their cutting down on labour intensive work.

That it was British economic and agricultural policies that were influencing the Ballybeg farmers was perhaps the most important factor in the local situation. It was, after all, the result of intense political activity over the previous fifty years; political activity that had been of vital significance in influencing the social environment of the Ballybeg people and their relationships with each other. We must not exaggerate the social upheavals they had experienced over these years; by comparison with many Continental communities they had after all been sheltered from the major convulsions of the twentieth century. Nevertheless many of the adults had considerable personal experience of political turmoil. From the beginning of the century the question of Home Rule for Ireland was to the forefront of people's minds. When by 1910 it became apparent that a Home Rule Bill would be forced through Parliament at Westminster, Ulster Protestants throughout the north responded by forming militant resistance groups; and militant Catholic groups had previously been active. The outbreak of the first world war delayed but did not ultimately prevent the development of virtual civil war, known euphemistically as 'the Troubles', which swept the whole of Ireland in the 1920's and was particularly intense in areas, like Ballybeg, close to the new border between the north and the south of Ireland.

Prior to the establishment of an independent Irish Free State this border had been a mere County boundary across which ties of economic relationships and kinship had run freely. Subsequently, although movement across it remained relatively free by the standards of most international boundaries, this line came to have real economic and social significance. Unlike some areas closer to the border Ballybeg did not have to reorganise its local life radically to fit in with the new boundary, but the border certainly exerted a definite influence on the pattern of social relationships in the area. Most vitally, perhaps, it crystallised the opposition to each other of Catholic and Protestant, for in general Catholic and Nationalist opinion refused to recognise the border's validity, whilst Protestants regarded its maintenance as essential to their freedom. The border, close physically and omnipresent psychologically, brought into sharp contrast not only those actually separated by it but those separated because their opinions about it were opposed.

The relationships of Catholic and Protestant in the Ballybeg area nevertheless cannot be understood simply by reference to the external political and economic environment. It is necessary to look at the social patterns within the area itself. Here what was significant was the distribution of Catholic and Protestant both spatially and socially. They were not distributed evenly in proportion to their overall numbers. On the contrary Catholics were in a majority in Ballybeg itself and in the hill district, whilst Protestants were in a majority in the lowland area. Furthermore, Protestants formed the majority of the more prosperous people; Catholics formed a majority of the poorer. These facts had great social significance.

3 Focus on a small district

To see what was the real social significance of the distribution of Catholics and Protestants I studied part of the Ballybeg area in considerable detail. I could not study the whole of the larger area in sufficient depth and I therefore chose for particular examination a small sector of lowland and hills that covered in all just under fourteen square miles, and contained a population of 383. This district was divided into twenty-one 'townlands'. Throughout Ireland the countryside was divided into small, named, territorial units, originally centering on tiny hamlets, and these units are called 'townlands'. They vary in size from 50 to 1,500 acres, usually being largest in hill districts. They are seldom of real administrative significance, but they retain considerable importance in the sentiments of the people. A farmer for instance will always be proud if he owns 'the whole townland' quite apart from the number of acres it contains. Of the townlands I studied in detail, six, covering just over seven square miles, were in the hill district and fifteen covering just under seven square miles, were in the lowlands. The population of the hill area was 153, and that of the infield townlands was 230.

Taking the population of this area as a whole the division between Catholic and Protestant was virtually equal but the distribution of the two groups was significantly different. Of the 197 Catholics 58 per cent lived in the hill area and 42 per cent lived in the lowlands. Of the 186 Protestants 78 per cent lived in the infield and only 22 per cent in the hills. Putting this in a different way, of the hill population 72 per cent were Catholic, and only 28 per cent were Protestant. Of the infield population on the other hand 65 per cent were Protestant and only 35 per cent Catholic. If we look at the way in which land was held the impression given by the overall distribution of the population is reinforced. In the hill townlands twenty-five farms were held by Catholics and eight by Protestants; in the infield townlands twenty-eight farms were held by Protestants and fifteen by Catholics. In percentage terms Catholics owned 75 per cent of the hill farms and Protestants 65 per cent of the lowland farms.

That these figures had social significance may be inferred from what has been said already about the difference between the two districts, for the hill area suffered from a number of disadvantages as compared with the lowlands. Although the hill farms were on average somewhat larger than the valley farms, the hill farms were nevertheless very limited in size, and their owners, trying to make a living under adverse ecological conditions, did not have acreages that were big enough to compensate for the drawbacks of soil and climate.

In certain respects hills and lowlands were socially alike, but the economic differences between them were very real. In both all cultivators were owner-occupiers and each farmer personally worked his own land; there were neither tenant-farmers nor gentlemen-farmers in either area. Nor was this pattern of land holding the result of recent changes, for although owner-occupation stemmed ultimately from the various Irish Land Reform Acts of the end of the nineteenth century, Ballybeg had not been held in vast estates, and by 1900 the biggest holding had been only 250 acres. Nevertheless despite such similarities in type of holding there were differences in income between the two regions. As might be expected even in the 1950's hill farmers were generally poorer than infield farmers. Hill farms, it is true, averaged eighty acres to the lowland farms sixty acres, but on lowland farms most of the land was assessed as of arable quality; in the hills only a third to a half of the land of the average farm came up to this standard. In previous decades the relative poverty of the hill farmers was even more marked because the hill areas were then virtually as densely populated as were the lowlands. Even as late as 1924 valuation returns show that over 65 per cent of the hill farms, as compared with 53 per cent of the lowland farms, consisted of holdings with less than twenty acres of arable quality land. Although the hill farmer derived some real advantage from the fact that his poor quality land usually included bog from which he could obtain his fuel, the fact remained that the higher its proportion the smaller the amount of productive farm land that he owned. Very generally, therefore, hill farmers were poorer than lowland farmers, and in the recent past this relative poverty had been even more marked than it was in the 1950's.

It was difficult to discover exactly what the farmers earned in a year since very few kept records, even for themselves, that would have allowed anyone to make a really accurate assessment of monetary gains and losses, let alone to calculate the value of own produce consumed as food and fuel. The local agricultural officer nevertheless thought that the money income of hill farmers varied from a lower limit of £150, on a few holdings where the income was helped out by some form of National Assistance, to about £800. The income of infield farmers varied, he thought, from £600 to £1,200, with most around the £800 mark.

All these variations between lowlands and hills were socially significant because they meant that there was a significant overall difference in the average incomes of Catholic and Protestant. These differences were translated to some extent into different patterns of life-styles which ultimately found some expression in concepts of own-group identity and in stereotypes. For this reason it is important to look quite carefully at what these styles of life were.

Speaking generally it was possible to distinguish three main patterns of living: first that of labourers and the poorer of the hill farmers; secondly a middle category of more prosperous hill farmers and the ordinary lowland farmers; and thirdly a category of lowland farmers who were both reasonably prosperous and who sought to copy the standards of middle-class people outside Ballybeg.

That people remained in the area to try to exist on the lowest incomes is probably to be explained by the fact that outgoings were minimal, especially for those who owned land. With the land went houses, which at a low standard were plentiful in this area of high emigration. Expenditure on fuel was minimal since turf generally supplied all the requirements for heating and cooking. For lighting the majority relied on oil lamps. Gas and electricity charges were therefore unknown. The poorest people seldom had to pay water-rates either; houses with any running water were infrequent even in the lowlands and very rare in the hills. The standard of services regarded as tolerable was perhaps best shown by the fact that not merely were the hill farms almost invariably without water-closets, a number of them were without any sanitary arrangements at all, if the cow-byre and the discreet hedge are excluded. Further, despite the growing involvement with the market the standard of living was such that families with some land, even labourers families, expected to rely to a considerable extent for food on what they produced themselves. The use of milk from the farm's own cow had declined when milk became subsidised, because it paid to send milk to the creamery and to buy it back in bottles; but the reliance on home-produced potatoes for the basic diet was considerable.

The poorest houses, single storey, small, rectangular cottages, were built of stone, the outside walls were covered with plaster, usually whitewashed each year, and they were roofed with thatch or corrugated iron. Usually they had four small rooms and were built to a traditional pattern. The kitchen, the largest room, lay in the middle of most houses and occupied the width of the house. A door led directly from the outside 'street', as the space before the house is called, to the extreme right of the kitchen. Across to the left was the inner chimney wall where there was formerly an open hearth and where now there often stood an iron range. In the far corner of that wall there was a door leading to the two bedrooms, one at the back and one at the front of the house, one leading out of the other. In the right-hand wall of the kitchen, towards the front of the house, a door led to the 'room'. From its general appearance this extension to the right of the kitchen seemed almost invariably to have been added to the main building at a later date and in the poorest houses there was still no extension to the right. 'The room' was normally used as a kind of parlour, although if the family were a large one it might be turned into an extra bedroom. In the largest houses of this type a partition was sometimes found at the back of the parlour, and behind it there was a permanent bedroom.

These rooms were decorated to different degrees. The bedrooms were generally distempered while the 'room' was covered with wallpaper. The kitchen was covered with a paper stretching from the ceiling to within four feet of the floor. Below, because of the speed at which it became dirty, the wall was distempered and in most homes was re-done once or twice a year, generally in some shade of green.

In the kitchen, where the family spent the bulk of its indoor waking hours, there was little furniture. The floor was generally of concrete or cement without any form of covering. A long oblong deal table stood under the window looking on to the 'street', and the table was very seldom moved even if this meant that all the family could not sit round it at one time. Usually there were four or five plain wooden chairs dotted about the room and, often, against the far wall was a long wooden bench capable of seating three or four people. Invariably a dresser was placed in the far corner of the right-hand wall. The only common piece of soft furnishing was one armchair drawn up near the hearth. In the walls there was commonly a niche made originally to hold the horse-collar, which had to be brought in out of the damp, but now it quite often held a wireless. On one of the doors a roller towel served both its usual purpose and as a communal handkerchief. Normally no secular pictures hung on the walls, except grocers' calendars; the other decorations were, according to religious and political affiliations, pictures of the saints or texts and pictures of the Royal Family.

The bedrooms were also somewhat scantily furnished. Iron bedsteads were usually covered with blankets but without sheets. Wardrobes were scarce and it was seldom that a house held more than one. Clothes were more commonly kept in old chests of drawers, while somewhere on the wall hung a mirror. The 'room', however, was more carefully furnished. It was used solely for entertaining important visitors, and the neighbours at marriages and funerals, and for this reason objects that enhanced prestige were kept here. The floor was covered with linoleum and there was generally a polished dining-room table with chairs to match, and in some cases a sideboard. The walls were damp from infrequent use, and from them dead and absent relatives glared down in company with bygone kings or popes.

The clothing of the people was in many ways in keeping with their homes. The men spent their working hours in ancient clothes covered with blue dungarees, while a pair of Wellington boots and a battered hat completed their outfit. It was only in the hottest weather that they removed their coats and they never worked without a shirt. Beside their working clothes it was usual for them to have a dark suit for Sundays and funerals, with a pair of shoes to match, and these might also be worn at fairs, although the majority of the younger men preferred flannels and a sports coat for these events. Only those without self-respect went out to the fair in their dungarees, and young and old always wore hats.

On the farm and around the house the woman wore a woollen frock or jumper and skirt, covered with a black or brown apron.

She also wore dark woollen stockings and ordinary or Wellington boots. For Sundays the woman had a fairly new coat and dress with lighter shoes and nylons, and similar garments, rather older, were used for shopping expeditions. In cold weather a common practice was to wear one of these frocks over the usual jumper and skirt, if a visit had to be made to the town.

Dressed for school, the children were for the most part warmly and neatly clad, the boys in dungarees and Wellington boots, the girls often in clothing inherited from elder sisters or cut down from their mothers' dresses. New frocks and suits were kept for church. What they wore indoors and at home did not matter and as soon as they came in from school the children changed into clothes that were generally ancient and often ragged, or they might wear their school clothes inside-out. In no circumstance, however, was a bare-footed child ever seen, although not many years before no boy wore shoes after the first of May without being made the object of scorn amongst his fellows.

Raggedness might have been common indoors but real dirt was not. There was little to obstruct frequent sweepings or to harbour vermin, though fleas were not uncommon. All self-respecting families put on some clean clothes every Sunday, and Monday was the washing day, and the women were beginning to use coupons for cheap packets of detergents. Personal cleanliness varied. The men washed irregularly and shaved before visiting town on Saturday nights, and for any visit of importance. The women washed more frequently and some houses possessed bath tubs that were sometimes used for people as well as clothes, although they were usually more likely to be used for children rather than adults.

Their food was simple. For breakfast the staple was bread, often home-made 'soda bread' with butter or jam; and there was tea drunk with plenty of milk and sugar. Only a few families commonly ate porridge at this meal. The main meal was the midday dinner. In living memory this had commonly consisted solely of potatoes and buttermilk; and the word 'dinner' was still synonymous with 'potatoes'. Often the flavour of potatoes was preferred to anything else, but some meat was normally added as a garnishing. Usually each person was served with a small piece of meat, part of a rasher of bacon, or half a sausage, and then each helped himself with a fork to potatoes which had been already placed in the centre of the table. Normally the potatoes were cooked in their skins and each person peeled his own on to the table. Sometimes, however, the woman mashed them all herself before the meal and mixed them with onions, when they were known as 'champ'. Other vegetables were few: carrots were often put in a stew along with onions; cabbage, after being boiled for a couple of hours and subsequently fried in bacon fat, was quite often eaten with bacon; but otherwise vegetables were almost entirely absent from the diet. From a dietary point of view, however, one good point about the dinner was that it was usual in most households for everyone to have at least one glass of milk along with the meal; a large jug of milk was put on the table and each person helped himself. After the main course some of the more sophisticated families ate a sweet. It was not a traditional part of the dinner but it had become quite a common habit to finish up the meal with boiled rice. If rice were not eaten there seemed to be no regular pattern in the selection of substitutes —a family might on an ordinary day have perhaps Birds Custard only; or if visitors were present tinned fruit was quite usual; and on one memorable occasion I was given a piece of tinned Christmas pudding surmounted by tinned apricots. But for the majority the only additions to the main course were biscuits and a cup of tea.

The two other meals of the day were both minor ones. Tea was eaten when the main work of the day was over. It was a very similar meal to breakfast, the chief item being bread and bought jam. Occasionally an egg was eaten at this time, but this was rare. Finally, just before going to bed the people helped themselves to porridge from a saucepan on the fire and they generally ate it with milk and sugar.

If there were school children in the house their times of eating tended to be slightly different. They had their breakfast with the family, but unless they lived very near the school and could get home at midday they had to wait for their dinners until half-past three as the local schools did not serve meals. The majority of children therefore took a bread and jam sandwich and the school provided a third of a pint of milk for them to drink. Once home, their dinner was the same as that of the adults, except that meat was not always saved for them. For the rest of the day there was no difference in the way that they were fed.

If we look at the next more prosperous section—those with cash incomes of more than £600—the greatest difference lies in the type of housing that was common among them. The houses were of two types: first there were a few old houses that dated from the last century which were of two storeys and had seven to ten rooms. The majority, however, were originally of the one-storeyed type but had had an additional storey built on to them in concrete blocks. Downstairs some of the partition walls had been taken out so that the two bedrooms had become a diningroom, while the 'room' was enlarged and spoken of as the 'lounge'. Upstairs there were generally three to four bedrooms, and where water had been brought to the house, a bathroom and a w.c. also. Many of these alterations were post-war, carried out with the help of a government subsidy.

Frequently, where the addition of the second storey was still recent, all of these rooms had not been fully furnished; that is to say the people themselves did not regard them as being so. Moreover, they did not seem to be fully occupied by the family. The 'room' furniture had been taken out and placed in the dining-room. The 'lounge' had its old mantelpiece replaced by a modern tiled one and a carpet placed on the floor. To replace the table a modern Chesterfield suite had been installed. But although the outward appearance of the room was transformed the uses to which it was put had scarcely been altered. The family photographs were kept on the walls and the door was still only opened on ceremonial occasions, although there was a slightly greater readiness to entertain visitors here than there had been before. Similarly, the dining-room was seldom used and its main function was to provide a place in which the children could do their homework—a real advantage, this.

In general the life of the family still centred on the kitchen. It was here that the bulk of the meals were eaten and the leisure hours were spent; and in this room the furniture had scarcely changed. Most of these kitchens still had no covering on the floor except an old sack that acted as a mat, and in most of the homes there was still only the one armchair. Even the position of these pieces of furniture had changed very little.

The clothing of the people in this category, in their working hours, was hardly to be distinguished from that of those already discussed, although any tendency to raggedness seemed to be reduced and the children were better dressed out of school. The main differences were to be found in the better quality and greater variety of the clothing that was worn for more important occasions. There was a particularly marked difference in the extent of the wardrobe of the women who dressed themselves with care before going out.

The standards of cleanliness were somewhat higher than were those of the preceding category. That is to say, washing was rather more frequent among the adults of both sexes, although the men did not often shave more than once or twice a week. Moreover, even when there was a bathroom in the house, baths were not frequently taken. Nevertheless, the washing and dusting of the house was a task which was not only rather more onerous because of the extra rooms and furniture, but one which assumed greater symbolic significance. In homes such as these a regular time, commonly Saturday mornings, was set aside in every week for 'doing the house'.

These people too had a somewhat different diet from that previously examined, mainly because it contained more protein. Often boiled eggs were eaten for breakfast and frequently there was something cooked for tea. Many of the attitudes to food seemed, however, to be the same in both categories. Thus the basis of the main meal of the day was still potatoes and meat and other protein foods seemed to be regarded primarily as garnishings; helpings of meat were very small even when the families were currently able to spend money on other things they regarded as luxuries. The cooked tea sometimes seemed more important because it signified the family's status than because of the food value it provided; I have, for instance, seen a small tin of baked beans regarded as a sufficient 'cooked tea' for six adults, three of whom were men who had been working outside all day. There was, moreover, little demand for variety in the food. I knew households with incomes of between £800 and £1,000 a year in which, when the wife was doing her share of farm-work in the busy planting season, meals for weeks on end consisted of eggs for breakfast, eggs and bacon for the midday meal and eggs for tea; this pattern of food consumption was not felt to be odd or unusual.

It was socially significant that behaviour at meals amongst these people was seldom very different from meal-time behaviour of the poorer category. A knife, fork and mug were set out for each person and plates were laid. When the meal was ready the members of the family sat down over a period of perhaps ten minutes, one after the other. Each speared a succession of potatoes from a collander in the centre of the table and, holding them up one by one on the end of a fork, peeled them in the air, the peel falling on the table. Each person, as he finished, got up and took a more comfortable position nearer the fire. Often the woman of the family did not sit at the table at all but remained near the fire ready to pass more potatoes from the hob should they be required.

School-children had their dinners separately when they got home in the afternoons. They, like the children from poorer homes, mostly took only bread and jam sandwiches to school with them for midday, so that this late afternoon meal was their main one. It was noticeable that it was seldom that parents showed any marked concern that children should eat high-protein foods; if a child were not interested in the egg or meat provided for it no attempt was made to encourage it to eat them; it would be happily served with some more potatoes instead. With the one exception of the provision of the late afternoon meal for school-children, meals for children generally were identical with, and served at the same time as, meals for adults.

In these more prosperous households the main difference in food provided lay in the amount and variety set out when visitors were expected. Even the poorest people made an attempt at lavish provision on such occasions, but the efforts of the better-off were naturally superior. Visitors were usually invited to tea. For a visitor's tea tinned meat or salmon and tomatoes began the meal and often there was tinned fruit as well. Besides this, although cakes played no part in the ordinary tea, it was the normal practice to put half a dozen varieties of cake on the table; it was in turn expected that a guest should take one of each variety. When the young Presbyterian minister introduced his newly married wife to his congregation by taking her to their homes in turn, they both suffered agonies of indigestion because they had to visit three or four households in an afternoon—in most lavish teas had been prepared and in most they were expected to conform to the 'one-of-each' rule.

Finally we may differentiate a third category of people where the cash income was certainly at least £700–£800 a year (over £1,000+ at today's values), but this category could not be differentiated from the last on the basis of income alone but rather in terms of the way in which this income was expended, and in the general style of life. All the farmers in this category were in the infield.

Outwardly there was not always any difference between size and appearance of the houses in this third group and those in the second, but a difference was apparent immediately the kitchen door was opened. This was principally because the floor was covered with coconut matting or rugs, a sure sign that men were expected not to spit; there was also a general impression of white and cream painted furniture. The use of the room was different also, for it was not so constantly used. Breakfast was almost always eaten here, because it was the one warm room in the house in the mornings, and sometimes tea as well, but the main midday meal, sometimes called 'lunch', was usually eaten in the dining-room. In the evenings the family could seldom be found sitting in the kitchen.

In these homes, indeed, the dining-room was the main living room of the house. Usually as well as a carpet and good mahogany dining-room furniture it had at least two comfortable armchairs for husband and wife. The sitting-room was commonly reserved for more formal occasions, but it was usually used at least once a week on Sundays. Water was laid on to all these homes and each had a bathroom and w.c.—the older type of fittings in these houses as compared with those few which did exist in other houses showed that most of their occupants had been accustomed to such luxuries even before the war.

The task of looking after these houses was substantial, for not only were there more rooms and furnishings to care for but also rooms other than the kitchen were used more often. Since this meant more frequent fires, always of peat, regular dusting was regarded as vital.

The clothes of the people were also different. Their better clothes differed not so much because more was spent on them or because more were possessed, although these were factors, but because they had not often been bought locally. The greatest difference was to be seen, however, in the working clothes, particularly those of the women. Some men, like other farmers, wore dungarees, although in a rather better condition than usual, but normally the men wore ordinary trousers or breeches and gaiters. The women never wore the thick stockings and boots that were common among the majority. If they had to go through mud, of course, they put on Wellingtons, but they did not work about the kitchen in them. Moreover, the clothes that they wore in their houses were seldom so old and never so grubby as those worn at home by the others and they favoured lighter aprons. Cleanliness was a most important principle with all these people and none of the men habitually went a day without a shave.

Their food was both more plentiful and more varied than that of any other section of the society. It was particularly the protein content of the meals that was higher. Moreover, the food eaten did not seem to be noticeably more scanty or less varied in busy seasons, nor did it vary very much if visitors were expected. I was both given special invitations to these homes and invited to stay for meals when I called unexpectedly, and there was very little difference in the food that was placed on the table. The children, if they had to take sandwiches to school, took not jam but meat and cheese. When they came home they were sometimes given the remains of the same meal that was served to the adults but quite commonly a meal was cooked especially for them.

The causes of the difference between the last two status types were complex. Certainly those in the last category tended to have relatively high incomes, yet it would be untrue to suggest that relative wealth alone could place a family in this category, although income did seem to be the main factor in deciding whether a household came within the first or second category. Even in these latter cases it was noticeable that other factors might influence a family's standard of living; a wife who had, for example, become used to relatively high living standards outside Ballybeg might exert such an influence that relatively high standards were maintained despite a very poor income. Much more certainly the standards of the third category were linked to other things than mere money. This seemed to be the case primarily because these standards could be maintained only if a woman could spend a fairly high proportion of her time on domestic tasks rather than farming chores. It was essentially women who were in some way 'outsiders' or whose husbands or fathers had in pre-war days employed labourers to do the yard work who had grown to expect to spend their time on domestic tasks. In the post-war world, when labourers had become 'difficult to pay' and maids almost impossible to get, few farmers' wives, no matter who they were, could avoid giving some help in yard work. Nevertheless in general the pressure to do yard work was greatest on the wives of poorer farmers in general and hill farmers in particular. The more 'mountainy' the farm and the poorer a man's equipment the more time he had to spend in his fields and the more essential it was for his womenfolk to do the yard work. If on the scale of values of the household and their kinsfolk yard work for a wife came before her domestic chores, she could never find time to do the things in the house that she would like to have done. If, by contrast, domestic tasks were highly valued and it was accepted that these might come before farming tasks, then there was the basic foundation for higher standards judged by clean-

liness, food values and general comfort in the home. If, for whatever reasons, the family's social reference group was the urban
middle class, then domestic goals became unusually high.

To give more details about these three types of life-styles and
to indicate the significance of the role of the woman of the house
in determining standards of living I will quote three particular
instances drawn from the three categories I have described. The
first is that of a Catholic hill-farm family where an 'outsider' mother
kept up on a low income standards that were considerably above
average; the second that of a Presbyterian hill-farm family where,
despite some relative prosperity, the standards maintained were
only average for the area; and finally the family of a Church of
Ireland farmer in the infield which maintained relatively very
high standards, despite the fact that the farmer had got into
financial difficulties that had made it necessary for a while to
mortgage the land. These examples will also enable us to see in
more detail the distinctive features of the different households.

Michael McKinleys' house (CD27)[1]

The first case was that of a hill farm owned by the McKinley family.
Mrs. McKinley (CC13) had come originally from Scotland, although
she was of Irish descent. Her father had been a skilled workman
with a good job and her background could be best described as
upper working class. She had found the transition to the very
rural life of Ballybeg rather difficult when she had first come to
Ballybeg with her husband, but when I knew her she had been
living in the area for over thirty years and she had long since
made the necessary adjustments. She had learned to cope with the
problems of life on a poor hill farm, but she had to a certain extent
withstood local custom and had maintained in her household a
standard of living that was relatively high. Perhaps she had stood
out against pressure to conform completely to local practice
because her husband had died not many years after returning to
the area, so that she had been master as well as mistress of the farm.

The farm was not very prosperous. It contained about 15 acres
of relatively good land, with another thirty acres of rough pasture
and ten acres of bog. It was reached by a steep, twisting, unmetalled
lane that led up from the main road about half a mile below. The
house lay a little back from the lane from which it was separated
by a rather scrawny hedge and an iron gate slung between the

[1] See kinship reference charts attached to the back cover.

D

traditional Ulster stone gate-pillars. One of these was beginning to crumble and needed repairing, but they were both smartly white-washed every year. The farm's outhouses had originally been two dwelling houses abandoned when their owners had emigrated. The houses were kept in good repair; one was used for the one horse, the pigs and calves and feed for the stock, and one had recently been converted to take hens kept intensively, under the so-called 'deep-litter' system. A few yards from the house stood the usual hay and corn ricks, and the midden. A rain-water barrel stood hopefully by the house, but as all the roofs were thatched, and therefore had no gutters, there was no efficient way of getting the water into the barrel. In fact the drinking water came from a well about a hundred yards above the house, and had to be fetched in buckets. No water was laid on in the house, nor was there either electricity or gas, and the family certainly could not afford to have either their own generator, or to use bottled gas. For heating and cooking they relied exclusively on the turf cut from their own bog. For lighting they had traditional paraffin lamps. There was one much brighter, modern pressure lamp, but this was not used in the house, instead it was kept outside with the hens, for the success of the intensive 'deep-litter' system depended on keeping the birds in a bright light until late every evening.

The house was the normal long rectangle with the narrow gable end towards the lane, the front of the house facing on to the 'street' and the outhouses opposite. Two small windows from the kitchen looked on to this 'street', and it was these that gave the first indica-tion that this was a slightly unusual household, for each window was draped with two spotless net curtains, and in the middle of each stood a pot with a flourishing geranium. The curtains and the pot plants were indications and symbols of the determination of Mrs. McKinley to maintain decent standards however trying the con-ditions under which she had to work. Her children had mainly left home but she still had there her eldest son, Michael, in his mid-thirties, and she was also looking after two grandchildren, a two-year old and one not quite a year old. As well as the children she often had young animals in her kitchen, young chicks or a weak piglet confined near the fire. She did quite a lot of work feeding stock in the yard and she seemed continually to be boiling potatoes for them as well as for humans. In the kitchen, typical of many farms in its plan, conditions could well have been squalid, but the house gave instead a well-cared-for impression.

The furniture in the kitchen was rather scanty. The usual deal table with chairs stood under the windows by the 'street' wall. Beyond stood, in the day-time, a baby's cot which acted in part as a kind of play-pen. Once there had been an open fire in the kitchen hearth, but now there was a black range with grate, water-boiler and single oven. Against each of the remaining two walls stood good-sized cupboards, one mainly for food, the other for china and kitchen utensils. Between them stood a small, square table under which was a large enamel washing-up basin, kept out of sight unless it was brought out to be used. On top of the table stood a wireless set. There were two armchairs in this kitchen.

What gave the room its air of relative prosperity was the fact that everything that could be dusted or polished was dusted or polished almost daily. Even the holy picture of the Sacred Heart on the wall seemed unusually well cared for, but what was really outstanding was the way in which the polished-brass fender shone, and the dust-free condition of the 'fire-board' with its two china King-Charles' spaniels. No-one in the circumstances could have kept the floor spotless, but its smooth cement surface was swept several times a day, and it was noticeable that when Michael came in he really made some effort to wipe his boots on the sack by the door. More-over, he left his dog outside. The half-door to the 'street' was barred against both dog and cat by Mrs. McKinley. She looked after these animals and saw that each got potatoes and a taste of milk regularly, but in her fight to keep squalor at bay muddy paw-marks seemed the last straw, and so she kept these animals out. What was even more significant was that at rushed seasons of the year, when most local women abandoned most ordinary house-work in their attempts to help their menfolk in the yard and in the work of the potato fields, Mrs. McKinley reacted in a way locally unheard-of. She got her sons up early enough to do their normal work in the yard before going off to the fields, or even to the Fair. Sometimes she had even roused them at 5 o'clock, although the normal hour for the hill farmer to get out of bed was about 8 o'clock. She did this because although she was willing to work hard she was not prepared to sacrifice her domestic standards to the livestock. (It was also noteworthy too that her son quite often fetched buckets of water for her, although this was usually considered a woman's task.) It was not only that Mrs. McKinley was not prepared to abandon her polishing and dusting at rushed seasons, cooking she also regarded as important. Potatoes were the staple in this house as in all the others in the neighbourhood, but to her it was important to 'eat well' and this meant that she put a higher value on meat and eggs than her neighbours. She had always tried to see that her sons had had something cooked for their tea after their day's work, or at least some cheese (a food that most people in the area totally ignored). Now she fussed over her grand-children, coddling eggs for them and patiently spending time in feeding them what she thought were the 'right' foods. She was in fact as busy as any of her neighbours but she made, and she had been in the position to make, an allocation of her time that was a little unusual for the district.

Paul Jamison's house (PD10)
A hill farm that contrasted with the McKinleys in a number of ways was that of the Presbytrian Jamisons. This household was definitely much more prosperous than the McKinleys and this fact exerted an influence on living standards. With the Jamisons standards of cleanliness were high and by comparison with some of the immediate neighbours they were a little extravagant on food, regularly eating eggs for breakfast, for example. Nevertheless there was not the marked difference in patterns of living that might have been anticipated, and the reasons, I suspect, was that the women of the house were local and had been brought up to accept local standards and the belief that a woman's place was in the farm-yard.

There were four people in this household, an elderly retired farmer, James (PB8), and his wife Elizabeth (PC10), and their son Paul and his wife Mary (PD19). Paul owned just over a hundred acres, of which forty acres were good land. The farmhouse was large for the district and lay only a stone's throw from the main road. Behind the house lay a range of substantial farm buildings, which were not converted dwelling houses but had been built as barns and byre. Most of the buildings dated from the end of the nineteenth century and when the house was first constructed it must have been particularly outstanding because it had been built with two storeys when almost every local dwelling had had only one storey, and it had been roofed with slates when most neighbour-ing houses were thatched.

The rooms of the house were outstanding for the area in their number and their size. There was a very large kitchen, about 20 feet long by 15 feet wide, and in addition a large separate scullery where all the work of washing-up and some of the preparation of food was done. From the kitchen a door led into a broad hall, lit through windows on either side of the front door of the house, that faced the road. On one side of the hall lay a dining-room, and on the other a sitting-room, and from the front of the hall stairs led up to the bedrooms. These were large, airy rooms, four in number, each with lino on the floor, and each fitted with a double bed, wardrobe, chest of drawers and a wash-stand with a full set of bedroom china.

Despite these particularly prosperous features no water was laid on to the house, nor was there much talk of having it laid on, although grants towards the cost of piping the water and providing indoor sanitation were available. The men remained quite content with more traditional arrangements. One of the bedrooms was unused and here there was a zinc bath-tub in which baths were taken on Saturdays. On the field side of the outbuildings was a privy; it was never, so far as I know, cleaned out or disinfected, but a small stream that ran in a little gully through the back of the hut was supposed to do the job, and indeed the possession of this privy was something of a prestige symbol.

Moreover, although the house was relatively large it was used in much the same way as most others in the area. Great pride was taken in the fact that instead of the traditional 'half-door' leading from the farmyard, which was the only entrance to most cottages, this house had a good, solid front door with a brass letter-slit and a knocker. In fact, nevertheless, this door was only used for funerals and weddings or visitors of incredible importance (and almost directly in front of it and only a few yards away was the big midden). In practice virtually everyone who came to the house came through the farmyard and entered the kitchen by the back door. Very few visitors indeed ever penetrated beyond the kitchen, for the sitting- and dining-rooms were used only on very formal or festive occasions. At Christmas-time or when the Minister was expected a fire would be lighted in the sitting-room. Then people would stand on the small hearth-rug, which was like an island on the lino-covered floor, or sit on the brown and upholstered green Chesterfield suite which was the family's pride. But normally all social life took place in the kitchen.

The kitchen had some features that testified to the relative affluence of the family. The main sign of this was the fact that there was electric light here, as there was in the sitting- and dining-rooms, for Paul owned an electric generator that he ran each evening. He used it for farm jobs, for example he ran his small grass-thresher from it, and he planned to use it more extensively in the future, but its main task was to supply light to the house. Other signs of affluence in the kitchen were the existence of two armchairs instead of one, and a long mahogany-backed sofa, of black leatherette stuffed with horse-hair. Most of the furniture in the room and its arrangement was, however, standard for the area. There was a black, twin-ovened range, which burnt turf from a great peat-stack which was built every autumn in the yard. On the 'fire-board' above the range stood the clock, flanked by ornamental trays and tea caddies, which were coronation souvenirs. A fender guarded the range, and by the fender stood a huge basket for hold-ing turf. The armchairs stood either side of the hearth, the sofa was placed along the internal wall of the kitchen, and in the traditional place a long deal table stood under the window that looked out on the yard, and it was only very seldom that the table was moved away from the wall to allow someone to sit on that side. Seating arrangements were formal: before the father had retired he had sat at one end and his wife at the other: now that Paul had taken over the farm it was he who sat opposite his father.

It would have been a great help to the women had water been laid on to the house. It was not far away since it had been led from a near-by spring to a barrel in the yard. This was a considerable advantage as compared, say, with the McKinley household, but it still meant that all water had to be carried by buckets across the yard, and it was carried by the women. This was important because a lot of water was needed: for boiling potatoes, which seemed to be always on the range, and were used extensively for humans and for farm stock; and the water was also needed for keeping the kitchen clean. The kitchen on this prosperous farm was inevitably an extremely busy place and therefore it got continuously dirty. The range always needed a good fire, and the white ash from the turf flew round the room in the draught caused by the opening of the outer door. The women and the men, visiting men as well as the men of the family, and their accompanying dogs traipsed in and out from the often muddy farmyard, and although a sack was placed hopefully by the door it did little to keep the mud out-side, especially as the men often ignored its existence. Every dinner time they sat with mud on their boots, and whenever the men smoked their pipes they spat on the floor—indeed it was clear from what they sometimes said that it was a puzzle to them to know how anyone could smoke a pipe without spitting.

With all this mess the women battled, but only when they could spare time from their own farm duties of helping with the milking and the feeding of the yard stock and the poultry. The floor of the kitchen was washed down at least once or twice a day, and the whole room was frequently dusted. Here, as in the McKinley household, it was possible to sit on a soft chair without picking up fleas. Other housework was done but it had to take a subordinate place because the women were kept so busy with their farm work. They kept pace with the housework by doing something at least fairly systematically. On Mondays, or Tuesdays at the latest, clothes were first boiled on the range and then put through an old wooden mangle in an outhouse. Friday was the day for baking and this household prided itself on its home-made soda-bread and apple cake, a kind of pie eaten for tea on Sundays. On very special occasions the women baked sponges. Normally, however, cooking occupied the least possible time and the almost unchanging midday meal consisted of stewed meat with cabbage and potatoes or bacon and egg with cabbage and potatoes. Saturdays, in preparation for the Sabbath, was the day for intensive household cleaning, when mother-in-law and daughter-in-law spent almost all the morning and much of the afternoon in dusting and polishing the rooms other than the kitchen.

Albert Baxter's house (PB15)

As an example of the household of a sophisticated, externally oriented family, I shall take that of the Baxters, who lived in the infield and were members of the Church of Ireland. The family consisted of the husband and wife (PC20) in their sixties and their young son Keith (PD30) who was in his early twenties. A daughter had recently married and left home. I had no reason to suppose that the family income was exceptionally high. The farm was just over a hundred acres, most of it reasonably good land, but it was subject to a mortgage; and as the father was not very robust and the son still somewhat inexperienced the cost of labour and some ill-judged experiments kept the farm from being as prosperous as it should have been. Nevertheless the standard of living was exceptionally high and the key to this seemed to be mainly the background of the wife.

Mrs. Baxter had been brought up in a rural rectory near Dublin.

She had trained as a nurse and had eventually become a Sister at a big Dublin hospital, where she had met her future husband. When on marriage she had found herself in the rural backwater of Ballybeg she had striven consciously to raise the standards of her new home. In this she had had the backing of her husband largely, I think, because, as will be explained later, several of his brothers and sisters had married sophisticated outsiders and their opinions, when they made family visits, mattered to him.

The Baxters' house, slightly larger than that of the Jamisons, dated mostly from the middle of the nineteenth century, although parts of it were older and there were odd passages and changes of levels that bore witness to the different additions that had been made to it. The house stood by a tarred lane which led, after three-quarters of a mile of twists and turns, on to the main road. Significantly Mrs. Baxter was sure that it was the spate of letters that she had written to the Council, complaining about the lane, that had led to its being tarred. From the outside the most striking difference between this house and most others, even of similar size, in the area, was that the entrance that led round to the front door lay through a proper garden, with a lawn and apple trees and rose bushes. Apart from the mowing of the grass, that was done by the son, Mrs. Baxter did all the work of the garden.

The Baxters used their front door rather more frequently than the Jamisons used theirs, but even so most people came round through the farm buildings to the kitchen door. Here there was a difference immediately apparent, for stone flags had been set outside the door and a boot-scraper had been cemented in and from the kitchen wall jutted out a tap for the cleaning of muddy boots. The boots themselves were normally, as a matter of course, taken off and left in the porch which protected the main kitchen door. The kitchen itself, slightly smaller than that of the Jamisons, stood out at once both because the stone-flagged floor was covered with coconut matting, and because of the lightness of its white painted walls and furniture. This lightness was emphasised by the fact that instead of the normal black range there was a large, white-enamelled Aga cooker, which not only provided four ovens but also heated the hot water for the household. There were only wooden chairs in the kitchen but these had gaily-coloured cushions tied to them. Against one wall a large, glass-doored dresser displayed china, and by another wall a large linen press held both table-linen and bed-linen, since this was the warmest room in the house.

Significantly the kitchen had two tables, a big round one for the family and a small one for any labourers who might be working.

What was particularly different about this household, and the reason for the absence of soft chairs from the kitchen, was that evening meals were eaten in the dining-room, which also served as the room in which the family relaxed. Here a turf fire was lit almost every day. There was a Wilton carpet, three smallish arm-chairs, and a slightly old-fashioned dining-room suite, with sherry in the sideboard for visitors. Over the Victorian caste-iron fireplace was a large water-colour of part of the Ulster coastline, and on the mantel-piece were family photographs. By one side of the hearth was a small book-case with a number of books, and a magazine rack for the *Radio Times,* the *Farmer and Stock-breeder,* and the *Woman's Weekly.* Near it was a stand for the wireless set. In the summer there was usually a bowl of flowers on the table. The room was far from being lavishly luxurious—the carpet was getting a little thin in places, the upholstery on the armchairs was a little worn, and Mrs. Baxter was worrying about renewing the old velvet curtains. But the very fact that the room was so well used indicated a way of life different from that of the Jamisons.

The Baxters too had their ceremonial room, the sitting-room. This was much less used, although they often sat here on Sunday afternoons even when there were no visitors. Here there was a Chinese carpet, carefully shielded from the sun on bright days, a three-piece bergere suite, with damask cushions, and a rather nice china display cabinet full of little figures, and odd plates from places like Bruges. A nest of coffee tables and a few odd small chairs were placed around the room. On the walls were a large, old-fashioned engraving of sailing ships in Dublin Bay, and a big framed photograph of Mrs. Baxter's Rector father. On the white-marble fire-place were large photographs of the daughter's wedding.

Upstairs there were four bedrooms, and what had once been the maid's bedroom had been converted into a bathroom and w.c. Damp had affected the ceilings in a couple of the bedrooms, the family fought a continuous war to prevent it getting in whenever a few of the old slates fell off in winter gales; but the bedrooms were comfortable with carpets and modern beds, and the room kept as the guest bedroom was particularly comfortable.

For the comfort of the house Mrs. Baxter was directly respon-sible, and she considered it her main responsibility. She did not divorce herself entirely from what went on in the farmyard. She had never grown to like hens, but she helped to manage the farm flock, which was kept in the 'deep-litter' system. Often in the evenings she spent a long time egg-cleaning. Nevertheless the house was her main concern, and she had persuaded her husband to install an old range in an out-building so that most of the preparation of food for the livestock could be done out there. To help her in the house she had a local woman who came in three mornings a week, but Mrs. Baxter herself spent a lot of her time on actual house-work, and she did all the cooking herself. For a woman in her sixties she led an extremely busy life.[1]

I have emphasised the role of women in determining the living standards of their families because I want to stress that income alone, and even income and place of residence together, were not the sole determinants of life-styles. Nevertheless location and income taken together were major factors in helping to decide people's patterns of living. This fact was important because despite the kind of individual variation just outlined most of the labourers and the poorer farmers had the lower standards of living described, and a majority of these people were Catholic; most of those with the better standards of living were Protestant. These facts, despite the great overlap in living standards that could be detected by an outsider, entered into the stereotypes that members of the two religious groups held about each other.

[1] It is difficult to find a really suitable term to apply to families of the Baxters' type. They were amongst the most sophisticated people in the area and mixed with outside professionals as social equals. The problem of finding the right term to describe them becomes apparent if Ballybeg is compared with 'Westrigg' (Littlejohn, 1964) a Scottish rural area in some respects akin to Ballybeg. For Westrigg Littlejohn distinguished upper middle-class 'gentlemen farmers' who owned 53 per cent of the parish with holdings of more than 6,000 acres, and lower middle-class 'working farmers'. The Baxters and those like them were clearly not 'gentlemen-farmers' in Littlejohn's sense; yet neither were they like his subordinate 'working farmers' since one of the important characteristics of those like the Baxters was that they knew no local social superiors and they judged their own social worth and responsibilities accordingly. It seems, therefore, preferable to avoid class terminology, and I refer to the Ballybeg Baxter-type family as 'yeomen'.

4 The common culture: relationships within the household

Despite the considerable variation in living standards depicted in the last chapter every farm in the area of Ballybeg was, by English standards, a small farm, for not one was over 150 acres. Not surprisingly at every level, even amongst the relatively prosperous, the pressures and the influences of the facts of small-farm life were felt by both Catholic and Protestant. This could be seen most clearly in family relationships and it is the influence of the farm organisation on these that I now want to examine. To avoid the possibility of exaggerating the situation I shall give a number of examples of households, chosen in such a way as to avoid distorting my material. To do this, I will describe further the household relationships of the three families already described, together with those of the households most closely associated with these three by neighbourhood and kinship.

Michael McKinley's household (CD27)
The household of Michael McKinley gives a good example of the structure of the family based on the very small 'mountainy' farm. Michael's father, Patrick (CC12), had been the son of a local farmer, himself from a small mountain farm, and most of Michael's father's siblings had emigrated to the United States. The father had gone to Glasgow looking for work, and it was there that he had met and married Michael's mother (CC13). It was her Scots' background that played a significant part in her housekeeping. Michael's father, having no special skills, had been dissatisfied with the work he could get in Glasgow, and shortly after his marriage he decided to return to Ballybeg where he was able to buy a small farm with his savings. Three boys and a girl were born, but it was not many years

before the father died. Michael, the eldest child, was then about twelve, and it was under Mrs. McKinley's strong-minded direction that the family had coped with a difficult situation, and the farm had continued to run and had gradually become quite prosperous for its size. This was the background to the authority she had wielded over her sons, her ability to get them up early in the morning, and most significantly her ability to organise the work of the farm in such a way as to leave her time for her housekeeping.

There was thus a direct relation between Mrs. McKinley's authority and the well-kept appearance of her home. There was also a relation between this authority and the predicament in which Michael now found himself. Mrs. McKinley had not cowed her sons; on the contrary it seemed that all her children were energetic and hard-working and those who had left home were doing quite well in the locality. Michael had stayed at home because as the eldest boy he had inherited the farm on his father's early death. He and his mother were running it quite efficiently, she looking after the profitable poultry and he after most of the rest of it, and they got on well together, for she was a good-tempered, kindly soul. Nevertheless Michael was already in his mid-thirties, and it was difficult to see how he could marry. Any woman he married would, as a farmer's wife, want to control the house and run the poultry, but Mrs. McKinley did not look as if she would be ready to give up either for some years, and Michael could scarcely try to remove her forcibly. The consequence was that he was not courting any girl seriously and it looked as if he were destined to be one of the districts many permanent bachelors.

Andy Stuart's household (PC100)
The Stuarts were the nearest neighbours of the McKinleys, and although the McKinleys were Catholics and the Stuarts were Church of Ireland they were good friends, as we shall see later. The Stuarts owned a similar small farm, and Andy Stuart's history probably foreshadowed that of Michael. The Stuart family consisted of brother and sister, Andy and Nelly, unmarried in their late fifties. Their mother had come from one of the other Protestant farms in the neighbourhood and had married, against her parents' wishes, a first cousin whose home was one of the smaller infield farms. Immediately on marriage she had moved down to her husband's family, although his father had not retired. For a while

she and her husband had lived in a dependent status in his home, but quarrels between him and his father had decided them to move back to the hill district where, because of the cheapness of the land, her husband had just been able to afford to buy a small farm. There had been several children of the marriage, but one by one most had left home. Two sons moved out and married locally, but Andy, remaining to help his parents, had been unable to get married. Nelly herself had left home and had worked in a hospital near Belfast. Eventually the father died and the mother became seriously ill, and Nelly had felt bound to return to nurse her mother in what proved to be her last illness. When the mother died Nelly felt too sorry for Andy to leave him on his own, and, against what she said were her own wishes, she had decided not to return to her old job but to remain with him on the farm. Everyone assumed that neither would now marry as they were past their youth and were able between them to cope with the man's and the woman's side of farming; why should they bother to marry?

Brian McFadden's household (CD8)
A second neighbouring household, very frequently visited by Michael McKinley (CD27), was that of another Catholic family, the McFaddens. The McFadden household consisted of Brian and his wife (CD2) and elder brother Tom (CD4), a bachelor. To understand this family it is essential again to know something of the history of the parents. Here, in contrast to the McKinley family, the father had lived to a good age after a late marriage. In fact the parents had married when the husband was in his late thirties and the wife in her early thirties. They had had five children and the parents had lived into their seventies. Tom, the eldest son, had taken his responsibilities seriously, feeling under an obligation to help his increasingly frail father. As a young man, in order to be able to earn some money for himself by rearing cattle, he had put savings he had made on a little cattle dealing into the purchase of a small local farm, but he had never felt free to take his independence and to marry. Instead he had stayed at home. At home he could not marry because his mother was still alive and in charge of the domestic side of the farm; moreover, his prospects were dim since the father had let it be known that he intended to give his land to his youngest son. In the end the youngest son Brian, who had been twenty-three when his father died, and twenty-eight when his mother died, did take over the farm and had married almost

immediately after his mother's death. There had been no conflict between him and his older brother, and although space was cramped after the birth of several children, it was accepted as natural that Tom should remain as a member of the household.

Peter O'Hanlin's household (CD14)

A somewhat similar family occupied the third farm at which Michael McKinley (CD27) was a very regular visitor, that of the Catholic O'Hanlins. Here the family consisted of an older brother Peter and his wife and children and an unmarried younger brother, Dan (CD15). Though the father had been primarily a mason and not a farmer he had owned a smallholding of five acres and the house that went with it, and his wife kept poultry in the same way as the wives of farmers. Because there was this inheritance of house and land the lives of his sons seemed to have been, at least to some extent, influenced by it. The parents of the present O'Hanlin brothers, Peter and Dan, were not from the immediate locality but had settled on this little, mountainy farm because it was cheap and near the main road. As a mason the father sought work all over the place and it did not matter to him greatly where he lived. There had been five children, three sons and two daughters. The eldest son, Micky (CD13), had learned his father's trade, and with the mobility that this gave him, he had been able to find a small house in Ballybeg itself and had married and settled down there before his father died. At the father's death the two daughters were already married to farmers in the district. When the mother also died a few years after the father, Peter, who had become a lorry driver, being without a woman in the house, soon married the girl he had been courting, the daughter of a neighbouring farmer who lived about half a mile away. Dan, the youngest boy, was still in his early twenties and, not yet married, he remained in his old home. Indeed, the farm had been left to Peter with the express provision that Dan should be allowed to remain until he got married. Dan, like his eldest brother, was a mason working under more senior men at various jobs round the countryside— usually indeed he worked with his mason brother. It seemed probable that the fact that he had this trade in his hands meant that when he wanted to he too would look for a cheap house and be able to marry without any difficulty. For the moment he was, however, enjoying his status as an eligible bachelor.

The contrast between the ease with which an unmarried man

could fit into a married brother's household, and the difficulties of an unmarried woman in such circumstances, was brought home to me by the attitudes shown in the house from which Peter O'Hanlin's wife Teresa (CD17) had come, a farm only a very short distance from the O'Hanlins'. Here there was as yet no difficulty but it was foreseen. Teresa's parents were both dead, the mother having died quite recently, and in charge of the farm was Teresa's brother, Kevin Whitelock (CD18), a man in his mid-twenties. Living with him was his *de facto* sister, actually a cousin who had been brought up in the family since birth when her own mother had died. This girl, Margaret (CE3), was nineteen and she most competently scrubbed and baked, looked after the family poultry and did the milking and the feeding round the farmyard. Kevin was busily courting a farmer's daughter, and although he was not yet engaged everyone expected that his engagement would soon be announced. It was significant, therefore, that Margaret assured me emphatically, and without seeming resentment, that the day Kevin did get married she would leave the farm—it would be quite impossible and improper for two sisters-in-law to live in the same household since there was bound to be friction between them over the running of the home and the hens. Interestingly Kevin's courtship attracted some slight resentment from the neighbours—on at least two occasions neighbouring boys drove his cattle over to the farm of his girl friend, giving him, they said, an excuse to go over to pay her another visit. I suspect that because Margaret was a local favourite people, almost without realising it, resented Kevin's courtship that would eventually drive her away. The fact remained that everyone to whom I mentioned the matter was quite sure that her plan to leave the farm was absolutely right. At least on a small farm wife and husband's sister could not remain together.

Having looked at the (predominantly Catholic) circle of small farms round the McKinleys I want to examine similarly the immediate associates of the Jamison family described earlier. In this case the household of Paul Jamison himself is particularly instructive, but the circumstances are complex, and I shall there-fore begin with others in his circle, made up of the three Protestant households with whom he regularly co-operated.

Campbell Wright's household (PC5)
The poorest of these farms, one having only fifteen acres of 'arable'

land, was owned by Campbell Wright. Not unexpectedly this was again a brother and sister household, Campbell being in his late sixties, and his sister ten years younger. They had had a number of brothers and sisters and since the farm was so small, they had all, when young, worked as hired help on the farms of the more prosperous infield farmers. Eventually, one by one, they had for the most part emigrated. Campbell himself and his sister, Mrs. Scott (PC4), had worked as labourer and maid respectively at a farm belonging to a Presbyterian farmer, Jim Davidson (PB19), near Ballybeg where they had 'lived in' in the farm house. Besides Campbell only one brother had remained in the district, and he had saved up enough money to buy a small infield farm. Campbell, however, when the last of his younger brothers left for America, in duty bound returned to help his parents and eventually took over the farm. There was no room for him to bring a wife to the small farmhouse that his mother still ran, and by the time she died Campbell had ceased to be very interested in getting married. After a short period on his own he was rescued from isolation and bachelor-catering by the return of his sister from America. She had been married out there to an Ulsterman, but her marriage had broken up and she had returned home with her two daughters, one of whom had since gone to work in Belfast.

Campbell Wright's household provided another example of a family in which the living standards were markedly higher than might have been expected from its income alone. This was because the sister, Mrs. Scott, first as a maid locally and then by her experience in the States, had learned household practices she tried to keep up against all odds. By hard work and ingenuity, and because she did not have to do all the yard-work that would have fallen to her lot had the farm been a busy and prosperous one, Mrs. Scott kept the house spotless and forced a tiny income to produce a diet richer in proteins than that of many farmers far better off.

The household was unusual in one other respect. Campbell was a member of the Church of Ireland, and Mrs. Scott had of course been brought up in the same denomination, but on marriage she had become a Presbyterian, because it was almost invariable for Protestant women who married men of a different denomination to change to their husband's church. This was the right and proper thing for them to do—it was not a matter for individual choice. What was remarkable was that the rule was so strongly held that despite the fact that Mrs. Scott said that she preferred the Church of Ireland service and despite her separation from her husband, she continued to take her daughters to the Presbyterian Church.

Bill Jamison's household (PD23)
The second farm with which Paul Jamison was closely associated was that of his cousin, Bill Jamison, who lived adjacent to Campbell Wright. This was an interesting household since it illustrated clearly the way in which small farms on the fringes of the 'mountainy' region could provide refuges of a kind for those from the more prosperous lowlands who were down on their luck but had no wish to emigrate. Bill Jamison's career is best understood in terms of his position in his father's family. His father William (PB9), Paul Jamison's father's brother, was a fairly prosperous man with a medium-sized infield farm. There were five children in this man's family, four boys and a girl. The youngest boy, Andy (PD27), was regarded as 'a bit simple', and as the father had thought him incapable of farming independently he was provided for in other ways. The father William was, therefore, concerned primarily with his other three sons and his daughter, and because he was relatively prosperous and the boys did not wish to leave the district he had sought to cater for them locally. William did not think that Bill, his eldest son, was cut out to be a farmer, and thought his best prospects lay in becoming an agricultural contractor, working with his own tractor and thresher on other people's farms. The second son, Robert (PD24), the father intended to place on a 'side farm' that he had bought, and the third son, John (PD25), was to get the family farm.

It had been intended that Bill should, for a while, continue to work from his family home. When he showed an obstinate determination to get married, however, temporarily he took over the house belonging to the side farm. At least he had been able to get married and he achieved a certain independence as master of his own house. Before long, though, his younger brother who worked the farm land wanted in his turn to get married, and Bill and his wife Ellen (PD28) had to move to another small, unused farmhouse (with the rate of emigration from the district it was not difficult to find a small dwelling). After a while, Bill became discouraged with lack of any great success in his contracting work and he sold his machinery and used his skill to get a job as a lorry driver. But it was not long before this job seemed tedious and unrewarding. Then his father retired, and Bill had another chance because of the provisions his father made. William made legally sure that three rooms in the large family farmhouse were reserved for him and his wife and the youngest boy, but as well as this the son John who took over the rest of the house and the farm was made to give each of his siblings a certain amount of money. Bill and his other brother did not get a great deal since they had already been helped financially by the father; indeed their sister Amy (PD26), who had recently got married, received rather more. Nevertheless with the money Bill did get and something he had managed to save from the sale of his machinery he was able to buy a small hill farm with twenty-five 'arable acres' plus rough pasture and bog, a farm which had the advantage of being not too far from his own family and quite near that of his cousin Paul (PD10). The move to the attached small cottage, with its primitive conditions, was, not surprisingly, regarded as being particularly hard on Bill's wife. She was in fact a niece of Albert Baxter (PB15), whose household has already been described, and before her marriage she had been used to a considerable degree of comfort in her home. To move up to this small farm with three young children was exceedingly difficult for her and she was still learning how to cope with her new situation.

Fred Richards' household (PD5)
The third house with which Paul was associated was that of Fred Richards, his neighbour and brother-in-law, the husband of his sister Rose (PD8). Fred's family had been associated with this farm for a hundred years, since it was in the 1860's that his great-grandfather had moved there from the lowlands; another case of a man without much money seeking a farm that was cheap. The farm was now fairly prosperous, with thirty-five acres of good land as well as grazing and bog. Its one disadvantage was that it lay down an unmetalled track a long way from the main road. Fred's position was different from any of those farmers who have so far been considered, for he was the only son of a late marriage, and his one sister, very intelligent as was Fred himself, had gone on to further education, which meant that she had had to leave the district whilst still in her teens, and she had never returned to it except for short visits, having got an excellent post in England. Both their parents had died whilst Fred was still in his mid-twenties. There had been no-one to stop Fred from getting married, nor had he had to mortgage his farm to pay his siblings their share when he took it over. Perhaps even more important, he had not

had to work for years as an unpaid helper under his father. Most sons who worked on their father's farm in fact received a mere pittance and, whatever the farm work they did, they had to rely for money on the odd bit of cattle dealing they were able to do. Significantly, of all the 'mountain' farmers I knew, Fred was the least interested in attending cattle fairs, though these were eagerly visited by most of the other men, whether or not they had animals for sale. This characteristic and certain aspects of his pattern of neighbourhood contacts, which will be discussed later, suggest the influence on his life of the fact that he had come early and easily into his small inheritance, and that even as a young man he had been master in his own house. To his wife Rose and their two children he was devoted, and he was more of a family man and less 'one of the boys' than any other farmer in that hill district—and this was not just my own opinion but that of the men and women who knew him best. The women thought him the model of the ideal husband, while the men would have mocked him had they not respected him for other reasons.

Paul Jamison's household (PD10)

The hill farmhouse owned by Paul Jamison has already been described and there it was stressed that the farm was very prosperous. The family as we saw consisted of Paul and his wife and his father and mother. The father James (PB8), now an invalid, had not been born in this house but down at the family farm in the infield where his brother William (PB9) still lived. James, the elder of the brothers, had as a young man been unwilling to remain at home completely dependent on his father, and had scraped together enough money to buy a small cheap farm about ten miles away from Ballybeg where he had lived, sometimes helped by a sister. As soon as he had enough money he had sold it and had moved back still to a 'mountainy' farm but to a larger and better one. At his stage he seemed to have hoped that he might eventually inherit the family farm. Indeed it was with this expectation that he married his wife, Elizabeth Richards (PC10), fifteen years his junior, and the daughter of a neighbouring farmer. In the end his hopes of being given his father's farm had been dashed; it had gone to his brother William and James remained on his 'mountainy' farm for the rest of his life. His wife had been bitterly disappointed and had blamed William for going behind her husband's back. The quarrel between their generation of the two families had never been fully healed, although their children were now quite friendly.

That disappointment apart, the marriage of James and Elizabeth had been in most ways very successful. They had had a large healthy family of three boys and four girls, all of whom were now married, most locally. All the girls had married respectable farmers within a radius of eight miles and the boys had done quite well. The eldest son, Henry (PD7), who was also the oldest of the family, had not wanted to remain at home dependent on his father, and he now had been helped to buy a small shop in the local big town. The youngest son, Tom (PD12), had been apprenticed as a mechanic in Belfast and he had a reasonable hope of soon acquiring his own small business. It was the middle son, Paul, who had taken over the family farm. The actual history of the processes by which Paul had acquired the right to marry, and control of the farm, illustrates all too clearly the problems associated with the transmission of property between the generations, problems that relative prosperity in some ways seemed to accentuate. Family relationships in the household were now under considerable strain, due partly to the characteristics of the individuals concerned, but much more to the situation in which they found themselves, over which, as individuals, they had very little control.

In the first place Paul had reason to feel somewhat resentful both against his father and against his brothers and sisters. He had been the one who had always stayed at home and helped his father. Whilst the two other brothers had gone off to earn money, Paul had had for years to make do either on small sums of money his father had chosen to give him, or on the occasional profit he was able to make from dealing a little in cattle on his own account. He had lived in fact as a dependant virtually without a wage. At last his father had agreed to let him marry and bring his wife home to their relatively large house but, although James was then nearly seventy, he had refused to hand the farm over to Paul, and Paul remained for another two years a married man but almost a pauper. At last, after many arguments and even quarrels, James did agree to transfer the farm but only at a price: each of Paul's brothers and sisters had to be given £250. Paul had accepted this as the right and proper thing, but nevertheless he resented the fact that in order to give them this money he had had to mortgage the farm and was now burdened with the repayments. This tax on him came at a time when he could ill afford it, since very soon after the farm was handed over his father suffered a stroke which effectively prevented him from doing any further work. Paul, therefore, had to employ a labourer regularly throughout the year at £3 a week and most meals, as well as an extra man at rushed seasons.

Paul's prospects were made the bleaker by the fact that his wife Mary (PD19) was childless and was likely to remain so. Much as he and his wife both wanted children, adoption was out of the question for them, for the whole countryside would have laughed at them for bringing in a stranger's bastard as an heir to such a farm and their relatives would have been outraged. Paul could therefore not look forward to any future slackening of the financial burdens of paying for labour.

The absence of children made more difficult the relationship between Paul's mother Elizabeth (PC10) and his wife, but the circumstances were such that it would have been a tense one in any case. Paul's mother was fifteen years younger than old James, and although he had been physically ready to retire for a year or so before he actually handed the farm over, Elizabeth was still an active, intelligent woman not yet sixty and it was she who had prevented her husband from retiring previously. This was very understandable since she was bound to suffer very much as a result of it. In the first place, the house as well as the farm had to be handed over. Had they saved enough money to have enabled them to have built a bungalow on the land things would have been better, but all their savings were put into the farm and all that the parents had legally reserved for themselves was their bedroom. On her husband's retirement, therefore, the mother-in-law had seen her home handed over to her daughter-in-law. Moreover, Paul's mother had been forced independently to hand the farm fowls over to her daughter-in-law.

On the farm there were about 250 free-range hens, plus young ones not yet laying, all kept in groups of fifty, and small flocks of ducks, geese and turkeys. Looking after the fowls took up a lot of the women's day. Their first task was to let them out and feed them, and they had to get them back in at night, always a particularly difficult job with the turkeys which never learnt any routine. Feeding the birds, watering them, giving them grit, picking up the eggs and cleaning them were daily chores which always took a good many hours. This was women's work essentially, and neither Paul nor his labourers ever dreamt of giving a hand in it. Once Mary did ask Jim Thompson (PC103), the hired man, to help her and he was furiously indignant—locally any male over about thirteen or fourteen would have considered himself insulted by such a request. The farmer's wife was therefore associated with the fowls very closely and for this reason alone would have found it hard to transfer responsibility for them to anyone else, but to understand the full significance of the demand made on Elizabeth after her husband's retirement we must look in even more detail at what these birds meant to the women.

The fowls were, in one sense, part of the farm stock, an integral part of the total farm economy and everyone agreed that no farm could be a paying proposition without them. Although they made a contribution to the running of the farm as a whole, however, it was the women who received any money from them. Virtually the whole of a woman's income came from selling eggs and birds. With this money, she bought food and clothes for her family, purchased household equipment and furniture and from time to time helped her husband pay his bills for feeding-stuffs for the other livestock. Ideally she coped almost entirely with the household's consumer demands, except her husband's clothes, whilst the man of the farm used any profit he made to reinvest in the farm in the form of more animals, machinery or land. In practice the woman was expected to manage almost entirely on her earnings from the hens and she received almost no other money for any purpose from the man. It is understandable, therefore, that Elizabeth should have put off as long as possible the day when she handed over the birds to her daughter-in-law Mary, as it was equally understandable that Mary was frustrated and dissatisfied until she got them.

Elizabeth had put off the evil day for two years after her husband's retirement, an unusual length of time. During this period Mary was in a very difficult position. She was a farmer's wife and titularly the mistress of the house but without the ability to make purchases for the family which were still done by her mother-in-law. Mary had in fact been very badly off financially ever since her marriage. Before it she had earned a little for herself as an assistant nurse in the County Town; after her marriage she worked —and that she worked hard all admitted—for her keep alone. For the first two years of her marriage Paul had no money even for himself, and even after the farm was handed over to him he gave her none. Indeed, it seemed not to have occurred to anyone that he was under any obligation to give her any cash, for in their experience farmers never did give housekeeping money to their wives. The result was that throughout this time if she needed any money for herself, to buy clothes for instance, she had to beg it from her father. This Mary found the more galling since she was well aware that her mother-in-law was spending much of the money she got from the hens on Paul's younger sisters still living at home, who were courting and spending more on themselves than they would ever again in their lives.

From Elizabeth's view-point, however, this was the last chance she would ever have to spend money she could call her own. She knew, as everyone knew, that before long she would have to hand over the birds, for there was no question of there being two flocks of poultry on one farm; she had built up the flocks but she had started from a nucleus which had been on the farm when she married into it. She stalled, in fact, until her youngest daughter was safely married and no longer needed money to spend on such things as going to the hairdressers. Even then she capitulated only in the face of a bitter quarrel with Paul, who was driven to demand the transfer from his mother by Mary's threat to leave him. It was then Elizabeth's turn to be penniless apart from what little money she had managed to put by, for she was too young to get a pension, and old James did not expect to share any of his with her.

Mother-in-law and daughter-in-law did their best not to quarrel openly, for in very different ways they were both well intentioned, hard-working women and each understood the position of the other, whilst feeling her own problems keenly. Nevertheless the strain between them was often great and the tensions were obvious to all. When Elizabeth, at Christmas time, killed a few chickens to send to her relatives in England as she always had done, without asking Mary's permission, Mary was silently furious, feeling the action as an affront and resenting the loss involved in gifts which were going to people better off than she and Paul were; although she was fair-minded enough to admit that the £10 she gave her mother-in-law at Christmas out of the sale of geese and turkeys was not enough for her year's work. Nevertheless it was significant that Mary, who in common with many others often saw misfortunes as Divine Judgement on wrongful behaviour, had many stories about the 'bad luck' that dogged the feet of those who treated their parents or parents-in-law badly; it was almost as if she needed to remind herself of these tales to make herself behave properly.

When we consider the enormous problems created by the presence of mother-in-law and daughter-in-law within the same household, it is not surprising that the son who is to take over the family land usually delays his marriage either until the death of his mother or until at least she is really willing to retire. It is not really essential to seek the explanation of this fact in particular psychological traits—the constraints are social and economic.

Albert Baxter's household (PB15)

The possession of a relatively valuable farm did not of course always lead to such problems linked to the transfer of property between the generations. Late marriage of the parents and the existence of only one or two siblings could make matters relatively simple. Such was the case with the Baxter family, whose house was earlier described. Old Albert Baxter had inherited his farm from his father. Malicious gossip locally maintained that Albert's father, George (PA), had risen from very poor beginnings; that as a boy the father had been sent merely to a 'hedge' school, not to the proper primary school because his family did not have the few pence needed to pay its fee. Albert's grandfather was said to have been a blacksmith and Albert's father was supposedly apprenticed to that trade. Whatever the truth of these statements, and they were in part undoubtedly due to the desire that the Baxters should be 'taken down a peg', Albert's father had certainly prospered. He had married the daughter of a schoolmaster at a grammar school in the market town. His three daughters had made socially excellent marriages: Jane (PB12) had married a baronet, Susan (PB11) a clergyman and Agatha (PB16) had married a very prosperous local shopkeeper, Nicholas Groves (PB17), now known, behind his back, to most people as Old Nick, but undoubtedly well off. There were four boys in the Baxter family. Fred (PB13) had become a doctor and practised nearby. Two of the sons, Morris (PB10) and Dick (PB14), had been helped to buy good substantial farms in the district, and Albert the youngest had eventually taken over the family farm and house. He had suffered some of the disadvantages already noted. He had not had initially to mortgage his farm to raise the cash to pay his brothers and sisters because the father had provided for them, but he had had to delay marrying until he was well into his forties and could take over the farm. Then he had married quickly. The farm had already been handed over to his only son, Keith, because Albert was already too old to be able to raise an essential mortgage on it.

Because of the different economy of the lowlands, with the

greater emphasis there on labour-saving machinery and the smaller significance of arable farming, Keith Baxter's (PD30) pattern of relationships differed from those of hill farmers. He neither co-operated very much with other farmers nor did he have that close relationship with his neighbours that found its expression in the hills in informal visiting, known as 'ceildhiing'. The one farmer with whom he worked quite regularly was his nearest neighbour, a young Catholic farmer of approximately the same age.

Jo McKinley's household (CD25)

This man was Jo McKinley. Jo's farm was smaller than the Baxters', being about forty acres all told; nevertheless his domestic position had a certain similarity. His father had married twice. The first wife had died in childbirth and Jo was the only child of the second marriage. His father had died comparatively young and Jo lived alone with his widowed mother (CB6), who was now in her seventies and not in good health. Their house had been of the old, small, single-storeyed type, but with his eye on matrimony Jo had applied for, and obtained, a government subsidy for house improvement. He had added a second storey to the original structure and a bathroom and internal sanitation had been installed (a condition for getting the subsidy). In Jo's case his mother was only too anxious to be relieved of household and farm chores which were really too heavy for her and she was propelling her son into marriage with all possible speed. Jo seemed to have some difficulty in making up his mind which girl to choose, for he was regarded as one of the most eligible young Catholic bachelors amongst the local farmers, and one of the most charming; he therefore had almost too much choice. Quite evidently, however, he was not going to be allowed to stay unmarried for very much longer.

Alec Laird's household (PC22)

The household closest to the Baxters' with which they had any kind of kin-based link was that of the Lairds, Mrs Laird being Albert Baxter's brother Dick's (PB14) niece by marriage. It was also the closest household that the Baxters regarded as their social equals. Mrs. Laird, indeed, had quite a close relationship with Mrs. Baxter; Mrs. Baxter drove and she and Mrs. Laird often went together to meetings of the Women's Institute in the nearby town of Kildrum. Albert Baxter and Alec Laird similarly tended to go together to meetings of the Farmers' Union.

Mrs. Laird had the most respectable of local connections. Her mother was a member of the Varley family, Church of Ireland people, without much money but with claims to aristocratic descent proved by two unusual possessions: a private burial ground, in which their relatives had to bury them or risk being haunted, and a banshee that wailed before any member of the family died. The first was visible to all and everyone believed in the latter. The family name had died out when the last Varley had only two daughters, one of whom married Dick Baxter. The other sister married an outsider, a farmer who came originally from Monaghan and settled in the area, buying a farm a stone's throw from his future wife's home. This man, Jim Davidson (PB19), a Presbyterian, was the farmer for whom Campbell Wright(PC5) and his sister had worked when young. There had been a number of Davidson children, three sons and four daughters. Of the daughters two married and left Northern Ireland, one, Marie (PD34), married Alec Black a local man and a cousin of one of Mrs. Mary Jamison's (PD19) cousins, and Betty (PD32), who was to become Mrs. Laird, remained at home unmarried. The father had intended his youngest son, James (PD33), to succeed him, and had provided for his two older sons by paying for them to be apprenticed to a reputable shopkeeper. They had long since left the district to set up in partnership as shopkeepers in a distant town. The boys, including James, had all been sent to nearby grammar schools. This probably was why James in the end did not take over the farm, for when the war came he volunteered and with his education he soon got a commission. After years as an army officer he found it impossible to settle down again to the rural backwater of a Ballybeg farm, and he went into business in England. Thus when her parents died Betty was left alone in charge of a very desirable farm and she soon married.

The Lairds seemed a very happy and contented couple, although their relationship both with each other and with outsiders appeared to be strongly influenced by the fact that the husband had married in. This was perhaps the more so since they had no children. It was noticeable that in the nicest possible way Betty tended to tell her husband what to do. 'We'll excuse you, Alec, if you want to turn the light out with the hens,' she suddenly said to him when we were all sitting and talking; an instruction to him that was particularly striking since most wives would not have dreamed of giving any kind of order to their husband, let alone

one connected with poultry. Other people often spoke about her almost as if she were still unmarried. Normally they were very strict in referring to all married women outside the immediate family as 'Mrs.——', but they often referred to Mrs. Laird as 'Betty Davidson' and then hastily corrected themselves.

Betty herself, without, I think, quite realising why she was acting differently, did not conform to the usual rules for Protestant married women with husbands of a different denomination. I have referred previously to the strictness with which women normally kept to this rule of attending the husband's church, but though Alec Laird was a member of the Church of Ireland Betty remained a Presbyterian like Jim Davidson her father. This had not passed unchallenged. She told me that in the week following the first Sunday after their wedding the Rector, an old friend of the family, had called to know, only half jocularly, why she had not been at his church the previous Sunday, but she had firmly snubbed him, telling him categorically that she had no intention of changing her allegiance. The Rector had appealed to Alec, who declined to try to argue with his wife. In fact she remained a most faithful Presbyterian. Amused gossip sometimes said that she kept going just because she was determined to maintain her right to lone occupation of the 'Davidson' family pew, and to keep out of it Old Nicholas Groves (PB17), who with his flourishing family of wife, son, daughter-in-law and grandchildren was squashed up in the 'Groves' family pew next door and casting expansionist eye on the 'Davidsons' '. (The fact that the Ballybeg Presbyterian church had abolished the system of paying pew rents many years previously had had no influence whatever on behaviour—each individual sat always in his or her family pew and trespass was a serious matter, the church seating arrangement giving concrete expression to the concept that a congregation was made up of family units, not unordered individuals.) This gossip, which implied slight criticism of her action, was significant just because it came from Presbyterians who might have been expected to support her stand. I have no doubt at all that had she married in to Alec Laird's farm in the usual way Betty would have been a normally conforming wife; that she was not was a measure of the lack of status of the in-marrying farmer.

II GENERALISATIONS ON THE FAMILY
Having now looked at a number of individual households in detail

it is possible to make generalisations about certain features of the family. I am not yet in a position to discuss all the relationships within the family because the most crucial, those between husbands and wives, and others of real significance, between adult brothers and brothers-in-law depended very much on the kind of relationships that the household had with those outside. Discussion of these patterns must therefore be delayed until we can look in more detail at the general system of links between a household and its neighbours and kinsfolk living elsewhere. Nevertheless some general statements can now be made.

The first thing that I want to emphasise is that within the elementary family relationships can be shown to depend less on religious adherence than on economic factors and on chance factors in the family history, that affected Catholics and Protestants apparently indiscriminately. If we look again at the structure of the households we have just examined we can see that crucial factors determining a man's life history are such things as whether or not he married and if so the age at which he married and the age at which he achieved financial independence. For farmers, whatever their religious persuasion, these matters were inextricably linked to the fact that there was a desire to inherit land, that almost all farmhouses were relatively small and unsuitable for two elementary families, that there was very seldom enough money to give other accommodation to retiring parents, and finally that the income of a farmer's wife was derived from her income from the sale of the products of the farm's poultry flock. Once this is acknowledged much that at first sight seems odd about the local family structure falls into place.

The man from a poor mountain farm was, other things being equal, more likely to remain unmarried than was the man from a better holding. Protestant Campbell Wright (PC5) and Andy Stuart (PC100), and Catholic Michael McKinley (CD27) and Tom McFadden (CD4) provided evidence for the kinds of pressure that could prevent marriage in such circumstances. Had relative wealth been the sole determinant of marital histories then, since the Catholic population was in general poorer than the Protestant, general differences between the family structures of the two religious groups would probably have been found. In practice, however, there were many factors operating to blur any such clear distinction. Such factors as the age at marriage of a man's parents, the age-gap between his father and his mother, the number of his siblings and his position in the birth order, the state of his parents' health and the ages to which his father and mother lived were all significant in influencing whether or not a man could acquire a farm and could marry at a reasonably early age. Mary Jamison's eldest brother Harry Christie (PD17) was a bachelor in his mid-thirties not because his father's farm was poor but because it was a good one that he had hopes of inheriting; but his father and mother had married young and were both living and his father, playing one son off against the other, would not retire. Fred Richards (PD5), the son of a poorer farmer, could get married early because he was the only son of parents who married late and died young. Michael McKinley (CD27) was kept from marriage because although he controlled his farm his mother was alive and active and the house was tiny; by contrast the young son of a nearby Protestant farmer was being hustled into matrimony because although both his parents were still alive and his father had no intention of retiring in his favour his mother had become incapacitated through arthritis, and his two sisters had already married and left home. The house was not very large but his parents were determined to make room for a wife for him; for as his mother said, her husband needed a woman about the house 'to look after the hens and to do the cooking and the washing'. A different kind of contrast to this household was provided by Paul Jamison's (PD10) family, for his marriage was in difficulties primarily because the comparative youthfulness of his mother made the relationship between her and her daughter-in-law almost intolerable. Given the basic economic background these kinds of contingent factors became crucial for family relationships.

Attitudes to children differed little between the religious groups. All farmers, whatever their faith, wanted children because their help was usually essential to the economic running of the farm; and the cost of children was very low since only a small minority of men spent much on their children for either their food, clothing or training. Moreover, money from family allowances made a welcome addition to the cash inflow of those who had only a very small monetary income. The allowances made little direct contribution to the standard of living of the children since most of it went ultimately to some kind of general farm expenditure; but these money subsidies were one reason why even some Protestant farmers showed very little sign of practising any form of birth control.

Children on all farms began to help from the time they were

about six. On the smaller farms particularly children rarely 'went to play' with any except their own brothers and sisters, partly because of the distances between the houses, but mostly because they were kept fairly busy at home. For the most part they appeared to enjoy the help they gave, for they were learning adult duties. Childhood was not sharply separated from adulthood; boys passed into their teens still anxious to learn more of adult farming techniques from their fathers and there was little sign of adolescent rebellion, although quarrels between father and sons in their late teens might develop over money. Pocket money was scarce and irregular even in sophisticated households; on the poorer farms children got little or nothing for the work they did, and for boys snaring rabbits was a favourite occupation just because it was one of their few ways of earning cash.

A man's relations with his daughters were always non-competitive and seldom difficult. If the daughters married locally they provided the father with useful sons-in-law and his relations with these men were usually good. A man's relations with his sons tended, by contrast, to become progressively more difficult once they reached their late teens.

A farmer's relations with his sons were influenced much more by economic considerations. The father owned property that in the normal course of events would be transmitted to a son *inter vivos*; but the father was free to select the succeeding son and could decide what, if anything, he should pay to his brothers and sisters when he succeeded. According to most people a father might choose any of his sons to succeed him; might, if it pleased him, select a son who had emigrated rather than one who had stayed behind to help him (Campbell Wright's brother John (PC3), when he died, had left his farm not to his son Eric (PD4), who had remained at home, but to one who had gone to the States, to whom rent for the farm was regularly sent). It was also said that a father was not under any obligation to make his intentions about succession known before the actual time when the farm was handed over on retirement or death. These were norms repeated to me by both Catholics and Protestants. In practice of course there were many constraints on a farmer's freedom of action.

In some families the choice of a succeeding son were made early because there were decisions about his education to be made; such decisions of course were mainly important to the more prosperous families. Keith Baxter (PD30) was an only son, but the decision

that he should become a farmer and not leave the land was nevertheless made during the course of his education, when his parents
removed him from school at sixteen to send him to an agricultural
college. More typically a nearby Church of Ireland farmer decided
which of his two sons should inherit when the eldest reached
fourteen. Both boys were then at grammar school, but 'to save his
father a man's wage' the elder was taken away at the earliest legal
moment to work on the farm. It was explicitly intended that the
younger boy should get the best education he could and leave the
land. Paul Jamison's (PD10) farming career was really decided when
he and his brothers were in their teens. The fact that his elder
brother was apprenticed to a shopkeeper and his younger brother
sent to train as a mechanic while Paul was kept at home meant
that despite all the later family arguments on the subject his moral
claim to take over the farm could not seriously be questioned;
the disputes really centred round the question of when he should
take over. Where the father organised no special education or
training for any of his sons this kind of explicit or implicit early
decision about succession was not essential; rather it could be
delayed until perhaps the father's ill-health or the threat of a son
to leave home eventually brought them to an agreement about who
was to succeed and when.

These differences of course produced variations in family
relationships, but they were variations correlated with income,
attitude to education and the desirability of the farm rather than
religious affiliation. Family relationships were clearly most easy
in those families in which the father's decision was taken early
and some education given to non-inheriting sons that effectually
removed them from farm life. This eased relationships both
between father and son and between brothers. Relationships could
by contrast become very difficult where no decision was taken
and where, because of the desirability of the farm, two or more sons
could be kept dangling, each hoping to succeed. Even when only
one son remained and it was virtually certain that he would take
over the farm, relations between him and his father could be
very difficult. The reasons were partly directly financial, and partly
due to the son's inability to marry until he gained control of the
farm. This latter point is one that, I think, became very clear in
the course of the earlier discussion on the structure of particular
households; but something more must be said about the financial
strains arising between father and son.

The basic factor again is the small size of local farms; even the most prosperous could scarcely pay adequately two adult men out of their profits. In fact it was not the custom for even the more sophisticated farmers to give a regular wage, however tiny, to a son who remained on the farm; it was precisely because the son 'saved a man's wage' that he was wanted at home. To acquire goods the son of a credit-worthy father might run up bills in the father's name at local shops, but this could lead to family rows. To acquire money the son could try his hand at local cattle dealing, or (a recent development) could use the father's tractor to do contract work for those without machinery. A successful son might aspire to achieve a measure of real independence by buying a good small farm of his own; a less successful son, who like Bill Jamison (PD23) valued independence at almost any price, might buy a farm very much below the standard of his father's holding. When it came to real competition between father and son the best card in the son's hand was his threat to leave his father, who in his absence would have to pay a labourer; the best card in the father's hand was the fact that a son lacking any but an elementary school education could not hope in the towns to get a job that would give him the kind of status he would eventually enjoy locally as a farmer. Paul Jamison, for instance, on the one occasion when he had quarrelled with his father and left home, had to think himself lucky to be taken on as a milkman in Belfast. Clearly the relationship between father and adult son at home was often fraught with difficulties.

The relationship of the mother with her children was not un-affected by eventual disputes over succession, but in general her links with her sons were less difficult.

Young children of course brought a great deal of work especially significant to those wives who were expected to spend a great deal of time in work round the farmyard. They were in themselves nevertheless usually regarded as adequate compensation for the work they brought. To have children meant not only that the mother was fulfilling her duty in providing her husband with his future workers, she was also increasing her own importance to the community, for on the mother, all agreed, rested the responsibility for instilling right values into her children and for turning them out as properly socialised new members of society. The behaviour of adolescent boys might be blamed on the father, as Bill Jamison (PD23) was held responsible for the mischief of his sons Nick (PE5) and Jim (PE6), but fundamentally their possession of right and proper attitudes was the mother's responsibility.

An older woman's social position depended very much on her children's careers. At best, if they married well locally she was brought into a steadily wider social circle and her importance grew. A woman like Elizabeth Jamison (PC10) who had a number of married children, especially daughters, living in the vicinity had a radically improved position. Instead of being isolated she was now at the centre of a complex kinship network within which her visiting was as frequent as her children could make it. Such a woman's daughters, especially if they were hill people, had strong motives for visiting their mother's home and visits by the mother were usually warmly welcomed—the young women were isolated and busy and the mother's visit was usually a very practical help to them.

It was not surprising that a mother with marriageable daughters was deeply concerned with their courting. She wanted them married, and ideally married to good farmers, and she gave them good advice about the character and financial background of the families of the young men they met. Elizabeth Jamison had certainly done so consistently and carefully. The one fear of all mothers was that a daughter might produce an illegitimate baby. Bastards, all agreed, were an undying disgrace and the responsibility for not producing them rested entirely on the girls. Boys, everyone knew, would go as far and as fast as the girls would let them and could not be blamed for doing so because, again as everyone knew, men were morally weaker than women; therefore all sexual restraint must come from the girls. If a girl knew enough about a boy's family to know he would marry her if she became pregnant, then this was a last card she could use to bring him to the point of matrimony; but it was a dangerous gamble and none would excuse a girl if she lost. A woman who, like Elizabeth Jamison, had all of her daughters not just safely married but well married locally had achieved a great deal. It was only sad that just when a woman had reached this point of triumph and social prominence a son was bound to be pressing to be allowed to bring home a wife who necessarily radically diminished the prestige of the mother-in-law.

F

5 The common culture: the social networks of households

The main purpose of this book is to discuss the relationships between Catholics and Protestants. Nevertheless to discuss these without seeing them in relation to the peoples' contacts with their co-religionists would distort reality. I shall therefore in this chapter discuss the general patterns of relationships maintained by the households which for the most part have already been described. I would like again to emphasise that these households were not specially selected for discussion because they display particularly striking features in their social networks. As I have said, to prevent myself from distorting my material through unconscious selection in writing it up, I began with three households and went on to study those closely linked to them by kinship or neighbourly contacts, omitting the remainder however interesting they seemed. From my first selection I have subsequently pruned some material for reasons of space. Some of the features which now appear to me to be important for an understanding of relationships between Catholics and Protestants only became apparent after I began to make this detailed analysis. This material I now present with little comment—it will be analysed later. The contacts maintained by each household are however sorted, at this stage into contacts with kin, contacts with unrelated co-religionists, and contacts with members of the opposed religious group.

Paul Jamison's network (PD10)

The household of Paul Jamison proved to be particularly interesting for two reasons both connected with the Jamisons' relative prosperity. On the one hand they had an unusually large number of kin in the locality, apparently because they were successful enough to buy up, or marry into, good local farms, which meant that their kin had stayed in the district instead of emigrating. At the same time because of their prosperity the Jamisons provided their immediate neighbourhood with certain services that kept them in touch with all or most of their neighbours. Because this prosperity was only relative, however, so that expensive labour-saving machinery was scarce, and because this hill farm demanded a lot of labouring, Paul was virtually forced into regular co-operation with others. It is these factors that shaped the social network of his household.

The Jamisons had many close kin in the district. As we have seen the father, James (PB8), had a brother, William (PB9), on a lowland farm not far away. The family quarrel over land, already described, had been maintained especially by the wives of the two brothers, and the fact that these two women would not visit each other had kept down contacts between their families. In recent years, never-theless, Paul had begun to see William's sons, quite often, and a real partnership had developed between Paul and his cousin Bill Jamison (PD23), particularly after Bill had bought the small neigh-bouring farm. The links with the family of Paul's mother Elizabeth (PC10) had always been strong. This was partly because they were close neighbours, and because Elizabeth's mother was still alive, though very elderly, and Elizabeth went regularly to visit her. Elizabeth's family farm had been taken over by her brother Willy Richards (PC9), who was married with teenage children, and links between her family and his were quite close. Elizabeth also had a sister Joan (PC11), married only four miles away to a man called James Woods (PC12), a prosperous farmer and agricultural con-tractor, whose services were often used. She had another useful kinsman living within a mile, a man called Robert McGregor (PC1) who owned a small farm but was primarily a mason. Donald McGregor (PC2), his brother, a full-time farmer, lived even closer. Donald, though married with a flourishing family, was a shy, retiring man and his wife seemed even more shy. They kept up no pattern of visiting with Elizabeth, and Paul thought of Donald merely as his mother's cousin rather than as a relative of his own, and no real kinship was thought to link them. Nevertheless the link with Robert was remembered when a mason's services were required.

The McGregors might indeed be better described as 'kith' than as kin. Kith tends to be a word of uncertain meaning whether used by laymen or by sociologists. The *Oxford Dictionary* defines the word broadly as 'friends, fellow-countrymen and neighbours— those who are known'. Significantly the word is derived from the same root that gave rise to 'couth', significantly, because this seems to imply that by definition non-kith are uncouth. By 'kith' I mean here those not regarded as true kin to ego but felt to be unusually close because each acknowledges ties of kinship or affinity either to the same individual or to individuals between whom ties of kinship or affinity are recognised. Thus Paul and the McGregor brothers both acknowledged kinship to old Mrs. Richards (PB6), Paul's grandmother and their aunt. Because Elizabeth's family had lived in this district for several generations she had in fact many in the area who could in this sense be called kith. For example Campbell Wright (PC5) was not kin to her, but his father's brother had married Elizabeth's mother's sister. This couple eventually emigrated and had since died, but while they were still living in the district Campbell and Elizabeth as children quite commonly met in their house as niece and nephew.

Of greatest significance for the social relationships of Paul Jamison's household were the local marriages contracted by his brothers and sisters. The pattern of their marriages is moreover itself of interest because it shows quite clearly that it was often in the homes of kinsfolk that future wives and husbands were first met. James and Elizabeth Jamison had had three sons and four daughters. Of these only the youngest boy, Tom (PD12), had married a stranger, a girl he had met in Belfast. Although she was respectable and a Presbyterian the family had their doubts about her, doubts that were understandable because all the other children had married into families well known to the parents. The eldest daughter, Rose (PD8), had married one of their nearest neighbours, Fred Richards (PD5), whose household has already been described. Fred was in fact Rose's second cousin through her mother, although in accordance with the usual local practice that thought that relationships ended with first cousins, he was asserted to be unrelated. Molly (PD9), the next sister, had married a farmer called Philip Aitken (PD6). He was Fred Richards' cousin, his mother's brother's son. The youngest daughter, Ruth (PD13), had married a farmer, Roddy Smiton (PD21), whose brother Ben (PD22) was married to her cousin Amy Jamison (PD26), the daughter of old William Jamison. The remaining daughter, Meg (PD11), was the only girl not to have married someone already closely linked, and even she had married a man, Bob Gilchrist (PD14), whose cousin—his father's sister's son, John Ritchie (PC13)—was married to the sister of James Woods (PC12), Meg's uncle by marriage. Paul had maintained this family pattern by marrying Mary (PD19), the sister of Eileen (PD18), the wife of his elder brother Henry, their parents-in-law being fairly prosperous, if somewhat old-fashioned, Presbyterian farmers who lived about five miles away. In these marriages could be seen the influence of the Jamisons' prosperity and their sound reputation as a family. Not only had all married into solid, respectable families, but the daughters had married not merely the sons of prosperous farmers but sons who were inheriting, or for whom farms had been purchased. Their husbands had no thoughts of emigrating.

Mary, Paul's wife, also had a number of kin not too far away, although her family presented a different pattern in that although all her brothers and sisters were now adult the only one besides herself to have married was her sister who had married Paul's brother. Both her parents were living, and still at home were two of her brothers, Harry (PD17) in his thirties and Jack (PD20) still in his twenties. She also had an unmarried sister, Annie (PD16), a determined, energetic spinster who was almost unique in her area in that she had bought, and was running, a small farm of her own, where she also lived. These relatives were living beyond the reach of easy visiting by Mary since public transport did not connect them and neither household had a car. Nevertheless visits could be made between them at the cost of a little effort and organisation; most commonly Mary's brothers visited her, since is usually seemed easier for a man to get away from a farm than for a woman to do so.

Paul Jamison was thus unusually well placed in having so many close kin and affines on farms that were, for a man, not too distant from his home. He had in fact six brothers-in-law, three first cousins, an uncle and an uncle-by-marriage all farming within a radius of ten miles, and some very close; even though relationships were traced effectively over only a short genealogical distance he therefore had plenty of kin in the district. In addition he had a brother with a shop in a nearby town.

With a few of his (spatially) nearest kith and kin Paul was brought into very regular contact because they worked together in a so-called 'swopping' ring, a co-operative work group. Paul had not simply taken over an existing arrangement from his father when he took over the farm. Old James (PB8) had, years previously, worked with his wife's father and brother, but because he had prospered and could afford his own two horses, and because he had had three growing sons to help with the work, his old 'swopping' arrangement had been amicably ended, the two households agreeing to work independently. Elizabeth's father had died fifteen years previously, and when her brother, Willy Richards (PC9), took over the farm he had linked up for co-operative work with his wife's brother. Paul, therefore, when he in turn took over his father's farm, found it more sensible to look elsewhere. He needed help, although he employed one full-time labourer, Jim Thompson (PC103). Paul was too hard up to buy labour-saving machinery and his farm needed a lot of labouring. He therefore turned to his nearest brother-in-law, Fred Richards (PD5), the husband of Rose. Fred was glad to work with Paul since this saved him the necessity of having to keep two horses, for when two were needed he could borrow one of Paul's; and he also needed extra hands as he had no sons of an age to help him.

In the beginning Paul and Fred proved ideal partners, but whilst I was in the area they ceased to work together so often and Paul began to co-operate much more with another relative, his cousin Bill Jamison (PD23). There was no serious quarrel between Paul and Fred, but practical considerations made them drift apart.

When Bill Jamison had first come to his hill farm he had had to swop with someone, for he could afford only one horse, and his sons were too young to help him. To start with Bill swopped with his neighbour Campbell Wright (PC5), who in his turn had had only one horse and had formerly co-operated with the previous owner of Bill's farm. Two years after Bill arrived, however, Campbell became old enough to draw a pension if he 'retired'. He therefore made his farm over officially to his sister. He continued to work it much as before, but to save awkward questions he felt obliged to sell his horse. This prevented him from being any longer a satisfactory partner for Bill yet Campbell himself needed to link up with some neighbour or neighbours who would do the horse work on his few acres for him in return for the work he could do for them. In the event Bill had turned to Paul and in effect brought Campbell along with him, so that when I first knew them Paul Jamison, Fred Richards, Campbell Wright and Bill Jamison were all working together, with Paul's labourer, Jim Thompson, as a kind of subsidiary partner since the group worked the couple of fields that Jim rented. Although this arrangement appeared to be working well Fred Richards became dissatisfied, and complaining that the group had become unwieldy he withdrew to work mainly on his own, though he sometimes worked in with Willy Richards who was, strictly speaking, his first cousin once removed.

Although Fred gave as his reason for his withdrawal the fact that the group had become unwieldy there was probably another reason, for his departure coincided with Paul's buying a tractor. Once he had done this Fred could no longer work with him on the basis of equality. In fact Paul had always been the slightly more influential partner, since he contributed not only his own labour but that of Jim Thompson as well. Moreover, his farm was bigger than Fred's, so that not surprisingly more work was always done at Paul's than at Fred's. Once Paul had bought the tractor his position *vis-à-vis* Fred was bound to become overwhelming. Paul's cousin Bill could still make a valuable contribution because with his background of agricultural contracting Bill was a skilled tractor operator and something of a mechanic. Paul thought of things from the angle of horses only (he seriously warned me never to put my car away while it was still hot on a winter's night, his explanation being that it would make the radiator freeze: a belief that seemed to arise from a kind of analogy with the disaster that could follow a chill in a sweating horse). Bill's skills therefore made a contribution almost as valuable as Paul's capital. Campbell stayed with the group because, given his circumstances, he was happy to take a subordinate position provided only that his partners would help him. Fred opted out, unwilling to take this role and probably suspecting that it would not be long before he would be asked to pay for the use of the tractor on his land.

These things are worth mentioning because they illustrate the very practical factors which determined who co-operated with whom in this area. Normally, if kin were available they, rather than unrelated outsiders, were chosen as swopping partners, but it was impossible on *a priori* grounds to be sure who would be selected as partners from amongst several kinsmen. These details also illustrate the way in which social relationships could be altered due to technological changes. What must be stressed is that Paul was drawn by necessity into working with other men and that these men were all kin or kith to him.

The frequency with which the group in fact worked together was of course socially significant. Naturally the extent of their co-operation varied with the season of the year and the work to be done. The tasks for which they joined together were, taking them through the year, the carting and spreading of manure, ploughing, the sowing of corn and the planting of potatoes, hay cutting, the cutting, drying and bringing home of the turf from the bogs, harvesting and carrying in the corn, and the lifting of potatoes. In the busy month of October when I was there the men of the group worked together on eleven days, a high figure considering the fact that for a complete week all field work was made virtually impossible by exceptionally heavy rain. In effect, therefore, the men co-operated on eleven out of only twenty possible field-working days. By contrast in February, before the start of the spring rush, they worked together on five occasions only. In addition there were also odd days on which some but not all members of the group worked together on minor tasks. On several occasions during October Fred and Paul and Paul's labourer, Jim, worked together thatching one another's corn ricks. On a different occasion Bill helped Paul with a cow that was calving. On two occasions in February, Paul, who owned an electrical generator, ran one of his special machines, a small grass thresher, and each time Bill was there both to help him and to put through his own grass—Bill alone of the group was there because none of the others had that year grown a crop of grass that was worth threshing. Others outside the immediate swopping ring who did have grass were on these days drawn in to take advantage of Paul's machine. Bill had told his brother John (PD25) of Paul's intentions, and John had sent his young brother up with grass seed to thresh on one of these days. On the other Paul's uncle, Willy Richards (PC9), turned up with his grass-seed.

Other kith and kin were drawn in when the work made particular demands on labour. Corn threshing was particularly the occasion for gathering as many helpers as possible, for the machine was always hired by the hour, and a rushed job meant a cheaper job. When Paul threshed his corn he always got James Woods (PC12), his uncle-by-marriage, to do the job. On these occasions Willy Richards (PC9) always turned up, partly because as kinsmen and neighbours they would probably have worked together in any case at this job, and partly because James Wood used Willy, his wife's brother, as a kind of agent amongst his clients in that neighbourhood; whenever James Woods sent a message telling a farmer of the day on which the thresher would arrive he sent it through Willy. When Willy came to help with Paul's threshing he brought along his teenage son, Dick (PE3), and also his own regular swopping partner, his wife's brother George (PC7). Fred Richards also brought a companion to help Paul with the threshing; this was Fred's elderly neighbour Ian Richards (PB1). Ian was not regarded as a kinsman but he was a first cousin of Paul's mother and of Fred's grand-father. He was too old to do much work, but threshing gave him an annual excuse to visit all his local kith and kin.

On every occasion when the men swopped they were fed, and usually stayed a long time talking, in the house of the farm where they worked. Thus the women were always to some extent involved on these occasions, although they did no actual field work except in connection with the planting and harvesting of potatoes. Campbell's sister, Mrs. Scott (PC4) and her daughter, for example, came to help Paul Jamison with lifting the potatoes, and his sister Rose (PD8) helped to plant them. Primarily, however, the women's contribution was centred on feeding the men.

Co-operative work was thus an important factor in bringing people, especially men, together. In Paul's case, those who came were primarily kinsmen.

Paul was often brought into contact with further kin and affines because, other things being equal, he turned to available kinsmen for many different services. As we have already seen, when he wanted a thresher he turned to an uncle-by-marriage, although there were others in the district whom he could have employed. Similarly, when he needed a new barn he chose, from a number of local masons, Robert McGregor (PC1), his mother's cousin. The use made of kin came out clearly in the great event of the winter in which I was in the district, Paul's purchase of a tractor. Previously Paul had occasionally borrowed a tractor through Bill, his swopping partner, from Bill's brother John (PD25). Perhaps it was not surprising, therefore, that when Paul heard of a likely tractor he took John along as his adviser in the matter. When Paul, having decided to buy it, went to fetch the machine a few days later his brother Henry, to whom he had in the meanwhile sent word, came to take him and their cousin Bill by car to the place where the tractor was. Then Bill drove it back with Paul a passenger, and it was Bill who spent almost the whole of the next day tuning it.

Kinship also played its part in the buying and selling of animals. When Mary wanted turkey chicks she bought them from the wife of Willy Richards. Paul sold fat cattle to ordinary dealers in the fairs, but with his foundation stock things were different. He had regularly to sell off and buy in heifers to bring fresh blood into his herd. In October he took a heifer into the Ballybeg fair, but he ended by selling her to Harry Christie (PD17), one of his wife's brothers; and the two heifers he bought in at the same time came from his wife's sister, Annie (PD16). He could not have sold to and bought from kin who lived nearby because their heifers were sired by Paul's bull; but though forced into transactions outside his immediate circle he still made use of 'kinship'. In the one emergency that occurred during this winter, when Mary's mother was taken suddenly ill, her family sent a message through to James Woods (PC12), Paul's uncle, and it was he who came over in his car to take Mary over to her mother.

Kith and kin who came on business were of course social visitors also. In addition other kin came on primarily social visits. In the two months of October and February Mary's youngest brother, Jack Christie (PD20), came over once in the first month and twice in the second. One of these visits was concerned with business because he came driving over the two heifers his sister had sold to Paul, but the other two visits seemed to be purely social; once for example he came bringing a gift of liver to Mary from their father who had just killed a pig. Each time Jack came he brought his cousin Sandy (PD15). Sandy was really only a second cousin of Jack and Mary, but he was a particularly close one since his mother (PC14) was a cousin of their father (PC15), and Sandy's father (PC17) was a cousin of their mother (PC16). Moreover, all their parents were still alive so that relationships were kept up between their families. Jack, although he lived with his parents, had a few acres he worked for himself, and since his relationships with his brother Harry (PD17) were sometimes difficult, he preferred to swop with Sandy. The two were therefore often together. More occasionally Mary's brother Harry came over, usually by himself. He came only once in the two months we are specially examining. Mary's sister Eileen (PD18), and her husband, Paul's brother Henry (PD7), came over on three occasions during these months, bringing their children. Paul's sisters also were keen to see their parents. During these two months Ruth's husband Roddy (PD21) came over on his own on one evening and in the slack month of February he brought Ruth and their chidren in his car to spend the whole afternoon and evening. Meg (PD11) also came over, alone, to spend a whole day with her parents in the same month. Paul's sisters Molly and Rose came over seldom, but in fact they saw their mother quite often. Rose's house was near, Molly was a frequent visitor since her husband Philip (PD6), being Fred's cousin, liked taking her there; and because of the tensions that sometimes arose between Elizabeth and her daughter-in-law in Paul's household, Elizabeth felt more at ease walking over to Rose's to see her daughters there.

There were two other visits by kin during these two months. Elizabeth's sister Joan (PC11) and her husband James Woods (PC12) came in for one social evening when they happened to be passing homeward in their car. On another occasion, that of the Presbyterian church's harvest festival, Mary, who had gone to church alone in the evening, brought back Bill Jamison's wife Ellen (PD28) to supper afterwards. This was a rare visit, and its formality was marked by the fact that a cloth was put on the table when supper was laid.

Visits to kith and kin were daily occurrences. Paul in the course of a working day commonly ate in the houses of either Bill or Campbell or Fred. At the same time as a man he had the privilege of visiting freely on winter evenings, and he commonly ended up in the houses of his nearby relatives. Occasionally he made longer journeys to see his wife's brothers, and though he usually took Mary with him he was on sufficiently good terms with them to go over to visit them without her, if for some reason she could not get away from the farm. His mother, sometimes alone and sometimes with her invalid husband, if he could be taken, regularly went to stay for days at a time with her married daughters during the slack farming season. Mary, by contrast, had to stay mainly at home. As a female in-law and not a kinswoman it was not considered right or proper for her to visit Paul's relatives unless she were formally invited, as at Christmas. Because of the difficulties involved in reaching her parents' home she went there seldom, during October and February she went only when her mother was taken ill—though once Paul had bought his tractor he began to take her over quite regularly on Sundays. During the two months under consideration, however, her only visits to kin were two occasions when she went to stay overnight with her sister in the big town easily reached by bus, and also one occasion when, by special invitation, she and Paul were taken over to visit James Woods and his wife for the evening. Though the women's visits to kin were limited, however, they were extremely important just because they saw far fewer non-kin than did the men.

There were in fact quite a lot of contacts, more or less of a business nature, between Paul's household and those in the neighbourhood because due to the Jamisons' relative prosperity people called to see them for various purposes. Of greatest importance was the fact that Paul kept the best bull for a good way round, and the only bull in his immediate neighbourhood. In the infield where most farmers were within easy reach of a telephone, most relied on artificial insemination carried out by vets of the Ministry of Agriculture. In the hill district the local bull was still important, partly because his services were cheaper. Everyone from the district, including for instance Michael McKinley (CD27), Peter O'Hanlin (CD14), Tom McFadden (CD4), Kevin Whitelock (CD18) and Andy Stuart (PC100), all brought their cows to Paul's bull. In addition Mary kept a fine turkey cock, and although his sway over the district was less, since he had local rivals, many women brought their turkey hens to the farm. Men bringing cows and women bringing hens seldom came inside the house, since the men were looking after unruly animals and no unrelated woman calling unexpectedly was a welcome visitor, it being always assumed that women were intensely critical of each other's housekeeping. Brief visits into the kitchen were, however, commonly made by the drivers of the lorries and vans that frequently came into the Jamisons' farmyard. As a matter of policy the Jamisons bought groceries and bread from both the main Protestant suppliers in Ballybeg, and they distributed their orders for animal feeding-stuffs between one of these grocers and the one Protestant specialist feed merchant. In addition the 'fowl man' called regularly for eggs and hens, and a lorry came to take pigs to the abattoir. The drivers were always invited in either for just a cup of tea or, if they called at meal-times, to join the family at their meal. Because the Jamisons had a reputation for giving a genuine welcome and enjoyable food the men were usually only too ready to accept the invitations, indeed they showed a suspicious tendency to call towards midday when the dinner would be ready. The Jamisons could, therefore, be said in some ways to have particularly good contacts with non-kin.

If we look, however, at the pattern of social visiting the contrast in the relationships between kin and non-kin becomes very apparent. If we take the same two months there were, apart from unrelated van drivers, just four occasions when unrelated Protestants had anything to eat or drink in the house. There was one visit by a woman who lived about four miles away. She had been a girlhood friend of Mary and was now a near neighbour of one of Paul's married sisters. She had been specially invited over, and her visit was a somewhat formal occasion on which Mary set out to impress, and prepared for it by doing a great deal of baking beforehand. Then there was an unexpected visit from an old man Arthur Little (PB100), a retired farmer and an elder of the Presbyterian Church, who usually came out a couple of times a year to visit his old friend James Jamison. The two other visits were each of a rather special nature. One was a formal visit made to the house by a newly married young couple, Archy and Jenny Wright. They were regarded as unrelated though their families were close, the girl (PE1) being a grand-daughter of Ian Richards (PB1), and the husband (PD1) a distant connection of Campbell Wright. They were Presbyterians, but not members of the Jamisons' church, for the Jamisons were on the borders of the catchment area of their church and Archy and Jenny belonged, like Fred Richards (PD5), to the Presbyterian church in Kildrum. This meant there had been less contact with them than would otherwise have been the case, but because they lived only half a mile away the Jamisons had sent them a wedding present. Mary and Elizabeth Jamison had then been invited to come to their house to view the display of presents, and in December after the wedding, Mary and Paul had been invited there to a dance, literally a barn dance, of kin and neighbours. Since then the new couple had been calling formally as man and wife on everyone living in their neighbourhood, and in February they reached the Jamisons.

The last visit was a most unusual one. When Paul bought his tractor he purchased it with the help of a government subsidy for which he needed the support of the local agricultural officer. The Sunday after he bought it he invited this man with his wife and children up to tea. This was the only occasion they had ever made such a visit and they were invited because the Jamisons felt they had to make a gesture of personal thanks.

It is against this background that contacts with Catholics should be set for social visits by unrelated Protestants were very few. If it is borne in mind that the religion of the agricultural officer did not determine the fact that an invitation to tea was given to him, and that in this hill district a newly married young couple were expected to call on all their near neighbours, whatever their religion, then there were really only two social visits in October and February by Protestants who were neither kith nor kin. In the same months there were two more or less social visits by Catholics to the Jamison home. In each case a woman who had come primarily to bring a hen turkey to Mary's cock parked her bird and ended by spending a couple of hours in the kitchen eating, drinking and gossiping. These visits were particularly noteworthy because so many barriers were normally erected against the unexpected visits of women.

These social visits by Catholics were only a small proportion of their total visits to the farm. Catholic lorry and van drivers were invited into the house in the same way as Protestant drivers—there were fewer Catholics than Protestants among these men because the Jamisons dealt with Protestant firms who mostly employed Protestants; but for example Peter O'Hanlin (CD14), whose household has been described, was a Catholic driver for the Protestant feed-merchant and there were a number of Catholics amongst the drivers of the pig-lorries. The 'fowl man' himself was a Catholic. Except for the fact that conversation on matters that might have a political significance were avoided, no-one could have detected any difference in the attitude or behaviour of the Jamison family to these men that could in any way be related to their religion.

Apart from these contacts the Jamison women had little occasion to come into contact with Catholics because women confined their social visiting mostly to kin. There were, of course, occasional visits by them to the homes of Catholic neighbours. For example, during the two months under review Mary went with Paul on one occasion by special invitation to spend an evening with the family of a neighbouring Catholic farmer. Later Elizabeth was asked to go over to help a nearby Catholic woman in a minor domestic crisis; the family's sewing machine had gone wrong and Elizabeth was known by everyone in the neighbourhood to be particularly skilled at repairing these gadgets. She therefore went along, put the machine right, and spent the whole afternoon there chatting afterwards.

The position of Paul was rather different in that he did have many more Catholic contacts which, though business based, were also socially important. All the local Catholic farmers brought their cows to his bull and his manner towards these men was no different from his manner towards Protestant farmers coming on the same errand. When Paul wanted his greyhound bitch mated he took her to the dog belonging to Jack Doherty (CD11), a Catholic neighbour, because this animal had the reputation of being the best in the district. When Paul wanted pedigrees for the resulting puppies, pedigrees to which he really had no title because his bitch was not pure bred, he got them from another Catholic farmer unknown to him but contacted through the good offices of a local postman. This farmer happened to have had a bitch that whelped at about the same time as Paul's; the necessary forms were therefore obligingly filled in and signed and sent along to Paul. Outside the immediate locality, when Paul happened to meet a Catholic neighbour at the Fair in Ballybeg or simply doing business in the place it was not at all uncommon for them to chat like old friends and go for a drink together. On one occasion, indeed, Paul returned home chuckling because he and a young Catholic neighbour had played a joke on Tom McFadden (CD4), a rather earnest office holder in the local Catholic temperance association. Paul and his neighbour, a member of the association, had been chatting when they saw Tom approaching; pretending not to have noticed him they set off for the nearest pub with Tom hotfoot after them. Only at its very door had Paul's friend, with histrionic gestures in Tom's direction, stopped in his tracks. The real sociological point of interest in this story is that Paul enjoyed the joke, because although Tom was a Catholic, Paul knew enough about his reputation for earnestness and lack of humour to enjoy helping another Catholic to tease him, and that these friends could join together to do so.

There were also occasions when Paul and his family recognised certain formal obligations to their Catholic neighbours as neighbours; these were the occasions of weddings and, especially, of funerals. Catholic wedding parties were attended and they were punctilious in observing the accepted neighbourly proprieties when a Catholic neighbour died. Broadly speaking, there were three obligations that might be owed on the occasion of a death: the obligation of attending the wake; the obligation of attending the funeral (to which men only might go); and thirdly, for near neighbours or kinsfolk, the obligation to refrain from all work in the fields between the day of the death and the funeral, which always took place three days later. These obligations were taken very seriously; for example Paul stopped work in the middle of threshing at his farm to attend the funeral of an old Protestant woman, Liza Gilchrist (PB7), who had lived about five miles away;

he had not had much contact with her personally but she was both the aunt of his brother-in-law Bob Gilchrist (PD14), and the mother-in-law of the sister of his uncle James Woods (PC12). Paul therefore dropped everything to go with James to the funeral, although, in the middle of threshing, time was money. Ties of kinship being non-existent, Paul did not of course attend as many Catholic funerals as he did Protestant ones. Nevertheless it was striking that when an elderly Catholic woman, living about three-quarters of a mile away, died just in the middle of all the excitement of the purchase of the tractor Paul, accompanied by Campbell Wright (PC5) and his labourer Jim Thompson, attended her wake, then Paul attended her funeral. It was even more striking that Paul put off using his tractor, although he was longing to try it out, until after her funeral in order to show his respect for the dead woman.

Although I have now described Paul's relationships with a number of Catholics with whom he was brought into contact through his farm I must say something further about his relationships with two of his closest Catholic neighbours. With neither did he have occasions for very regular contacts because links of kinship and kithship bound him in co-operative ties to Protestants rather than Catholics. Nevertheless the links his household did maintain with them are instructive.

With the more distant of the two, the McIlhaggars, the Jamisons' links were rather casual. Peter McIlhaggar brought his cows to Paul's bull, but this was their only normal business contact. Otherwise the men sometimes met in neighbours' houses; the women gossiped when they met occasionally going into or out of Ballybeg on the bus and as representatives of their households they met each other at neighbourhood activities. Because they were near neighbours of the young Presbyterian couple, Archy and Jenny Wright, the McIlhaggars gave a party for them after their marriage to which Paul and Mary Jamison were invited. More often than weddings, wakes brought them together; for example when Lizzie Wright's (PB4) brother, Willy John, died, as near neighbours both the Jamisons and the McIlhaggars spent a lot of time in the house prior to the funeral. Clearly also there was considerable knowledge of the McIlhaggars' domestic affairs; they were neighbours to the extent that it was interesting to gossip about them. Peter McIlhaggar's wife's elder sister, a widow, usually stayed with them, but she was a woman with a somewhat difficult temperament who had never really reconciled herself to the loss of her own home, which as she was childless she had given up after her husband's death. Periodically she would have a row with her sister and brother-in-law and leave them to go to stay with other relations, always asserting that she was never going to come back. Her goings and comings were matters for amused observation by the Jamisons.

Although the Jamisons had relatively little actual contact with their other Catholic neighbours, the McCurdys, their relationships with each other were in a subtle sense much closer than could ever have been guessed from a mere counting of the time they spent in each other's company. The two farms faced each other across a shallow valley and each family could see what the other was doing. To get any kind of statistical evidence for the nature of their relationship it would, I think, have been necessary to have counted the number of times the McCurdys' name cropped up in the Jamisons' conversation. Despite their lack of frequent visiting and lack of co-operation over work, their attitudes towards each other were based on a generation of respect. Old James Jamison and old Patrick McCurdy had reckoned themselves, and had been reckoned by their neighbours, to be the two best farmers in their neighbourhood. Old Patrick was still actively farming with his son and it was clear that Paul to some extent regarded the old man's activities as the standard by which to judge his own, as indeed did other members of the household. Time and again Paul or his mother would look over the valley and comment on what Patrick was doing in his fields, and often there was the implicit thought that either Paul ought to do the same or that he ought to have a good reason for not doing so. Not only was Patrick McCurdy looked up to as a first-class farmer in the fields, but the condition of his beasts caused admiring comments and 'McCurdy's great yellow dogs' were the best sheepherders for miles. His acquisition of a subsidised tractor had fired Paul's ambitions.

When I was in the district the greatest cause for admiring the McCurdys was the fact that they were the first in the area to claim the government subsidy for improving their house by building a second storey and installing plumbing. The Jamisons, including old James for whom special arrangements were made, were invited over to the subsequent house-warming party, which began to raise ideas about plumbing in the minds of the Jamison women. Apart from this one event there was little visiting between the households. They did visit at Christmas and Patrick McCurdy's two unmarried

o

daughters, who were working in Belfast, usually slipped over at least once when they had holidays at home to visit the Jamisons. Apart from this, actual contacts were of the usual kind: special neighbourhood gatherings, chance meetings on the road, and the occasions when Patrick's son brought cows to Paul's bull. The respect and affection in which the McCurdy household was held by the Jamisons could not really, however, be judged by such things alone. A small clue was given by the fact that Mary Jamison, more conscious of social distance than the others because she was young and a female and a stranger, habitually referred to Patrick McCurdy as 'Mr. McCurdy', a term of unusual deference. I must repeat, nevertheless, that it was the attitude shown in conversation about the McCurdys rather than the frequency of contact with them that really revealed the opinion of them held by the Jamisons.

Each of the other members of Paul Jamison's swopping group had patterns of relationship with others that presented a fair degree of contrast with Paul's own. Principally they differed in having fewer kin with whom they interacted, but there were other points of contrast as well.

Fred Richard's network (PD5)

Fred Richards, Paul's neighbour and brother-in-law, had very few in the area whom he regarded as truly his kin. Although his family had been a long time in the district his kinsfolk both in this and previous generations had either emigrated or been childless, or had had only a few children. His only sister had gone too far for him to maintain more than sporadic contact with her; his parents were dead, and neither of them had had either brother or sister who had remained to marry and bring up a number of children in the area. He had, in fact, just one first cousin, Philip Aitken (PD6). With him Fred's ties were close, and it was not by chance that they were married to two sisters. Apart from his links with Philip, Fred's most important 'kin' links were with his in-laws, the Jamisons, through whom he was brought into contact with a wide range of their kin. His mother-in-law came over usually at least a couple of times a week, and Paul Jamison rarely let a week go by without visiting Fred's farm, even when there was no co-operative work to take him over there. He also regarded Willy Richards (PC9) as almost a kinsman because Fred's father had been Willy's cousin, and because Willy was his wife's uncle. Fred and Rose often visited and were visited by Willy Richards and his family.

What distinguished Fred's social life from most of his neighbours was that he restricted his evening visiting, virtually going only with his wife to visit kin. Fred belonged to organisations of which she was not a member, the significance of which will be discussed later, but the important point is that he did not often go visiting at night on his own, although such visiting was a pattern maintained by most of the hill farmers. As I have previously suggested, I suspect that this was due to the fact that Fred had very early become master of his own house. Fred was always happy to be visited there, but it was difficult to get him to leave his own hearth.

Because Fred's farm was rather remote from the main road, and because he was not prosperous enough to be in a position to offer special services to his neighbours, there were relatively few occasions for others than members of his swopping group to come there. As I have already pointed out, moreover, Fred was not a man to frequent fairs, whether at Ballybeg or elsewhere. He was, to Paul's constant wonder, quite content to sell his cattle to regular dealers who came round to his farm annually, and did not take stock to Ballybeg to sell them amid all the bustle of the fair. All this meant that although he was a perfectly friendly neighbour he had relatively little occasion for contact with others in the area including the Catholics. Of course as a man he saw more of them than his wife did, but there was little occasion for him to do more than pass the time of day with them when they met on the roads.

Campbell Wright's network (PC5)

Campbell Wright and his sister, Mrs. Scott, were in the same way short of kin locally. Although they and their father and their mother had all come from families with many siblings their only near kinsman in the district was a brother's son. This man, Eric Wright (PD4), was again from a sizeable family since he had had four brothers and sisters, but they had all emigrated. With Eric, however, Campbell and his sister had relatively little to do, for they regarded him as an unreliable individual, and he had little interest in maintaining links with them. He was unmarried; he had bought a farm but had had to sell it because he got into considerable debt, and he lived on government benefits.

Most of Campbell's visitors were the members of his swopping group, who came on many evenings in the winter, primarily, I think, because the house was a welcoming place. Campbell and his sister got on with each other very well, his sister's housekeeping standards were very high considering the tiny income that she had, and she enjoyed having visitors, finding the farm otherwise very quiet after her American experiences. The two houses of Bill Jamison (PD23) and Jim Thompson (PC103) were almost adjacent to Campbell's. Jim's wife, however, was not a very good manager and there was nothing about his house to attract the men there; Bill's wife, Ellen (PD28), had not yet accepted her changed situation and visitors to her house could not but sense her unhappiness and resentment. Domestic tension was also sometimes high in Paul's house. It was not surprising, therefore, that the men met most commonly at Campbell's.

Campbell himself seldom went out far at nights. He sometimes looked in briefly to his nearest neighbours, the Thompsons and Bill Jamisons. He less often called in to see his next nearest Protestant neighbours, the McGregors (PC2), but usually only attendance at a wake took him out of his own house. There was, however, a strong link between this household and that of Willy Richards (PC9). Willy and Mrs. Scott (PC4) had been contemporaries at school and Sunday school and also as children they had met often at the house of old John Richards (PB5), Willy's uncle, whose wife Sarah (PB2) had been the Wright children's aunt. Now with no female kin at all in the area, Mrs. Scott had made a great friend of Willy Richard's wife, Alice (PC8). Mrs. Scott refused to keep to the conventions that unrelated women did not visit, and it had become accepted that she could often call round at the Richards' house. When Alice Richards embarked on knitting a rather adventurous cardigan Mrs. Scott went round to knit the required rows of fair-isle stitches, and her daughter crocheted the button-holes; all excuses for visits were taken.

The household's social field tended to be circumscribed in every direction by their lack of kin and by their poverty. Apart from their links with Willy Richards by far their most important social ties were with Campbell's swopping group. With Catholics their links were rather limited, although perhaps less so than Fred's, for they lived adjacent to the main road. Being friendly people they took many opportunities for roadside gossip with all their neighbours, including the Catholics. Mrs. Scott's daughter, Jean (PD3), had been of school-age when she first came to the district and had attended the local Catholic primary school. She had made quite a number of friends among Catholic girls of her own age and they had visited in each others' homes quite regularly. She still maintained quite a close relationship with Kevin Whitelock's adopted sister, Margaret (CE3), who lived nearby. Campbell himself, as a lifelong resident attended Catholic wakes and funerals with a real sense that he was fulfilling a neighbourly obligation. If for some reason a Catholic came round to the farm he was invited in quite naturally. In fact, however, the occasions for close contacts were scarce. Campbell and Mrs. Scott might not have actual kin locally, but they were part of a small Protestant enclave with whose members they had such kith links that it was natural for most significant ties to be with them.

Bill Jamison's network (PD23)
About the contacts maintained by Bill Jamison's family so much has been said already that there is little more to add. We have already seen the close contacts that Bill maintained with Paul Jamison on the one hand and his brothers, especially his brother John (PD25), on the other. His wife's relationships with her kin were significant, though, in illustrating the fact that kinship links might not survive marked differences in social status. Bill's wife, Ellen (PD28), in fact seldom saw her brother Derek (PD29) or her uncle, Albert Baxter (PB15). She visited her brother at Christmas but they did not come to see her, nor did she want them to do so. Because on her marriage she had changed from being a member of the Church of Ireland to the Presbyterian Church she did not have occasion to see them even at church. She at least saw her Presbyterian aunt, Mrs. Nicholas Groves (PB16), and her Groves cousin at church, but they seldom did more than greet each other. The one cousin who did try to maintain contact with her was her mother's sister's daughter, Mrs. Betty Laird (PD32). Mrs. Laird and Ellen Jamison usually gossiped after church, and Betty Laird made a point of inviting Ellen's two sons to stay for some period of every summer when she had visits from her nephews, her brother's children.

Of all Bill Jamison's household it was his children who had most contact with Catholics because they went to the nearby school that was Catholic run. This was in contrast to their lowland cousins who, although they lived almost on the doorstep of this school and were only seven and eight years old, had daily to walk in and out the three miles to Ballybeg where there was a Protestant school; this was largely for religious reasons, but partly because it was considered educationally superior. All the hill Protestant children went to the Catholic school because they lived further out and because at the end of the day they would have had the steep climb up to their homes at the end of a three mile walk. Bill's boys, Nick and Jim, therefore, knew the local Catholic children very well indeed—they had been at this school from the beginning and expected to stay there till they left school altogether at the age of fourteen, so they had had plenty of time to get to know their neighbours' sons and daughters. How far they formed strong friendships with Catholic children it was difficult to judge because children in this society seldom went round playing together. Out of school they were expected to help their parents round the farmyards or to do something useful like rabbit snaring, not to go cavorting over the countryside. It was nevertheless significant that on the one occasion when I did see Nick and Jim go out mischief bent with lads of more or less their own age, they chose to go with a group of Protestant boys. This was on Hallowe'en, still an occasion for licensed jesting. They went out to play pranks on neighbours, led by Jim Thompson's son, a fellow in his early twenties, and accompanied by the only other Protestant boy from their class at school, and by the slightly older Dick Richards (PE3), Willy's son. At least, however, they were very familiar with the Catholic children amongst whom they were growing up. The targets of their mischief were the irascible, both Protestant and Catholic.

Their father too had quite good contacts with local Catholics. He was not a resident of long standing in the neighbourhood like Paul or Campbell or even Jim Thompson. Bill, therefore, did not attend Catholic wakes and funerals so punctiliously. Nevertheless he was a cheerful, friendly person, glad of an excuse for the odd pint with any neighbour, whatever his religion, and the local Catholics seemed to regard him with amused tolerance. As Peter McIlhaggar (CC2) said, 'Bill was the sort of lad to put the Union Jack up on St. Patrick's Day and the tricolour up on the Twelfth, just to set neighbours at each other'; but this was said with a reminiscent grin rather than with irritation.

Andy Stuart's network (PC100)
As I have said previously it was significant for the links of all these Protestants that they lived in a small Protestant enclave, and it is useful to compare their relationships with Catholics with that of a Protestant farmer living rather isolated from other Protestants as well as being isolated from his own kinsmen. This was the position

of Andy and Nelly Stuart, whose household has already been described.

To understand their situation and relationships it is also essential to say something about the neighbourhood in which they lived. It was only on the other side of the main road from the farms that have just been discussed, but here the land rose more steeply to high, heather-clad hills. In the earlier part of the nineteenth century the people who had lived here had mainly been not independent small-holders but cottagers who were employed on the estate of the local landlord. The pattern of smaller than average farms had lingered here. Steep, winding, unmetalled tracks led to cottages in the hollows. Houses on the same lane had fairly easy communications with each other but real co-operation between households on different lanes was far from easy. This point was significant in determining who actually co-operated with whom.

Andy and Nelly had kin in the area. Their mother had come, as we saw, from a nearby farm, though on a different lane. She had married their father, her first cousin, against her parents' wishes; and the quarrel between kin that had marked that marriage had never been really made up. Eventually the mother's parents had left their farm to a niece who was now living there with a husband who had married in. The two families had for long scarcely been on visiting terms. The siblings of both their parents had either emigrated from the district or had died unmarried or childless, so that Andy and Nelly knew of only two first cousins still in Northern Ireland, and they lived in a distant town.

The relationships of Andy and Nelly with their own siblings was instructive. While their parents were alive the children had tried to see them with some regularity, so that Andy had had a lot of visits from his siblings. But after the death of the parents these visits had dropped off for various reasons. An older brother had, until a couple of years previously, lived fairly close, though on a different lane, where he had bought a vacant holding and where he had married. He could only afford one horse and had had to co-operate with someone, so finding it difficult to work with his father and brother he had healed the family rift, so far as he was concerned, and began to swop with the husband of his mother's cousin, who had inherited the mother's parents' farm. While he lived in the area he visited Andy and Nelly quite often (it was easier for a man to scramble across boggy patches and over walls than it was to take a horse and horse machinery that way). Recently, however, the brother had sold his land (for £300) and had moved to the infield where he had taken on the job of caretaker to the local Orange Hall. He and Andy saw each other quite often in Ballybeg but he did not come up to their farm for months on end.

Andy and Nelly also had two sisters who were married locally. One had married a farmer who lived some distance from Ballybeg. As they were not on a bus route and had no car they seldom saw this sister, though Andy, who loved to attend fairs, saw his brother-in-law quite often and family gossip was exchanged. The other sister had married a small farmer who lived very near Ballybeg itself. Until recently they had seen this sister quite often. She and her husband had come out regularly while the mother was alive, and even after she had died they continued to get the bus out and walk up the lane. Recently, however, the husband had been in poor health and the steep walk to their farm had proved impossible for him. The sister was reluctant to leave her husband alone and so these visits had almost ceased. Again such contact as there now was was between Andy and his brother-in-law who often saw one another in Ballybeg.

There was also a younger brother, Graham, but with him there was scarcely any contact, although he lived in Ballybeg. He was regarded as the black sheep of the family because he had made a Catholic girl pregnant and had felt forced to marry her and he now had five Catholic children. Andy and Nelly knew the children's names but that was all—there was virtually no other contact between the families, although Andy would stop and exchange a few words with his brother when he met him in Ballybeg. What has to be emphasised here is that the lack of contact was not due to any abnormal bigotry on the part of Andy and Nelly. On the one hand their sister-in-law desired no closer links since she wanted nothing to disturb her children's attachment to their church. On the other hand, Andy and Nelly had particularly good and close links with their Catholic neighbours.

In the first place, Andy's regular swopping partner was Michael McKinley (CD27), the Catholic neighbour we have already met. Each man had one horse only. When they needed two horses the animals were put together and when working singly if one were sick or lame the other horse was borrowed as a matter of course. When Michael wanted to help a Catholic neighbour, down on his luck, who needed two horses for ploughing, he naturally borrowed

Andy's as well. Even when horses were not being used Andy and Michael worked together. Thus they worked together at planting potatoes and sowing corn. Michael was a skilled sower, whether from a sheet, or from the special hand-sowing device, the 'fiddle'. He therefore regularly scattered the seed whilst Andy harrowed the land after him. Subsequently throughout the year they helped each other, at hay-making and corn harvest and at potato lifting. Each worked also with other people. Both, for example, were helped by Peter Brooks (CD10), a poor but very active Catholic neighbour who also was unable to afford a horse of his own. He got Michael and Andy to come with their horses to work his land, and in return, rather as Campbell helped Paul, so this man repaid them by doing a considerable amount of labouring for them. Naturally just as in the earlier cases described, the men always expected to be, and were, fed in the house of the man for whom they were working that day, so that the womenfolk were always to some extent involved in these 'swopping' arrangements and especially so at potato planting and potato lifting, when the women not responsible for the cooking usually turned out to give a hand in the fields, or in preparing the eyes of the potatoes for planting. Andy and Michael also had their individual responsibilities to their kinsfolk—in particular, for instance, Andy regarded himself as being under an obligation to help his semi-invalid brother-in-law in the summer to cut and prepare turf, but for the most part these neighbours worked with each other.

Andy's companionship with his Catholic neighbours was not limited to work situations. It was common for him in the winter months to walk down the lane at night to spend an hour or two either in Michael's house or with one or other of the neighbours who lived further down towards the main road. Because Andy and Nelly lived in the house highest up the lane they saw visitors in their own house rather more rarely, but they were known to be hospitable and welcoming, and their neighbours did come to them from time to time, especially as Nelly's housekeeping was of an unusually high standard. Indeed, on one occasion I arrived in the afternoon to find Nelly in the midst of a great baking session. She explained that she was expecting six neighbours, all in fact Catholics, the next night. They were coming up for a special card party because one of them, Jack Doherty (CD11), the man who owned the sire of Paul's pups, had acquired some Eire Hospital sweepstake tickets, and he wanted to put them up as prizes in a game of poker. For one reason or another all the men involved felt that Nelly was likely to offer them a warmer welcome than they would get in their own homes, so it was in her kitchen that they wanted to play.

Andy and Nelly were thus in a very different social situation from the Protestants in Paul Jamison's district. Socially isolated from their kith and kin, yet in a situation in which co-operation with neighbours was essential, they valued their contacts with Catholics both from a practical viewpoint and because they sincerely valued these relationships for their own sake. They could not ignore the local rules prohibiting completely free contact between Protestants and Catholics—their brother who broke the ultimate taboo was ostracised—but within accepted limits their relationships with their Catholic neighbours were excellent. It is, moreover, important to notice that in maintaining these relationships, Andy and Nelly themselves were breaking no rules in the eyes of fellow Protestants. They were thought somewhat unfortunate in having none of 'their own people' nearer, but they were not criticised for their friendships with Catholics which, in the circumstances, were thought to be perfectly natural; though the danger in the situation from the Protestant viewpoint was shown by the marriage of Graham.

Michael McKinley's network (CD27)

Michael McKinley's practice of co-operating with Andy was also clearly related to an absence, initially at least, of kin in the area. Because his mother came from Scotland he was without any local kin on her side. The only one of his father's siblings who lived locally was a sister who lived in Ballybeg (and since his mother thought her undesirable she had discouraged even ordinary social contacts with her family). Michael's brothers were not really in a position to co-operate with him either, or at least could not do so regularly. Brian (CD28), the brother next in age to Michael, had managed to buy himself a small farm and had married, but the farm was too distant to make swopping possible. Pat (CD29), his younger brother, now in his middle twenties, had not moved so far away, but even so he was too distant and too busy with other things to make co-operation practicable. Pat had moved up to help an old bachelor farmer, with the expectation of eventually being left the farm, and in the meanwhile he had acquired a tractor with which he was trying to build up a business by doing tractor work for others for payment. Charging only about £2.10 an acre for ploughing he was a little cheaper than some others and his business was expanding. Michael sometimes helped him in his work in return for cash, but Michael's fields were so small that it would not have paid him to employ his brother, even at a cut rate, on his own farm. Michael also had a sister married locally. She was young and her husband, Sean Mulligan, was a lad still only in his early twenties. He lived in a cottage on his father's land and he was not an independent farmer. While Michael gave his young brother-in-law some help in earning money for himself, going down, for example, to help him kill a pig and then organising the sale of pork for him, there was no intention as yet on Michael's part of changing swopping partners; in any case this brother-in-law lived along a different lane.

Michael's mother (cc13) had few contacts other than with the men, especially Andy, who dropped in to see Michael, and she herself seldom went out except to Mass. At the beginning of March she told me she had not had a woman visitor other than her daughter in her house since before Christmas. Being the strong-minded woman that she was she had taken steps to ensure that her son and daughter did visit her regularly; she had firmly taken a child from each. Her married son, Brian, had twin boys, and his wife was expecting another baby. Mrs. McKinley asserted that her daughter-in-law, having a lot of farm work to do, could not possibly look after both her toddlers, and so she kept one. Then at the beginning of the winter her daughter had come up with her husband and baby to visit her. Mrs. McKinley made the excuse that the night was too cold to risk exposing the baby to it and had hung on to her that night. Since then she had continued to cling to it, and she had the satisfaction that her daughter, and often her son-in-law, now had the habit of coming up to see her every night.

Apart from Andy, with whom he had much in common in family position and in outlook, Michael had little occasion for much contact with Protestants, although he knew Paul Jamison, of course, since he had occasionally to take a cow over to his farm. For the most part, in any case, his informal social world was centred on the three houses of the Stuarts, the O'Hanlins and the McFaddens, in all of which he was very much at his ease. His interests beyond this were primarily in his own townland and the people in it were overwhelmingly Catholic.

Peter O'Hanlin's network (CD14)

The pattern of informal relationships maintained by the O'Hanlin household was slightly different from their neighbours because neither Peter nor his brother Dan (CD15) were primarily farmers, although Peter worked his small-holding on a part-time basis. Peter, it will be remembered, worked as a driver for a Ballybeg firm and his brother Dan worked as a mason. This exerted an influence as we shall see, but domestically the significance of kin and kith was still strong.

The brothers had useful connection to nearby farmers. Their brother, Micky (CD13), living in Ballybeg was married to the daughter of John McIlhaggar (CC3), one of the most prosperous Catholic farmers in their locality. One of their elder sisters had married a farmer several miles distant and they seldom saw her family, but the other had married a local farmer, Jack Doherty (CD11) (the owner of the greyhound). Although this sister had died she had left several children, now all in their teens. Therefore although the parents of the O'Hanlins had not come from the district but had moved here for the sake of the house, Peter and Dan had acquired local ties. Through his wife, Teresa Whitelock (CD17), moreover, Peter was brought into kithship with a number of other local residents. Teresa had near at hand her brother Kevin (CD18), and cousin Margaret (CE3). Her three older sisters had married and were living in towns some distance away, but Margaret assiduously kept in touch with them. A near neighbour was an old man called John Donaghue (CB3), not a recognised kinsman, but in fact Teresa's father's cousin. Tom and Brian McFadden (CD4 and CD8), who have already been mentioned, were likewise not 'kin' to Teresa but were her father's cousins' sons. Through Margaret, Teresa traced a kind of kithship with the McKinley's, for Michael (CD27) and Margaret (CE3) were what outsiders would have called second cousins. Teresa also had another very important link through Margaret with a woman called Mrs. Devine (CC9), the wife of the local blacksmith. Mrs. Devine was Margaret's aunt, her father's sister who had taken a very close interest in Margaret's welfare ever since she was a baby, and had been a constant visitor in the Whitelock household in consequence, with the other members of which she was on very friendly terms.

It was these people who for the most part formed the local social world of the O'Hanlins. Peter did not need to swop very much because the farm was not his main concern. When work had to be done, however, he either worked with Kevin Whitelock, his brother-in-law, or he hired Pat McKinley or one of his Doherty nephews (CE1 and 2) to do his work. The constant visitors to the house were Margaret, Michael McKinley, the McFadden brothers, old John Donaghue and Jack Doherty. The McKinleys and the McFaddens were the families that Peter principally visited. Dan (CD15), looking for younger and more lively company, as befitted his age and unmarried status, found it in the household of his brother-in-law, John McIlhaggar, and in that of the Dohertys, where his nephews were almost his own age; he was also very friendly with Mrs. Devine's son, James (CD22). How far these contacts were based on kinship and kithship, and how far on ties of propinquity, it was impossible to determine, and they themselves were not sure. Teresa, Peter's wife, had links that were much more circumscribed because she was tied to the house with small children. While her parents were alive she had made regular visits to see them and necessarily saw her brother Kevin and Margaret as well; now it was Margaret who visited her and she saw Kevin in her house really only when he had been working with her husband. Margaret's aunt, Mrs. Devine, had proved a real help to Teresa when she had been unwell during her last pregnancy, but now that she was better Mrs. Devine came rather seldom. The Devines' house, however, was by the roadside on the way in to Ballybeg, and if Teresa did go there she usually managed to call in to see Mrs. Devine.

Both the O'Hanlin brothers had unusually close contacts with Protestants. Though he had only two cows, Peter, like his neighbours, took them to Paul's bull, but this fact was relatively insignificant. What was much more important was that he worked for a Protestant firm in Ballybeg, where the rest of his work-mates were Protestants. Dan likewise had, through his work, unusually close links with Protestants. His father, as a mason, had had friendly relationships with Robert McGregor (PC1), the local Protestant mason. This may seem surprising since it might appear that these two men must have been rivals. But, in fact, each expected to work primarily for co-religionists, and since both accepted this division of their market each felt more the competition of masons who were co-religionists. Occasionally, if very rushed, each had recommended the other to clients in a hurry; it was better to do this than to recommend a co-religionist, for he might become a client's first choice next time. After Dan's father died, although Dan worked mostly with his brother in Ballybeg, Robert McGregor had employed him from time to time. They naturally worked on jobs round Protestant farms, and in this way Dan had got to know a number of these farmers unusually well. Robert was widely regarded as an interesting man; Robert's wife was friendly and welcoming and Dan, and sometimes Peter as well, dropped in to his home on winter evenings quite frequently. Indeed it was a house at which Protestants and Catholics were perhaps more likely to be found together in the evenings than anywhere else in that hill district, because all enjoyed the McGregors' company; it was, for example, one of the few houses to which old Patrick McCurdy (CB100), Paul's neighbour, regularly went.

Brian McFadden's network (CD8)
The McFaddens were like the O'Hanlins in some ways, though their links with others were in general more limited. Their parents' siblings had left the district or had had no surviving children, so that the brothers had no recognised cousins in the area, although of course they had the more distant cousin links already described. Of their own two brothers they saw rather little although both had remained fairly close at hand. The elder, Patsy (CD6), had bought a farm about twelve miles away and had married a girl from that district; now that his parents were dead most of his contacts were with his wife's family rather than with his brothers, whom it was difficult to visit without a car, which he could not afford. Their other brother, Jo (CD7), had married a girl from only about three miles away and was living in Ballybeg, but they thought him rather a disgrace. He did no settled work and lived on what his brothers called 'the dole' and the money his six children brought him in family allowances. His brothers had little patience with a man they regarded as deliberately idle, and whilst they saw him and his family from time to time they made no particular efforts to keep up contacts. In fact their most important links were with the household of their married sister, Angela (CD5), for here there was a double link. Angela had married a respectable Catholic farmer about two miles away over the hill, and the brothers-in-law had begun to co-operate a little. They were obviously too far apart to work regularly together, but they did join up for turf-cutting, co-operation that made sense because the bog they cut lay between their homes. Four years after their sister

married, Brian had married Angela's husband's sister, Kathleen (CD2). Naturally the two families often got together.

The McFaddens moved mainly in the same small group within which Michael McKinley (CD27) circulated. There was nothing in their lives which brought them into particular contact with Protestants except in the casual course of contact within the wider neighbourhood. Andy Stuart (PC100) was the one Protestant they knew really well; so far as the other Protestant households I have described are concerned, the McFadden brothers knew the men quite well but not intimately, and the women less well or not at all, depending primarily on whether they had been born locally and had gone to the local school, or whether they had married in from some distance. Like the other Catholics whom I have described they were meticulous in giving to Protestants the respect due to all neighbours at funerals. When, in the course of this study, I attended the wake of an old Protestant, the brother of Lizzie Wright (PB4), who lived not far from the Jamisons, I found amongst the crowd gathered there that Michael McKinley and Tom McFadden had walked up with Andy Stuart. Brian McFadden and the O'Hanlins were expecting to come later, although they had not then arrived, and Kevin Whitelock and Margaret had been earlier but had gone. These things were undeniably important just because they symbolised the significance of the role of 'neighbour', apart from the role of religious group member. It could not disguise the fact that links with neighbours who were not co-religionists were normally limited.

Pat Devine's network (CC10)

This household is included here because its contacts closely linked these Catholic hill farmers with those in the infield. The contacts of the Devines were significantly affected by the fact that the husband was a smith and not a farmer, and as the only smith in that locality Pat Devine had good contacts with almost everyone. He had been born outside the district, first coming to Ballybeg when he had got a job as a young man with a local smith. He had married a girl, Kate O'Hara (CC9), who came from the district, and he had made it his home. Pat had no local kinsfolk at all and had not bothered to keep up with those in the area in which he was born, about twenty miles away. Mrs. Devine had had a sister married locally, but she had died. With her brother, Bernard (CC8), she was somewhat distant; he was Margaret's father and she blamed him for not taking enough interest in her. The brother had married again and was so wrapt up in his new wife and their children that he had given insufficient attention, so Mrs. Devine thought, to his daughter by his first wife, allowing her to be brought up by his sister-in-law. Mrs. Devine, however, was in general an extremely friendly person who was always ready to welcome to her house anyone who came. Though she saw little of her brother, his children, now teenagers and the same age as her own youngsters, came often on their way in and out of Ballybeg. She had also kept up quite a close relationship with the family of the man she continued to regard as her brother-in-law, Joseph McKinley (CB5), the husband of her sister who had died. This sister had died at the birth of her first child and the baby had died too; Mrs. Devine therefore had no actual niece or nephew in his household. He had married again, however, and his second wife, Annie (CB6), was kith to Mrs. Devine, in that she was her second cousin (and in fact also a second cousin of Michael McKinley). There was one child, a boy, of this second marriage; this was the Jo McKinley (CD26) whose household has been described. Though his father was now dead, Mrs. Devine continued to treat him as if he had been her nephew and a cousin of her children. He seldom passed her house without calling in. The way in which Mrs. Devine kept up her links with her niece Margaret and with Teresa O'Hanlin has already been described.

Pat Devine had a son James (CD22) in his early twenties, and this boy provided all the help that Pat needed. James was contented to learn from and assist his father, partly I suspect because the father, getting regular cash payments for the work he did and not under the same necessity as a farmer to plough money back on stock, was more free in giving James regular sums of money for his help. Nothing equivalent to a swopping ring bound Pat to any particular small set of his neighbours; instead everyone was his potential customer, and he sought to be on good terms with all.

One thing, however, did bind this household to a relatively small group. Pat and Mrs. Devine liked a game of cards, and since she was so welcoming and the house was by the roadside, their kitchen was the regular meeting ground of a so-called poker 'school'. Those who came most regularly seemed to be those who were otherwise somewhat isolated. One man, a Catholic, Paddy Sullivan (CC103), had moved in from a district about twenty miles away. He had bought a farm which, in the infield manner, he worked with his sons without having established any regular swopping arrangement with his neighbours. His wife, though local herself, had no relative in the area closer than a first cousin. The Devine household was the only one to which Paddy regularly came. It was symptomatic of the comparatively egalitarian relationships that existed between the generations throughout this community, that his son Owen, a lad of fourteen, often came to the Devines to play cards with his father. Another regular player was Barney James (CD100), a Catholic from the Republic who had come to the area originally as a farm labourer, but had then taken a job in the quarry near Ballybeg; he was another kinless man. A third very regular visitor was in somewhat similar circumstances. This was Jack Doherty (CD11). He too had come from outside to take a farm in the infield and, as I have said, he was a widower. He now had local ties through his in-laws and through his children, but the Devines were his chief friends. Jack's brother-in-law, Dan O'Hanlin (CD15), the young bachelor mason, also played regularly.

Not surprisingly the Devines had a lot of links with Protestants, one or two of whom were regular poker players. There was Eric Wright (PD4), Campbell Wright's unsatisfactory nephew, whose house was nearby. Mrs. Devine was sorry for him and blamed all his farming misfortunes on his lack of a wife; without a wife, she said, he had not been able to make a success of the poultry so that it was no wonder he got into debt. Another regular caller was a young Presbyterian farmer, also a bachelor. He was Harold Heath (PD102), a nephew of Arthur Little (PB100), the church elder who had come out to visit old James Jamison (PB8). Harold's uncle did not approve of these visits of his nephew to the Devines, really because the uncle did not approve of card playing; but as Pat and his son were repairers of all sorts of machinery it was not difficult for Harold to excuse his many visits to the smith. Other Protestants if they were walking or cycling out of Ballybeg, having equally so many reasons for seeing the smith on business, also often stopped either for a few minutes' chat or for a rest and a cup of tea. Indeed just because the majority of Pat Devine's best customers, the larger farmers, were Protestant he was naturally particularly friendly towards them.

Jo McKinley's network (CD26)
Jo McKinley, Mrs. Devine's 'adopted' nephew, had a position in his neighbourhood somewhat akin to that of Andy Stuart (PC100), for Jo's neighbours were for the most part Protestants. Moreover,

his kin links were limited. He had neither brother nor sister, nor did he have first cousins. His father had been the youngest of a large family but all but he had emigrated. His mother had had one brother and one sister, but the brother had gone away to become a priest, and came only on rare visits, and the sister, who had remained unmarried, had failed to make a success of a small shop she had tried to run in Ballybeg and had gone to a job in Belfast, and they had lost track of her. For these reasons Jo valued his ties with the Devines and visited the family very regularly. Through these links he was also on particularly good terms with their cousins.

Because he lived in the infield, where the conditions of farming were different from the hill district, Jo had no swopping partnership in the normal sense; he had no farming kin. What he had developed was a pattern of co-operation with Keith Baxter (PD30), his nearest Protestant neighbour. Jo had neither horse nor tractor of his own, but Keith had a tractor. Jo told me he 'swopped' with Keith, but Keith denied that he swopped with anyone, when I asked him about this. What happened was that Keith used his tractor on Jo's land without asking for any payment, and Jo in return worked on Keith's fields for nothing. For example, the day after Keith cut Jo's hay Jo spent the whole day thinning Keith's beet for him. There was much friendliness between them, and Keith would put himself out to do Jo's tractor work. Moreover, a greater symmetry was introduced into their relationship because Jo did own an old car, whilst Keith had not yet bought one for himself and could not always have his parents' car. Sometimes Keith borrowed Jo's car, not always remembering to refill it with petrol. There was therefore a great deal of friendliness, and of equality in this working arrangement. Yet Keith was right in denying that he 'swopped' with Jo, for this term implied more than mere co-operative working; as we have seen from the hill farm examples, those who swopped there went freely in and out of each other's homes and were regarded as equals. For reasons that we shall see, Jo did not go freely into Keith's home. In fact the only Protestant household into which Jo could go with almost complete freedom was, significantly, the home of a hill farmer who had moved down to the infield near Jo. This man, Martin Wright (PC104), found the infield a stiff unfriendly place in which neighbours were not neighbourly. He loved nothing better than for neighbouring men to visit his kitchen in the evenings, where he always sat. Jo did not go there very often, but when he did so he was a welcome visitor and made to 'feel at home'.

Albert Baxter's network (PB15)
Why Jo did not feel at home in the Baxters' household becomes very apparent if we examine the relationships this family maintained. As we know Keith's mother, Victoria (PC20), was a Dubliner without any kin in the North of Ireland. Albert Baxter on the other hand had a number of local kinsfolk. He had no cousins because his mother too had been an outsider and his father's siblings had all left the area. Nevertheless, he had had three brothers married locally, and though one had since died the other two, one of whom was a farmer, were not far distant. He also had one sister who had married locally to the prosperous 'Old Nick' Groves (PB17). These kin were all socially important in the district and they played a part in the Baxter family's social life in a sense greater than did kin in the lives of many of the hill farmers, because they were amongst the few people locally whom the Baxters regarded unhesitatingly as their social equals. There was a simple objective test of this fact; these people were amongst the few whom, in an evening, the Baxters would invite unhesitatingly into the dining-room where they usually sat, and who could be there at their ease. On one occasion, by contrast, I met Willy Richards (PC9) and his wife in that room, but they were sitting bolt upright on the very edges of their chairs. Taking Ballybeg as a whole there were a number of people from different households who could pass this test, but in the immediate neighbourhood of the Baxter home there were only two families in this category: one household, like the Baxters, were members of the Church of Ireland, the husband being indeed the Vicar's Warden; the other was that of the Lairds (PC22).

With none of their kin, however, did the Baxter family co-operate on farming tasks. Formerly Albert had run the farm entirely with the help of labourers. It had only just over seventy-five acres of arable land, so the demand for labour was not excessive, but until the war they had grown flax, a labour intensive crop, and had usually employed three men. When help was needed for a rushed job he had hired extra hands from the hill district on a purely temporary basis. This was the common local pattern amongst many farmers, so that there was little tradition of neighbourhood co-operation. Today things were different. Keith had to run the farm with the help of one labourer only, a Catholic immigrant from the Republic, and labour-saving machinery, the tractor and the milking machine. It was clearly to his advantage to have developed a pattern of co-operation with Jo McKinley, but it was obvious that for Keith it was in a sense an unfortunate necessity forced on him by the high cost of labour.

It would be quite wrong to suggest that when they were working together Keith treated Jo as his inferior, or indeed that in that context he even thought of Jo as socially beneath him. Nevertheless it was obvious that if when they were working together I went to talk to them Keith immediately, and largely I think unconsciously, tried to demonstrate by speech and behaviour that he was not just an ordinary countryman like his companion. This was scarcely surprising since this was indeed quite true. His parents, and especially his mother, for whom the locals were yokels, had tried to see that Keith did not become a country bumpkin. They had sent him to a good grammar school—it was in no sense an English public school but it had ensured that most of his school friends had not come from the Ballybeg district. After he left there he had been sent away to an agricultural college for two years. Subsequently his mother had done her best to see that Keith's friends, of both sexes, were relatively sophisticated and she tried to discourage any tendency he showed of developing really close ties with any except a chosen few of his neighbours, whatever their religious persuasion. Mrs. Baxter had even tried to provide Keith with a really nice friend by allowing the local curate to live with them (though he had proved a great disappointment as he began almost immediately courting the daughter of a Ballybeg shopkeeper, and he had had little time to spend with Keith). Mrs. Baxter was not antagonistic to Jo McKinley; she liked him because she thought him quite enterprising, and she recognised how useful his help often was. Nevertheless if he happened to call round in the evening he was not invited in to sit with the family in the dining-room—Keith came out to him and they sat chatting in the kitchen, but usually for a limited period only. It was not long before Jo thought of taking his leave.

It was interesting that although, as I shall show, almost every Protestant man was a member of the Orange Order, neither Keith nor his father belonged—Mrs. Baxter had seen to that. Her principal complaint against the movement was that it was too egalitarian. The members insisted that all Brethren were equal, and she did not approve, as she said quite explicitly, of farmers and their labourers sitting down together. She also thought that many of her poorer Protestant neighbours were ridiculously bigoted against the Catholics and that the Orange Order encouraged this. As an example of this bigotry she quoted a case which had happened in the immediate neighbourhood, for almost on their doorstep lived a widow, a Church of Ireland woman, who was the cleaner of their local church. Recently at the harvest festival some of the local Catholics had asked her to show them the decorated church and she had done so, and on these grounds there had been quite an agitation amongst some of the local Protestants to get the Rector to dismiss her.

This was a fascinating story, for as I came to piece it together it seemed that it was only Mrs. Baxter's exclusion from local gossip which had led her to believe that this was a piece of local bigotry. On the contrary, it was probably a nice piece of local Catholic–Protestant co-operation designed to get rid of a woman believed to have the evil eye! The plan was thwarted only by the Rector's unexpected intransigence. The woman, Mrs. Thompson (the widow of a cousin of Jim Thompson, Paul Jamison's (PD10) labourer), was the one local Protestant whom Jo McKinley thoroughly disliked and it is significant that one of his main objections to her was that 'she never stood in the church'; she cleaned it but never went to the services, a sinister characteristic in his view. Then all sorts of odd things happened to those who went against her. Jo said a friend of his, a fiddler, who had been afraid to go in and play to her when she had asked him, found that three nights running he got a puncture in his bicycle tyre when he rode past her house, so the third night he went in and did as she told him. Then, Jo said, Keith had asked her to take some hens off his land so that he could plough the field which he had been allowing her to use, and, said she, 'maybe you will and maybe you won't plough the field', and that night Keith forgot to drain his tractor and, with the freezing weather, the radiator burst, and he was weeks before he got it repaired! 'Where did she get the power to do that now?' Jo and his mother, and their friends were so upset that the Rector had not taken the responsibility of getting the woman to move 'though his church people tried to persuade him to', that I became convinced that the whole episode of the row over the Catholic visit to the church was a put-up job between them and another of their Church of Ireland neighbours, Martin Wright

(PC104), the man who had moved down to the area from a hill farm and loved visitors. He shared the McKinleys' fear of the evil eye and had led the agitation for the woman's removal.

That Mrs. Baxter was unaware of the local gossip was not surprising, for she had little to do with people just because they were neighbours, but chose her friends on the basis of status and outlook. She thought that by any cultured standards her neighbours were often ignorant and boorish, and far from clean, and she had too little in common with them to make her wish to try to develop friendships with the majority. She objected to Catholics as 'low class people', and she scarcely knew most of her Catholic neighbours except by sight. Indeed, what was most noteworthy about the Baxters' association with Catholics was that in general the Catholics they knew best were labourers about the farm or maids or daily women. They had from time to time employed a Protestant in these roles but most had been Catholic. Moreover, there were very few Catholics amongst the people they thought of as their social equals. As we shall see, this coloured their attitudes to Catholics even though, in principle, they adopted a 'liberal' attitude to Catholics in general.

Alec Laird's network (PC22)

Finally we may consider the relations maintained by the Lairds. In many ways their style of life was similar to that of the Baxters, largely because Betty Laird (PD32) had been brought up in the same tradition, that in which labourers and maids were employed and domestic living standards were relatively high; it was not that the Lairds were in any sense wealthy farmers. Like the Baxters they had ceased, so far as practicable, to labour their land because of the costs of employing men; their main income came from poultry and from a good flock of fifty pedigree ewes. Betty as well as her husband worked round the farmyard, but she had maintained the tradition of spending the evening in a more comfortable room than the kitchen. Moreover, even when they ate in the kitchen, if they were employing a labourer, as they did from time to time, he ate at a separate table, a thing undreamed of by, say, Mary Jamison (PD19). Nevertheless, because Betty Laird, in contrast to Mrs. Baxter, had been brought up in the district and had at least a few kin locally at different social levels, there was perhaps less of a sense of separation between this household and most others.

Betty's husband had no local kin. Betty herself, as we know, had two cousins on her mother's side, Ellen (PD28), the wife of Bill Jamison, and Derek, Ellen's brother. With the brother, a Church of Ireland member, who disapproved of the fact that Betty had remained a Presbyterian after her marriage, Betty had little to do. That she tried to maintain some kind of contact with Ellen, I have already mentioned. There was also, not too far away, a cousin on her father's side, but again there was little contact between the families, though they visited each other occasionally, and regularly at Christmas. Her most frequent contacts were with her sister, Marie (PD34), married to Mary Jamison's cousin's cousin. Because Betty had lived a long time unmarried at her family home she had developed quite strong friendships with several other unmarried women and girls in Ballybeg with similar backgrounds to her own, but these relationships had not been kept up much after her marriage.

With the neighbours the Lairds maintained no very regular co-operative relationships. When they did work in with anyone it was most often with Harold (PD102), the young bachelor farmer whom we have met playing cards at the Devines (CC10). Alec Laird worked with Harold, for example, at turf cutting and potato lifting. But Harold's interests, as a young man in his twenties, were not those of the Lairds in their forties, and he seldom visited them in the evenings. At threshing, when co-operation over a wider number of farms was essential, the Lairds regularly worked with a Catholic neighbour, Liam McDermott (CC101), who came over to help, bringing his labourer with him. Difference in life style, however, seemed to prevent their relationship becoming really socially significant. Liam and his family, although they had a house as large as the Lairds, were just like Paul Jamison's family, a kitchen-based household, clearly within the second type of household described. They did not think very much of each other's way of life. To the McDermotts the Lairds, though not as bad as the Baxters, were still 'a bit standoffish'. To the Lairds the McDermotts seemed penny-pinching and rather neglectful of their children because they let them 'come home from school to a heap of potatoes and a wee bit of bacon, and only give them an egg on Sundays', although they were 'well off' and sent 'hundreds of eggs each week to the packing station'.

Because Alec Laird was both an outsider and no doubt felt a slight sense of inadequacy at being an in-marrying husband, he had really very few contacts with other men in the district except

Albert Baxter. Because Betty's kin were rather limited this meant that for the most part this was a household in which husband and wife spent most evenings alone in each other's company.

Interestingly, however, although she had really few close contacts with her neighbours, Betty Laird was anxious to stress to me both that the links with the neighbours were quite close and, most significantly, that her relationships with her Catholic neighbours were very good also. In reality, her relations with Mrs. Devine (cc9) were sufficiently good, for example, for Betty to grumble to her about the behaviour of some Protestant boys who after a dance had thrown their beerbottles into the Presbyterian Minister's garden. But so far as I could tell, Mrs. Laird had only ever had one really close Catholic friend, a Scots girl temporarily resident in Ballybeg during the war. With her she had been on terms of close friendship, but this kind of relationship had not developed with Ballybeg Catholics.

II GENERALISATIONS ON KINSHIP AND THE NEIGHBOURHOOD

Having discussed these detailed cases depicting the pattern of relationships between particular households and their kin and neighbours, we must now consider these relationships at a more general level.

The first point to be made is that links with neighbours were important both for their own sake and because they influenced the household's ties with its kin elsewhere and, crucially, because they influenced the kind of relationships existing between members of the same household, especially the husband and wife. As the pattern of ties with neighbours varied according to the district in which it was situated, so too did the pattern of family relationships.

In the hill area 'swopping' was the regular practice for most farmers, as it was, for instance, for Paul Jamison (pd10) and Michael McKinley (cd27) and their circles. 'Swopping' involved two or more men, usually living close together, in regular co-operative work whether they were working with horses or without them. In the lowlands, by contrast, co-operation between farmers when it did take place was rather different in character. In this area farmers had depended primarily on regular paid labour and on the seasonally hired gang of 'boon' labourers. When, during and after the war, labour became hard to get and difficult to pay, neighbouring farmers in the lowlands began to work together, but co-operation was usually connected with the sharing of machines. I knew cases in which adjacent farmers in the infield co-operated quite regularly in the sense that they regularly borrowed machines from each other, and yet the men themselves rarely worked together. Significantly, lowland farmers who had such co-operative relationships, even when these involved a certain amount of work-ing with a neighbour, might, like Keith Baxter (PD30), indignantly deny that they ever 'swopped'. This was a 'mountainy' thing to do and they could not accept that the kind of co-operation into which they had been forced was really the same thing. I felt that there were many respects in which they were right to make a distinction; the infield pattern of co-operation was not only different in origin, there were real differences in the kind of tie that linked the partners. In particular there was the fact that 'swopping' in the hills was essentially an egalitarian partnership between neighbours of the same social status. Infield co-operation, in so far as it was based on the use of tractors and other expensive equipment, might well link those who had very different social statuses, for the partners to the arrangement might not contribute equal amounts of capital. Where the energy used was literally horsepower it was likely that each partner in the hills would bring his horse. When the energy used was only metaphorically horse-power and the tractor was used, there could not be the same kind of equality between the man who supplied that and his partner who supplied only manpower. Under these circumstances there appeared the kind of inequality that characterised the relationship of Keith Baxter and Jo McKinley (CD26). With greater capitalisa-tion this kind of inequality was, it seemed likely, going to spread to the hills. Indeed I think it was to avoid such a change in their social relationships that Fred Richards (PD5) opted out of Paul Jamison's swopping circle when Paul bought his tractor. At the time this study was made, however, the pattern of egalitarian partnerships between poor hill farmers was still very strong.

Other social features could be correlated with these different patterns of neighbourly co-operation. In the hills neighbouring men often visited one another's houses especially on winter even-ings, dropping in casually and unannounced. Michael McKinley, for example, was so well known in the house of his nearest neigh-bours, the McFaddens (CD8), that he would regularly walk into their kitchen in the evenings without knocking. Indeed, I have seen him, if the McFaddens were talking about a matter that was not his concern, settle himself comfortably in a chair, without a word picking up the paper to read as if he had been in some club. All the other men I knew in that area, apart from Fred Richards, passed their time very commonly in the houses of their neighbours; and although Fred himself did not go out much I have seen Willy Richards come in to Fred's house and, immersing himself in a Western, make himself quite as much at home as Michael McKinley did with the McFaddens.

It was, in fact, clear that in the hill district if a man were used to visiting another's house it caused no comment for him to enter and sit down for an almost silent evening. Good manners did not require the hosts to give any special greeting to their visitor. It seemed that when there was real familiarity there was no obligation on visitors or hosts to talk to one another even though they might be together for several hours.[1] Generally these casual visitors, whether or not they chatted, set off for home a little short of midnight; but the length of time they might stay was a matter for slightly rueful pride, at least when hill people were talking about the custom. It was said that sometimes the only way to get rid of a late stayer was pointedly to wind the clock. But a farmer assured me that on one occasion, years previously, he had become so absorbed with a book he was reading in a neighbour's house that he did not look up till he had finished it—and by that time, he discovered, it was early in the morning, all his fellow visitors had already left, the family had gone to bed, and he was alone in the kitchen!

By contrast, in the lowlands the pattern of visiting was different. There this informal visiting, 'ceildhiing' (kaileying), was explicitly regarded as an old-fashioned habit, too time consuming to be indulged in by busy farmers. It was argued by both Protestant and Catholic that people with a lot to do simply did not want to visit in this way and certainly were not prepared to welcome all and sundry to their houses. There were exceptions: the Protestant farmer, Martin Wright (pc104), loved to see neighbours dropping in, but as has already been mentioned, he had moved down from the hill district and missed the friendliness he had been used to there; the Devines (cc10), as we have seen, welcomed a lot of visitors who came mostly to play cards, but they were not a farm family. Indeed households that had such visits were not merely

[1] See Littlejohn (1964), p. 105, for similar behaviour in Westrigg.

few in number but slightly odd—at least this was the attitude of other farmers to Martin Wright, who was laughed at behind his back. For example, when I mentioned to a farmer that I intended to call round there he told me with a grin to go early to be sure of getting a seat, their kitchen was so crowded.

It was in fact my own reception at the different homes when I first began my field-work that originally alerted me to the difference in visiting patterns between the two areas. In the 'mountainy' area I found no problems in making easy contacts with the people. Although I was a woman and in general visits by non-related women were not welcomed, I, with a visitor's licence (and perhaps because as an outsider my gossip was not feared), could walk into any house to chat and reckon that in the evenings I would be welcome to stay for hours. This was quite regardless of the religious affiliation of the household. In the infield on the contrary, I found that I had to try to engineer special invitations. This was particularly true of the farmers and the more prosperous generally. I was almost always received in a friendly fashion, but it was obvious in many households that if I came unannounced in the evenings I was felt to be intruding on the family's private activities. I had to ask specific questions and be ready to leave quite quickly if I were not to outstay my welcome. This attitude did not seem to be greatly influenced by the religious affiliations of the particular household.

That differences in attitude should exist between the two districts was not really surprising.[2] When the infield farmers said they were too busy to go visiting at night there was truth in this. Because they were more prosperous and concentrated more on dairying they had more milking to do in the morning; they even had to finish their milking earlier than the hill farmers because the milk lorry made two runs each morning, and went first through the lowland district. Hill farmers, who for the most part started work only just in time to get the milk ready for collection by the lorry, did in fact get up in the morning from one or two hours later than lowland farmers, and could afford to sit up later at night.

Even more significant were social factors. Visiting was often fostered by swopping relationships between neighbours, and there was swopping only in the hills. Most influential of all, I think, was the fact that social distinctions in the lowlands were more marked than they were in the hills and these distinctions made impossible

[2] Ibid.

the visiting pattern of the 'mountain', for this was essentially based on visiting between social equals. In the hill district there were, of course, differences in affluence, but so long as a family, however wealthy, spent most of its time in the kitchen, poorer neighbours could visit the household and be visited on equal terms. But when a family ate its meals and spent its leisure hours in other rooms, this sense of equality was lost. The neighbour who called round to borrow something in the evening from such a household very commonly did not come into the room where the family would be sitting but stayed in the kitchen and kept his visit short. This is something on which I have already commented in connection with the relationship of Jo McKinley (CD26) and Keith Baxter (PD30), but it was a widespread pattern and was to be found between co-religionists as well as between Catholic and Protestant. Even when neighbours were invited into the inner room the sense of social distinctions could be very strong. Most farm kitchens were relatively similar despite differences in cleanliness and brightness. Differences in living standards became more obvious to the eye in the furnishings of sitting- and dining-rooms. Moreover, to those who kept such rooms for very ceremonial occasions only, the mere invitation to talk to the family in such a setting could cause distinct uneasiness.

There were other differences too between the 'mountain' and the 'infield' that were also connected with neighbourly behaviour; these differences also, to a considerable extent, operated independently of religious affiliation. In the hills both Catholics and Protestants accepted that neighbours owed one another formal obligations at weddings, and especially at funerals, whereas in the lowlands the obligations were less onerous. A generation previously in the hill district a wedding had been the occasion for a commonly riotous, neighbourhood party. People from a wide district used to turn up for drinks offered by the bride's parents, bonfires were lighted, sometimes deliberately planned to try to scare the horse bringing the newly married pair home; and there were various activities by the local lads designed quite explicitly to disturb the new couple's first night of marriage. With the change brought about by the spread of the habit of honeymoons, the occasion for the wildest part of these activities has been removed. It was, however, still the custom for the bride's parents to give a party for the couple on their return from their honeymoon, and to this were invited, besides kinfolk, all the neighbours, whatever their religion, in the parents' townlands, and others regarded as near neighbours in adjacent townlands. Subsequently kin and a few of the nearest neighbours held their own parties for the newly-married couple. For example, when the Presbyterian Archy (PD1) and Jenny Wright were married, several parties were given for them, not only by their kin but by a few neighbours, including two Catholic neighbours. They also, as we saw, called formally on every person living in their own and adjacent townlands.

In the hills it was even more important to mark the death of a neighbour. People living within a mile or two miles of the bereaved house would come to pay their respects by visiting the family between the death and the day of the funeral, which took place invariably three days later. Men and women went to the wake; not to go was unthinkable. Moreover, although the custom of general all-night wakes was declining, it was felt that close neighbours as well as close kin should, at least in the person of one representative of the household, sit up for one night with the family. Social pressure to do this was strong, and sometimes people conformed against their will; for example, I heard Dan O'Hanlin (CD15) complain bitterly that he had gone to a neighbour's wake and had got himself stuck so far from the door that he could not inconspicuously slip out, and in consequence he had had to stay there all night, a great nuisance. When Lizzie Wright's (PB4) brother died, Paul Jamison (PD10) and Campbell Wright (PC5), as near neighbours, stayed up all night although they would far sooner have been in their beds; they felt they had no choice in the matter.

A funeral itself called for other formal kinds of recognition from neighbours, as well as kin and kith. Quite explicitly farmers in sight of a bereaved house, and those farming in the same townland or living not far distant in adjoining townlands, were under an obligation to do no work between the time they were notified of the death (and couriers were sent round to give the news formally to all) and the funeral three days later. We have seen with what strictness Paul Jamison abided by this rule, even though the death concerned was that of a woman who was a Catholic and had lived not in sight of his own farm nor in the same townland, but a little distance away; he even forbore to use his new tractor despite his anxiety to try it out. Again, Paul as the representative of his family attended the woman's funeral. Only men go to funerals, but their attendance is regarded as a most important way of expressing respect for, and sympathy with, the bereaved. Even tenuous links of kithship are enough to make a man turn out, as Paul went to the funeral of the mother-in-law of the sister of his uncle by marriage; equally men are expected to attend the funeral of any 'neighbour' within one to two miles, whatever their religious persuasion.

In the lowlands practices with regard to both weddings and funerals were somewhat different. It was not essential to ask everyone within a given radius to the wedding—status differences affected the matter, and a few families like the Baxters gave quite formal receptions to which only relatives and neighbours of acceptable status were invited. Other families issued wider invitaions, but it was very unusual for anyone to give a return party just because of being a neighbour. Funerals were more widely significant: all in the same and adjacent townlands normally visited the bereaved family once before the day of the funeral, but it was very rare for even relatives to sit up all night, perhaps partly for the same reason that infield farmers did not visit normally very late at night, for there was urgent work to be done in the morning. Attendance at the funeral was normally very important, and most neighbouring men as well as male relatives did attend the funeral; but it was not expected that neighbours should cease work between the death and the funeral; even in the same townland farmers went about their usual business except on the day of the funeral itself. Again this may have been due primarily to the different pattern of farming; since the infield man concentrated so much on livestock rather than on arable farming, more of his time was taken up with stock who had to be carefully tended, whatever happened to neighbouring human beings. From all these minor differences, nevertheless, it followed naturally that the concept 'neighbour' and 'neighbourhood' meant rather different things in the hills and the lowlands, and the relationship was distinctly less close in the lowlands.

A further aspect of this type of behaviour, in which variation related apparently more to the district than to the religious affiliations of the people concerned, was the system of the division of labour by sex. The roles of men and women were more sharply defined in the hill district than in the lowlands. This was very apparent in connection with poultry. On mountain farms males, after the age of about fourteen, would not work with poultry; nor could a labourer be expected to help the farmer's wife with such tasks, and when Mary Jamison (PD19) as was mentioned asked Jim Thompson to help her with some hens, he indignantly refused and asked her if she were trying to turn him into a woman—it was not work for a man. Certainly farmers never helped their women-folk with such chores as cleaning the eggs before sending them to the packing stations. In the infield, by contrast, some men at least took a real interest: Jo McKinley (CD26) had gone so far as to risk the jeers of his friends and had joined the Poultry Club, which most of them thought to be only for women. Another go-ahead Catholic farmer I knew encouraged his sister (he was unmarried) with her first-class poultry flock in which he took openly a very great interest; Alec Laird (PC22) took an equal share of the work entailed in putting the hens on his farm in a 'deep-litter' barn; Albert Baxter (PB15) used regularly to help his wife in the chore of cleaning eggs. The involvement of such men with the poultry was due in part simply to the greater commercial orientation of the valley farms; the income to be derived from hens rose sharply in the early 1950's, due to new techniques of intensive egg pro-duction, and men here saw and valued the new income to be derived from it. Often, by contrast, a 'mountainy' farmer did not have enough capital to convert an old barn for intensive egg pro-duction, so the hens were less profitable and he had less incentive to concern himself actively with them. Even on those hill farms on which the new technique had been introduced it was, however, noticeable that men took no part in any work connected with the poultry; hens and women were conceptually so linked that a man who concerned himself with hens would have become the laughing stock of his neighbours.

With regard to work in the fields, the situation was somewhat different. Women on hill farms worked with the men at certain tasks, specifically the planting and harvesting of potatoes. It was usually a woman's task to prepare the eyes of seed potatoes for planting; and again it was usually women who worked in the fields dropping these potatoes whilst the men opened and then closed the drills. When the potatoes were harvested the women were there to gather them into baskets and carry them to the clamps to be stored. Infield women, on the other hand, very seldom worked in the fields.

The difference between the two areas was due partly, I think, to the greater demand for labour in the hills where a greater proportion of the land had to be regularly ploughed because of the rapid deterioration of the pasture; but primarily I think the differences were due to social factors, to considerations of status. As we saw earlier, the infield farmer, until recently, had coped with periods of rushed work by employing at cheap rates gangs of men and women from the nearby hills. In the lowlands it was simply 'not done' for the wife or daughter of a farmer with any social pretensions to give a hand with such work, because the whole family would lose in esteem. Thus Betty Laird (PD32) told me that although as a girl she had been taught to milk so that she could help in the dairy on the maid's day off, her father had never allowed her to do any work in the fields: 'he had labourers to do that'. This attitude showed no sign of changing; when I asked the athletic, teen-age daughter of a sophisticated infield farmer if she had ever lent a hand at hay-making, she was quite simply shocked at the mere suggestion, for in her eyes hay-making was labourers' work. In the hills, on the other hand, there was no such fear of losing face, since every family expected its women to help with the potatoes. Hill Protestants conformed to the hill pattern in this as in other things. The wives and daughters of the infield Jamisons (PB9) helped at such work only very occasionally, but Paul Jamison's (PD10) potatoes were regularly dropped by his sister Rose (PD8) and a girl cousin, James Wood's (PC12) daughter (his mother and wife being fully taken up with preparing food for all the helpers); and Mrs. Scott (PC4), Campbell Wright's sister, came to help to cut the seed potatoes. The willingness of the women in the hills to help with these tasks may have been due in part to the very considerable part that potatoes played in the food of the hill people. The planting and harvesting of potatoes was so directly and importantly related to the provision of the family's food supply that the women were ready to co-operate by doing the necessary work for them in the fields.

There was, however, a paradox in this pattern of the division of labour between men and women; infield women who never worked in the fields knew much more about their husbands' work than did the hill women who sometimes worked in the fields beside their menfolk. This difference in knowledge and interest was something that I came to realise when for a period of several months I kept a work diary of the daily activities of a number of farmers in both districts. Consistently I found that in the infield I could, if necessary, get a great deal of information about a man's activities from his wife. On hill farms, on the other hand, I had to find the farmer himself before I could get the information, for wives and sisters were often quite unable to tell me what tasks their husbands and brothers had been doing, at least in any detail. Interestingly, the only time I heard a woman on a hill farm ask a question that showed real technical concern in a man's work was when I heard Elizabeth Jamison (PC10) ask Paul what he was doing about spraying his potatoes—if he left it too late, she said, it would spoil their flavour. This remark was perhaps merely another example of the fact that potatoes lay within the women's sphere of interest.

All these differences in household and neighbourly relationships were clearly connected with differences in the relationship between husband and wife in the two areas, and this too was a difference that apparently ran independently of the religious divisions of the community. Naturally actual relationships between husband and wife varied very considerably within each area. As we have seen, even in the hills a few men, like Fred Richards, spent most of their spare time in their own homes. Nevertheless it was not expected in the 'mountainy' area that a husband after work should be primarily his wife's companion. On infield farms by contrast the companionate aspect of marriage was much stronger. The divergence in relationships between the two areas seemed linked to the pattern of neighbourhood relationships. In the hills, as we have seen, men commonly went visiting especially on winter evenings, leaving their wives behind. Not merely was this the case, but it was the norm that their womenfolk should not cross-question them about where they had been. Of course the women sometimes found out, and in private they may well have asked questions, but they explicitly denied doing so, it was something they 'wouldn't dream of'. This was quite as true of Protestant hill families as it was of Catholics in the same area. It has also to be remembered that the pattern of visiting meant not only that a husband was often out leaving his wife alone, but that when he was at home she had no right to the privacy of the fireside with him. Neighbouring men might come in and sit down without knocking, let alone without invitation. I am not suggesting that wives resented this because the pattern of visiting was one accepted as normal, but it necessarily influenced the marriage relationship in any household affected by it. In the infield where farmers did not have the same visiting pattern, the number of hours that husband and wife spent primarily in each other's company was normally much greater whatever the actual content of their

I

relationship. This was true also even of those farm families who spent most of their evenings in their kitchens, because even there the family was for the most part together and alone. My impression was that wives in the infield knew more about their husbands' work than did the wives of hill farmers because the infield husband had to talk about it to someone and usually his wife was the only other adult in the house.

Summing up, therefore, I would argue that the relationship between a man and his wife was influenced not so much by their religious persuasion as by the area in which they lived, for on this depended the strictness of the dichotomy between men's work and women's work, and the kind of ties that a man had with his neighbours. The closer a man's links with his neighbours the less his wife saw of him or saw of him alone.

The general social life of women appeared similarly to be more influenced by the area in which they lived than by whether they were Catholics or Protestants. Whatever her religious affiliation the wife of a hill farmer could be particularly isolated, for whilst the social pattern of the hills tended to deprive her of her husband's companionship, local norms made it improper for her to visit any except kin on her own account. Indeed only the most sophisticated of the infield women as a rule mixed much with non-kin. That women in the hills did not visit neighbours was expressed in the local saying that 'women love a wake just because it gives them the chance to visit neighbours' homes', from which they were normally of course excluded. The isolation of the wife who had moved a mile or two on marriage was something else brought home to me when I first began my field-work, for I found such women usually quite incapable of giving me clear directions about short-cuts between farms. They had, of course, visited most of the nearest houses when they were first married and for wakes, but their visits to unrelated households took place so seldom, and then normally after dark in company with their husbands, that they had never really learnt their own way about the local paths. For such women visits from kin and their own visits to kin were of very great importance. This was especially so since the shops had begun to send their goods round the district in vans, thus helping the women in some ways but at the same time depriving them of any excuse to get away from their own homes into Ballybeg.

It was, I felt, of the greatest benefit to such women particularly that one of the norms of the area most strictly influencing every farmer was that no work should be done on a Sunday. Catholic and Protestant differed as to what they might do by way of recreation, and the Protestants were 'Sabbatarians' in the way that the Catholics were not. Nevertheless, all work except looking after the essential needs of stock was strictly taboo (so strictly that I have seen Paul Jamison very anxious about his corn rick because he had been unable to thatch it on the Saturday, yet waiting over a wet Sunday for the Monday before doing anything to keep the weather out). As almost all, Catholic and Protestant alike, were completely indifferent to the demands of their respective clergy that they should go to church or chapel on Sunday evenings, Sunday after the midday meal was the day given over to the visiting of kin, especially by the wife. It was felt that the husband on this day should try to help her visit if he could, and it was a day of real social value to the wife.

Relationships with other kin, both in the household and outside it, were also to some extent influenced by the kind of neighbourhood relationships in which the household was enmeshed.

Relationships between adult brothers varied considerably. In each area a similar range of factors could be seen influencing individuals. Their links with one another depended on such factors as whether they were married or not, living at home or living elsewhere in the district, and on whether each was a farmer or not. Their relationship also depended on the events which had led or were leading to succession to the home farm by one of the brothers.

Unmarried brothers living at home usually co-operated unless uncertainties over succession caused quarrels between them. A bachelor brother might continue to live at home with a married brother who had succeeded to the parents' farm. The bachelor seemed glad to have his sister-in-law to do the woman's work around the place, as in the cases of the O'Hanlins and the McFaddens. It was my impression, however, that this kind of arrangement would have worked less well in those infield households where a man's interests were more centred on his wife and children and where wives were less willing to share the privacy of the home with outsiders. No case existed in the area of the infield I studied of a bachelor brother living at home with a married brother.

Ties between brothers in separate households also varied. A brother who had moved out almost invariably visited his home, and therefore any brothers still at home, while his parents were still alive. The causes for quarrels between brothers were, however, so obvious, arising from disputes as to who was to inherit family land, and as to what the inheriting brother should pay to his non-inheriting siblings, that there was often strain between brothers; and as we have seen in the case of the Jamisons, a man's wife might carry on the quarrel with his family even when he himself was prepared to forget the matter. Without being able to prove it statistically, it was my impression that the greater the desirability of the farm concerned, the more likely brothers were to quarrel. If their relationship were unmarred by quarrels, however, then neighbouring brothers who were farmers were the most obvious partners for co-operative work.

Apart from the influence of straightforward economic interests on the nature of the tie between brothers, however, another significant factor was the type of neighbourhood in which the men were living. Where ties between neighbours were strong and there was much local visiting in the evening men did not seem to seek out their brothers purely for companionship—men like Bill Jamison, Michael McKinley and Andy Stuart seemed to enjoy such relaxed, friendly relations with those near them that they did not make efforts to visit their brothers further afield. On the other hand, Albert Baxter went to visit his doctor brother at weekends purely for social reasons.

Economic and neighbourhood factors similarly influenced relations between adult brother and sister. The crucial factors were whether or not the brother was living with the parents, whether or not he was married and, if the sister were married, whom she had married. If the brother inherited the farm and married, his sister moved out immediately since the woman's role on the farm made the presence of both wife and sister impossible—as Kevin Whitelock's (CD18) adopted sister, Margaret (CE3), told me, she would move out the same day Kevin took a wife. If the sister married a farmer living nearby, then very often close relations developed between the brothers-in-law that kept the households in constant contact. Our cases showed how often brothers-in-law did co-operate. In part this was due to the fact that a man's sister was more likely to marry a nearby farmer's son than his brother was to be able to buy a farm close at hand. More men, therefore, had a sister's husband near them than had a brother. I suspect also, however, that brother/sister relations were less competitive than brother/brother relations, and that this was a factor leading to lasting contacts. Where 'swopping' was important, obviously co-operation with brothers-in-law was more important, so that the area in which the individual lived significantly influenced these relationships.

It is worthwhile remarking that relations between brothers-in-law seemed sometimes to be important irrespective of the kind of relations existing between husband and wife; this suggests that too much emphasis should not be placed on the idea that a man develops strong ties with his sister's husband because of his emotional involvement with his sister. Paul Jamison's (PD10) relations with his brothers-in-law are instructive here. His relations with his wife were difficult, but that did not stop him or her brothers from seeking each other's company even although they lived too far distant from each other to co-operate regularly. It seemed indeed that the relationship was valued partly because it gave each man useful contacts in an area just outside his own, contacts that proved valuable in local dealing, in trading at the fair, and indeed in the occasional drunken brawl.

Relations between locally married sisters were usually important to the women concerned. All the factors that conspired to make visiting in other houses difficult pushed sisters into close relations with each other. Quite often they involved their husbands in this relationship, so that the men too were in and out of each other's houses and sometimes formed semi-permanent co-operative links.

Kinship relations, strictly understood, were very limited outside the immediate circle of parents and siblings because, as we saw repeatedly, kinship connections with the children of first cousins were not recognised. Within the small recognised circle factors influencing behaviour were multifarious: the distance separating individuals and their methods of transport, their occupations and the family history of quarrels or friendship between the linking kin. There seemed to be a tendency for the children of a brother and sister and of two sisters to have better relations than the children of brothers, for all the reasons we have discussed—Paul Jamison had better relations with the household of his mother's brother, Willy Richards (PC9), than with that of his father's brother William Jamison (PB9), partly at least because of the old quarrel between William and James. Conversely, where a regular swopping arrangement had existed between brothers-in-law their children might remain in contact because they had inherited the arrangement. Kevin Whitelock (CD18) co-operated with his mother's sister's son because their fathers, as brothers-in-law, had swopped, and the sons kept up the arrangement.

Kinship outside the circle of the nuclear family was less significantly influenced by the area, hills or lowlands, in which the household was located. Basically everyone throughout the district was similar in that whatever links did exist with cousins were rather tenuous. Differences in relationships with cousins according to where a household was situated were marginally evident, but only in the same way as were differences in the relationship of brothers in separate households. If male cousins lived close together in the hills, then the general necessity for 'swopping' might lead to the development of strong links between them. For this reason, links between cousins living close together might be stronger in the hills than in the lowlands. On the other hand, the fact that men in the infield lacked close neighbourly ties meant that they sometimes sought out their cousins for purely social contacts in a way uncommon amongst the hill farmers. Keith Baxter (PD30) made a point of visiting his cousins at Christmas and periodically throughout the year simply to maintain social contacts with them; Paul Jamison's (PD10) contacts with his cousins were rather different, and from our point of view significant. Until a few years previously his contacts with the children of old William Jamison (PB9), his father's brother, had been minimal because of the family quarrel over land. Then his cousin, Bill (PD23), moving to a neighbouring hill farm had activated his links with Paul. Paul's readiness to help was interesting because Paul had the help of his brother-in-law to rely on and did not really need Bill as a swopping partner. Paul may have perceived that a link with Bill would improve his ties with Bill's more affluent and influential brothers in the infield. But there is no need here to be too cynical; almost certainly part of the reason that Paul did help Bill was that Bill was in need and Paul recognised that he had a cousinly duty to help him. That being the case, the necessity for repeated acts of co-operation between them had led in a short time to their being linked by very strong ties. The relationships between women and their cousins tended to have some social significance in both areas just because all kin tended to be significant to women because they could be more freely visited than others.

Despite the formal difference betwen Catholics and Protestants regarding the permissibility of marriages with cousins, in practice such difference had little effect. Despite all the intermarriage of local families the marriage of known first cousins was regarded as bad and risky even by Protestants. Andy Stuart's (pc100) parents were first cousins, for example, but their marriage caused a very serious family quarrel. It was widely believed that such marriages produced physical and mental weaknesses in the children and ought to be avoided.

In theory, again, because kinship links more distant than first cousins officially bar marriage for Catholics they might have been expected to have shown clearer recognition of these relatively distant relationships than did others. In practice, there seemed to be very little difference indeed. With Catholics, just as with Protestants, I found when I was talking about genealogies and suggested to informants that certain links I had discovered made them kin to particular individuals, I was told firmly: 'Oh no! Our fathers were cousins but we're not related.' John Donaghue (cb3) and the wife of Peter Brooks (cd9) were respectively Teresa O'Hanlin's (cd17) first cousin once removed and second cousin once removed; the links were admitted to exist but they were certainly not thought of as 'really' kin. The attitude seemed to be almost precisely identical with the attitude amongst Protestants. True kinship was felt to exist outside the household only between parents and parents' siblings and married children, between married siblings and their children, and between in-laws, especially the wife's brother and the sister's husband. In one case I suspected that church rules played at least some part in the strength of a relationship, for the fact a Catholic had an affinal relationship with a deceased wife's sister which was permanent, surviving the latter's death, was a factor in the close links betwen Mrs. Devine (cc9) and Jo McKinley (cd26), her deceased sister's husband's son by a subsequent wife. Nevertheless, this difference was a very slight one. The fact that dispensations to marry kin more distant than first cousins were fairly easily obtainable, undoubtedly relaxed a rule that would otherwise have made the recognition of such people as second cousins crucial for Catholics.

Finally it is perhaps necessary to stress that one point of similarity between the kinship patterns of both Catholic and Protestant is the very considerable difficulty that is found if one seeks to generalise about the 'significance of kinship' to either group. Obviously I have just made a number of general statements about the extent of kinship recognised and the social factors influencing kinship behaviour. This is different from saying that kinship in general has such and such a significance for the people as a whole or for any group as a whole. We are dealing with an area that has experienced prolonged and heavy emigration, and this emigration has not affected each household uniformly. In consequence, families have varied enormously in their possession of locally living kinsfolk. The families most likely to proliferate in the neighbourhood appear to be those in which the parents are relatively prosperous but not so sophisticated as to think of educating their children for good jobs outside the area. For the children of such parents the best chance of social and economic success lies in inheriting, buying or marrying into good local farms, and they were well equipped to succeed in such an enterprise. The children of poorer or more educationally ambitious families seem more likely to travel. Nevertheless, chance factors have easily brought about very great variations in individual cases; that is why in discussing particular households I have thought it essential to consider how many kinsfolk lived locally before trying to understand why the members did or did not have a lot of kin-based contacts.

6 The common culture: values and attitudes

Because later on I shall stress the differences between Protestants and Catholics, the ways in which they tend to be socially separated and their mutual antagonisms, it is important here to stress the extent to which the members of the two religious groups shared a common outlook.

In the first place, it is only necessary to review what has already been said in previous chapters. Whilst it has been essential to make certain distinctions between the hill area and the lowland area, and whilst it is important that there was a preponderance of Catholics amongst the hill farmers and the poorer members of the district, there has been ample evidence that the differences manifested by the poor and the people of the hill area cannot be explained primarily in religious terms, but were shown by Protestants as well as Catholics in the same economic and environmental situation.

Thus, as I have already sought to show, types of relationships with neighbours and with kin and with affines cannot be associated in any exclusive way with particular religious groups. This is obvious in the case of ties with neighbours since these ties to some extent cross cut the religious divisions. Even in the case of kinship, however, where the religious boundary forms a boundary for kin links also, although particular ties of kinship are not traced across this division the pattern of kin ties is identical on both sides of the social border.

Besides those characteristics already discussed, there were other significant social patterns also that showed the similarity in behaviour and outlook of Catholics and Protestants.

One general characteristic of the area was that it was in many ways very egalitarian. As I have already indicated, this egalitarianism was more pronounced in the hills than in the infield, but it was not something that distinguished one religious group from another.

The egalitarianism of the hills was most evident in the relationships there between the farmer and his labourer. If we take the case of the relationship between Paul Jamison (PD10) and his labourer Jim Thompson (PC103), it is clear that the emphasis on at least formal equality was very strong. I must emphasise that there was no disputing the fact that Jim was 'only a labourer' and not a small farmer down on his luck. People laughed at Jim behind his back because he was 'a big blow', pretending to be what he was not, and one of the things they quoted against him was that for a little while he had claimed to be a proper farmer, owning some fields, but then the real owner had come back to the district and it was apparent to all that in fact Jim had only rented a little land and had never bought any. It was the ownership of land that counted; the fact that Jim rented a couple of tiny fields and grew a few potatoes on them did not make him any less a labourer in local opinion. Nevertheless, not merely did Jim eat at the same table as the family, but the Jamisons did their best to avoid marking out his status as inferior. He was brought into Paul's swopping group as a kind of partner; for example, when his potatoes were ready for lifting he was allowed time off to go to prepare his field, and then the whole group went down to work for him, and that day they were all fed in his house by his wife. On Ballybeg Fair days, although he stayed at the farm long enough to finish the yard work and did not go to the Fair as early as did Paul, Jim always went in the end; it would have been unthinkable either to stop him from going or to dock his pay, for to attend the Fair was the right of every man. Out of hours his role was primarily that of a neighbour. On one occasion, for example, Paul's brothers-in-law, Harry and Jack Christie (PD17 and 20), turned up late one afternoon when Paul was away from the farm, and Jim immediately assumed the role of resident male; to prevent them from having nothing but the company of women, he sat several hours in the Jamisons' kitchen chatting to them instead of going home. Sometimes Jim would come up even on a Sunday, when of course he never worked, to go visiting with Paul to Paul's kin. If there were a local wake then, as a neighbour, he was likely to attend in company with Paul or some other member of the swopping group. All the men of this group, it must be emphasised, he called by their Christian names. When Jim became chronically ill and Paul replaced him with a Catholic labourer, there were some inevitable differences in the relationship, for the new labourer was young and a stranger from an entirely different district, and he was un-married, living with friends some little distance away. Nevertheless, he still ate at the same table, addressed all the men by their Christian names, and attended fairs as Jim had done. Hill farmers never sought to stress their social superiority to their hired men.

The situation was different on most infield farms. For example, Jim Thompson's son, David (PD100), was employed in the infield by John Jamison (PD25), Paul's cousin. He ate at the same table as the rest of the family and he called the men of the family by their Christian names; but he was not allowed time off to attend the Ballybeg Fair, nor was he a neighbour in the same sense. Not only did he not live so near at hand, but even had he done so he would not have mixed socially with his employers in quite the same way, for Paul's cousins did not live in an area of neighbour-hood 'ceildhiing' or of neighbourhood wakes; the occasions there-fore for them to meet in the role of neighbour in other people's houses were virtually non-existent. In the case of the Baxters (PB15), the social distance between them and their labourer was much more pronounced. As we have seen, the labourer ate at a separate table when they ate their meals in the same room, and he was expected to call Albert Baxter 'Mr. Baxter'. This was significant in itself, for the use of this title was rather rare.

Patterns of address used in the district were interesting and in themselves suggested that we are here dealing with an area that despite all its social divisions had a kind of common culture. The most noticeable feature was the tendency for almost everyone, except unrelated married women, to be addressed by their Christian names. Even the terms 'uncle' and 'aunt' were used only by young children; adolescents addressed their uncles and aunts by their Christian names and thought it babyish to do anything else.

No matter how young the speaker, outside kin contexts all men and unmarried women were called by their Christian names, what-ever the age of the person addressed. On the other hand, married women had to be addressed as 'Mrs. ——' by all except close relatives, or exceedingly close friends in the more sophisticated circles. When a girl married, everyone, even female school-friends, had to change their mode of address or be considered very insulting.

For example, when Jenny (PE1) at sixteen married Archy Wright (PD1) she at once became 'Mrs. Wright' to everyone, even to old Lizzie Wright (PB4), her seventy-year-old neighbour, whom Jenny continued to address as 'Lizzie'. Similarly, young Annie McKinley (CD30) was as immediately and as universally transformed into Mrs. Mulligan in her circle.

The only other people invariably given a handle to their names were the professionals. Medical men were always 'Doctor'; solicitors and bank managers were 'Mr.'; teachers were 'Master' or 'Miss' according to sex; clergymen were referred to as 'Father' or 'Reverend', and addressed as 'Father' or 'Mr.' or 'Rector' according to denomination. These patterns of address and reference clearly separated those with distinct, clear-cut statuses, who were for the most part also outsiders to the district.

What was most interesting, however, was that there were a few exceptions to the rule that all men who were non-professionals were addressed by their Christian names. There were a few men who enjoyed special esteem, either within a small neighbourhood or throughout the district, and if they were also over the age of about fifty they might be addressed and referred to as 'Mr.', especially by women and the younger men. What was so interesting was that the pattern was similar for Catholics and Protestants; a man so honoured was normally addressed as 'Mr.' by members of both groups, and the characteristics leading to the title seemed to be identical.

To merit the dignity of formal address it seemed that a man had to be no longer young; he had to have achieved success as a farmer or as a shopkeeper; he had to be married; and he had to be known to be sensible, sober, to have time for social contacts, and perhaps above all to be 'modest'.

It is not easy to convey briefly all that is meant by the term 'modest'. It means more than a mere absence of bombast. A quiet well-behaved dog is a 'modest' dog, and this perhaps gives us a clue. The word really implies an absence of any tendency to thrust oneself forward, the absence of any apparent desire to call attention to oneself, and especially the absence of any tendency to order one's fellows around. Perhaps this stress on 'modesty' reflects generations of hostility to external authority which was often felt, even by Protestants, to be alien and dictatorial in its attitudes to local people. Certainly today 'modesty' is valued for its own sake. Indeed in my experience it was the cardinal virtue recognised in the district. For example, when Philip Carter, a popular lowland farmer, was killed in an accident and his death became the main topic of conversation, it was his 'modesty' that I heard emphasised time and again in these verbal obituaries. 'Modesty' was valued by Catholics and Protestants alike.

The result of all these attitudes could be seen in the use of the term 'Mr.'. No man, however high the status group to which he belonged, was willingly given this title if he did not fulfil these conditions. At the most he might be called 'Mr.' to his face by women or by men considerably younger than himself, but he would be known by his Christian name behind his back. Thus Albert Baxter was grudgingly called 'Mr. Baxter' to his face because he demanded this, but behind his back he was 'Wee Bertie', even to women, who because of the social distance imposed by their sex were always the first to reflect attitudes of respect in their speech. By contrast, the younger man, Philip Carter, was 'Mr. Carter' to all the women and to men younger than himself.

It was noticeable also that the term 'Mr.' was not given only to the affluent infield farmers. A relatively prosperous hill farmer who had no social pretensions to being a 'yeoman' might in his old-age achieve the dignity of being accorded the title of 'Mr.', at least in his own area. Moreover, what was particularly interesting was that these respect attitudes cut across religious boundaries. Women, both Catholic and Protestant, tended to address and refer to old James Jamison as 'Mr. Jamison'. Similarly to these same women old Patrick McCurdy was 'Mr. McCurdy', never 'Paddy', although other men of the same age and apparently quite prosperous were always called by their Christian names. Clearly esteem for individuals existed to some extent at least independently of the religious divisions.

It will be apparent by now that Ballybeg was a district in which social pretentiousness was very unpopular. Indeed, perhaps the most interesting set of attitudes shared in common by both Catholic and Protestant was the antagonism felt in varying degrees by most other people for those farmers who were not only relatively prosperous but had adopted styles of life which served to cut them off somewhat, even if unintentionally, from the rest of the inhabitants. These were those whom I have called 'yeomen', whose most important single distinguishing characteristic was their habit of using their sitting- and dining-rooms where most people used the kitchen.

Any behaviour thought to have been adopted by anyone with the deliberate intention of marking social distinctions was deeply resented. For example, the accent of the 'yeomen' sometimes aroused antagonism. The degree of difference was not nearly as clearly marked as it would have been in England or parts of Scotland, since no-one spoke with a standard English accent. Almost everyone had been educated at the local primary schools, and even those who had gone away to boarding schools had attended ordinary grammar schools which had boarding houses for the benefit of children from the depths of the country. None of the local children had been to a public school in the English sense. There were variations in the local accent between the hill people and the valley people, and even when the latter had no particular social pretensions they regarded their accent as less 'ignorant' than that of the hills. This slight difference was, however, accepted and roused no resentment. What really was resented were the conscious attempts by 'yeomen' to alter their accent or vocabulary when talking to educated outsiders. Others knew that the speaker was, in effect, proclaiming his membership of the sophisticated outside world and his separation from his neighbours. Jo McKinley, for example, asked me whether I had noticed the way Keith Baxter always tried to speak with a 'posh accent' when he talked to me. Jo said Keith always did this when he talked to a visitor; and Jo stressed his 'amusement' at such airs—'I can never help laughing at Keith when he does that.'

We have already seen that resentment was aroused at the attempts some 'yeomen' made to claim a handle to their names, when they had not been popularly accorded any such title. This resentment boiled over, however, if they wanted titles other than the simple Mr., Mrs. or Miss. For example, I found Mary Jamison one day furiously indignant; she had been into Ballybeg and heard at the grocers that Albert Baxter's sister, Jane (PB12) (who had married the baronet), had come into the shop and on being addressed by the assistant as 'Mrs. Smythe' promptly reminded the girl she was talking to 'Lady Smythe'—'Don't you think she's terrible ill-mannered to do a thing like that?' Mary demanded. Even more interesting was the case of the retired regular army captain who came from a local family and was now living locally. He expected, perhaps not unnaturally, to be addressed as 'Captain'. This caused considerable indignation amongst his neighbours. If he had wanted to be called 'Mr.' they might have grudgingly acknowledged his right to the title, but this strange claim to social distinction really annoyed them. Neighbouring farmers felt obliged to give way to his wish themselves because they wanted to remain on good terms with him, but these same men, mainly Protestants, encouraged their Catholic labourers to 'take a rise out' of the 'Captain' by addressing him as 'Jack'.

It was especially the 'yeowomen', if we can use this phrase, to whom the others objected, and their complaints were probably well founded. Ordinary people said that when they met the men involved, especially when they were away from their wives outside their houses, they could talk and mix freely with them. It was the women who were so snobbish that it was impossible to get on well with them. The women just did not want their neighbours in their houses or to have anything much to do with them outside, and they were always giving themselves airs. In view of all that has been said of the significance of the role of women's work in influencing the pattern of household organisation, and in view of what we have seen of the general lack of contact between women and their neighbours, it is not surprising that those who felt them-selves slighted by the yeomen should blame their wives and sisters.

It would be wrong to exaggerate the amount of antagonism felt for the 'yeomen'. Nevertheless it must be emphasised that most people strongly resented any attempt to impose even mild social distinctions such as would be regarded as normal in much of the rest of the British Isles. It was a culture in which it was regarded as perfectly normal for quite close kin to have very different positions in the hierarchy of occupational status. No-one, for instance, thought it really surprising that Mrs. Bill Jamison should have such a different position from that of the Baxters, or that a cousin of the most prosperous shopkeeper in Ballybeg should be merely a lorry driver, for it was common even for brothers them-selves to vary in the prestige attaching to their work, simply because on farms the kind of opportunities a boy got varied so greatly with his position in the family. Against this background, differences in wealth were acceptable, but snobbery, except perhaps that of farmers in respect of farm labourers, did arouse antagonism.

It was unusual for people to have their poor relations used to denigrate them. That I heard many people say that Albert Baxter's father (PA) had been 'only a smith', and had 'only been to a hedge school', was indicative of the hostility aroused by his social pretensions.

Even outsiders were not immune to criticism and adverse gossip if they were over pretentious. The Catholic doctor was constantly criticised for asserting what were regarded as unwarranted claims to superiority. People picked on what they described as his habit of arriving late for Mass, saying that he then walked ostentatiously to the front of the church and that his short, pompous figure, an object of amusement in itself, would then be seen meticulously placing gloves, hat and stick on the seat behind him before kneeling. I was told that on one occasion, to take him down a peg, the boys got hold of these offending articles and, to the suppressed mirth of the congregation, passed them to each other, behind the doctor's unconscious back, until they reached the rear of the church. Unkind gossip said that the doctor came from 'only a very small farm', and I even heard it said that his brother was a priest who had been 'unfrocked' for drunken driving. 'He's got nothing to boast about' was a common comment. That these statements were probably false does not detract from their interest; on the contrary, if false the attitude they expressed was particularly significant.

Of even more interest for our main concern, the relations of Catholics and Protestants, was the fact that all, whatever their religious affiliation, showed a very similar attitude to the world of officials outside their district. Everyone showed irritation because Ballybeg formed part of a political and economic system over which its inhabitants had very little influence; yet this external world imposed all sorts of regulations affecting the lives of the local people. There was distrust and dislike of the officials who came into the area enforcing rules about health, about schooling, and about the running of the farms. It mattered little what a man's religious affiliation was—his attitude to the official who condemned his byre as insanitary, or who came to check on his, often over-optimistic, claim for a government subsidy, was usually tinged with hostility.

In part much irritation and misunderstanding stemmed from the failure of local people to comprehend the impersonal attitudes of bureaucracy. Local relationships were always on a face-to-face basis, and were largely with people known as individuals in a number of different contexts. It was not surprising that the people did not believe that the decisions of officials were reached in accordance with the demands of impersonal rules.

Most people believed that officials could and should bend rules to suit local people; if they did not do so it could only be out of antagonism to particular individuals. Officials, it was tacitly accepted, should adapt their behaviour to suit the particular circumstances of the particular individual with whom they were dealing. It was also firmly assumed that if the individual could only go about things the right way and contact the right official through the right channel, then anything that was required could be done; it was simply a matter of really knowing the ropes. It was perhaps an extreme case of this attitude that when formerly scarce foodstuffs became unrestricted, Mary Jamison (PD19) commented in all seriousness that this was the wrong time for the grocers to try to get people to buy more of these goods; they should have got hold of them and offered them round when everything was rationed and people needed these foods more! Mary's comment was, however, only slightly more exaggerated than many others of a similar nature that all expressed total lack of understanding of a 'bureaucratic' attitude.

It was noticeable, for instance, that precisely the same kind of irritation was expressed separately to me by the Unionist Mrs. Baxter (PC20) and the Nationalist wife of a Catholic shop-keeper in Ballybeg, both of whom were independently made furious by the behaviour of customs officers at a nearby border post. In fact all the officials had done was to ask each woman to open her case for inspection; neither could accept this because each felt the official should have recognised in *her* the kind of respectable person who would not attempt to smuggle. That a rule had to be rigidly applied to all seemed to them simply absurd.

In a similar instance, Jo McKinley's mother was furious with the police sergeant for having stopped Jo near the border one night when he was hurrying to fetch a vet for a sick cow. Mrs. McKinley argued that the sergeant knew Jo and he ought not to have stopped Jo when he could see he was in such a hurry; no doubt the very fact that made the policeman suspicious.

When Keith Baxter (PD30) drove out on to the main road without stopping, his usual practice, and was flagged down by a new constable who asked to see his driving licence, Keith was furious; he might have thought of many excuses for his indignation, but what he actually said was that a policeman had no business stopping anyone until he had learnt enough about the district not to have to ask for the names of people who were almost in their own farmyards, and demand licences of those who obviously possessed them!

K

Granted the existence of this kind of attitude, it can readily be seen that the refusal or agreement of an official or external authority to a request for a grant, or planning permission, or the acceptance or rejection by any outside organisation of an application for a job, was immediately assumed to be due not to an impartial assessment of the case, but to the attitude of some particular official to the applicant considered as an individual. Whilst this meant that any refusal to a Catholic was often assumed to be due to his Catholicism, it did not follow that a Protestant who had been refused thought his own case had been objectively judged.

Often it was thought to be very important to make a request for some favour through a good intermediary. Indeed, it was clear from conversations that in the local opinion one of the main duties of clergymen and other professional people was to act as negotiators with the outside world. The results of this belief were not always happy. If the intermediaries were unsuccessful they could be blamed for letting people down, even when what was requested was simply beyond their powers to accomplish; yet a blunt refusal to try to help resulted in even greater resentment. The new young Presbyterian minister, reared in the bureaucratic atmosphere of Belfast to the belief that officials worked according to objective rules and regulations, and that the interference of outsiders could do no good, incurred resentment when he refused to try to assist members of his congregation in matters where he thought such interference would be useless. The importance attached to the use of the proper intermediary was clearly indicated by the fact that a number of Ballybeg's Catholics habitually consulted the Church of Ireland Rector for advice and for letters of support in their dealings with officialdom. They told him they did this because they did not want their parish priest to know all about their financial affairs, and this was perhaps part of the truth; but it seemed equally certain that in approaching the Rector rather than their priest they thought they were pulling a more useful string.[1]

It is necessary to emphasise again that Protestants shared with Catholics a very general hostility to outside government officials, and even the government itself. The government was Unionist and Protestants were Unionists, but over the forty years the party had been in office it had inevitably been responsible for much legislation that was unpopular with both groups. Catholics may have suspected that official policy was designed to help Protestants rather

[1] See Harris (1961).

than Catholics, but Protestants in this area believed it helped not them but those nearer Belfast. They certainly did not think of themselves as forming a favoured group. Catholics were particularly ready to damn the police and maintain that they favoured Protestants, but few ordinary Protestants thought of the police as their especial friends. Of Paul Jamison's (PD10) group, for example, it was only Fred Richards (PD5) who trusted the police to be fair. Paul and the other men explicitly thought the police were out to get people for trifles, just to keep up their scores of arrests and convictions,[2] Mary Jamison (PD19) thought that nothing could be worse than giving information to the police, and even said, in the context of a discussion about a particularly unpleasant Ulster murder, that no-one should give information to them even in such a case; 'you'd have no luck after'—her stock phrase for hinting that supernatural sanctions would follow particularly heinous offences.

When we consider all that has been said about the conditions of farming life, and its influence on neighbourly relations and family structure, about patterns of polite behaviour and values, and even about attitude to the outside world, we can see that there was a considerable area within which Catholics and Protestants shared a common culture. Yet it remained true that the two groups were in many respects remarkably distinct. We must now consider, therefore, the extent of the social separation between them.

[2] Significantly, although Paul and Bill Jamison and Fred Richards had all been 'B' Specials during the war only Fred was still a member of the force.

7 The social separation of Catholic and Protestant

Despite the fact that Catholics and Protestants lived side by side throughout the area studied, and despite the fact that their relationships with each other were in many contexts both close and friendly, it must also be emphasised that there were a great many contexts also in which their social spheres remained quite distinct. Often this was due not so much to the fact that they sought to exclude each other from their activities, but because each group tended to share in relationships from which the members of the other group excluded themselves.

In the first place it is obvious that the majority of the people were involved in religious and political organisations in which members of 'the other side' had, by definition, no wish to participate.

Roman Catholics almost invariably attended Mass once each Sunday. In Ballybeg this did not mean that all the Catholics in the area met together each week, for there was not only the main Catholic church in Ballybeg itself, but a chapel had been built nearer the hill area to which most of the people from that district went. Moreover, even those who attended the same church did not necessarily meet since there were usually two and sometimes three Masses performed in each place each Sunday. Nevertheless, the opportunities for Catholics to meet other Catholics regularly were obviously great; and they were increased by the holding of special services on saints days that the more devout attended. These, mainly women like Mrs. Devine (cc9), also met when they attended evening 'Devotions' held especially in Lent.

By comparison, Protestants were brought somewhat less into contact with each other by their church attendance. This was partly because Protestant men were rather less regular church attenders (although very active church-goers by English standards) and partly because amongst Protestants there were denominational divisions that reduced the chances of common participation in a church service. Nevertheless, even amongst Protestants, at least one adult member of a household normally attended church each week. Moreover, and this was extremely important for the formation of social relationships amongst the young, the Protestant community expected children until well into their 'teens to attend their church Sunday School each week. Since a family was very strongly criticised if the children were not sent, most children had very good records of Sunday School attendance. (Indeed in general for both Catholic and Protestant children their first experience of membership of groups outside the family was a 'religious' experience of this kind, since church attendance began very young.)

Women had their most important non-kin ties with other members of their churches with whom they were brought into contact through actual church services. Men were commonly also brought into contact with their fellow co-religionists through politically oriented groups.

Protestant men whatever their denominational allegiance had for the most part close ties with the local Orange Lodge and/or the Free Masons. The significance of the Orange Order is something that will be discussed in detail later. Here it is sufficient to say that although the groups met comparatively infrequently, and a man was seldom involved in a meeting more often than once a month, the influence of the groups was the greater because there was a strong element of emotional attachment to a particular lodge, and a sense of loyalty to fellow lodge members. It is important to note that this was not only based on antagonism to Catholics, but on their sense of local pride *vis-à-vis* other Protestants. This competitive spirit of the lodges in relation to one another was displayed in the preparations each lodge made for its participation in the annual large Orange demonstrations, especially that of the Twelfth of July. Members, and to some extent their wives, spent much time beforehand in activities designed to enable 'their' lodge to put on a good display. Each lodge had its band, which practised for months for its public performance. But even those not involved as players were active. The strong inter-lodge competitive element focused on the acquisition of good instruments and fine uniforms for the band, and the purchase of the huge painted banners that led each band on the most important public occasions. Alongside the convivial lodge meetings, therefore, a lot of effort was put into the collection of money that could often be ill-afforded. All this was inevitably involved joint activity.

Some of the Catholic men belonged to the 'Ancient Order of Hibernians', a moderate Nationalist organisation that in appearance was very similar to the Orange Order. In this organisation, too, there was a stress on bands and banners and traditional demonstrations and attendance at lodge meetings. For reasons that will become apparent, however, the Hibernian Order was less significant for the Catholics than the Orange Order was for the Protestants, and its reputation for political moderation had perhaps lost it some local support. At any rate, it did not appear that membership of the Hibernian Order was particularly high, nor was the attachment to fellow Lodge members particularly intense. There were, however, other activities that did serve to unite Catholic men. Many of the younger ones were brought together through their interest in the Pioneers, the Catholic temperance movement. Many of these, as well as others, were united through their interest in sport.

It was, and is, a feature of Northern Ireland that Protestant and Catholic children seldom learn to play the same games. Non-team games such as badminton and table-tennis were usually associated with Protestant youth clubs and were played mostly by the sophisticated; youngsters like Keith Baxter (PD30) and his friends. In rural Ulster, in general, it was in fact only golf and, to a lesser extent, tennis (games that demand considerable expense in laying out their playing areas) that ever drew people from both religious groups. Golf courses and tennis courts were, however, not a feature of the Ballybeg countryside; they were found only some miles away in the bigger towns and it was only the very unusual Ballybeg resident, whether Catholic or Protestant, who went there to play.

The Catholic/Protestant division was even more marked in relation to team games. It would have been quite impossible to have had a 'Ballybeg' football team representing the district as a whole. The games Protestants learnt were soccer, rugby and hockey, whilst Catholic children learnt Gaelic football, hurley and camogie —this was the result of sectarian schooling and the association of Nationalism with the 'Gaelic revival'. Protestant boys were, in fact, not much involved with team games of any kind. The local Protestant school had no sports field and most of the parents would have considered time spent in playing football a waste. Only those boys and girls who went on to grammar schools elsewhere ever became really keen on such games. It seemed indeed evidence of the Protestant lack of involvement in sports generally that a Protestant committee, planning children's sports as part of the Coronation fête, expressed fears that Catholic children would come along and infuriatingly scoop up all the prizes (to which only Protestants had contributed) because with the much greater emphasis on games at their school they would be in much better practice for athletics.

There was, conversely, considerable enthusiasm amongst Catholic young men for Gaelic football. This was partly because of its association with Irish nationalism; and it was in part because of this association that they were encouraged and actively supported by the rest of the Catholic community, both men and young women. Many attended the Sunday matches when the Ballybeg team was playing at home, and some even went by coach when the team was playing away. Some local Protestants would ask interestedly after the results, and were obviously quite pleased if the local team won. Nevertheless, the connection of the game with Nationalism meant that not only did Protestants not play as members of the team, but that it was rare for them even to watch a match. This was partly because the matches were always played on Sundays, which Protestants considered unsuitable; more important, however, was the fact that the whole activity was suspect to the Protestants just because of its symbolic significance. Sometimes they suggested that the matches might well provide occasions for the rallying of I.R.A. members from different districts. More common, however, was the feeling simply that the Protestant, even if he wanted to watch, would be regarded as an interloper and be made to feel self-conscious and uncomfortable. For all these reasons attendance at Gaelic football matches held regularly throughout the winter months was almost as much a purely Catholic activity as was attendance at Mass.

Just as teams and fans were recruited on a religious basis, so were the audiences at the local film shows; and partly for the same reasons. There was no cinema in the normal commercial sense in Ballybeg, a fact of some importance at this time since there was only one television set in the place. Film shows were, however, given regularly once a week, but only on Sunday nights and only in the Parochial Hall of the Catholic Church. The only Protestants who attended these shows were a few lads in their late teens and early twenties. These young men were severely criticised by other Protestants. Their basic fear was that they would become involved with Catholic girls, but the criticism openly voiced was that to break the Sabbath so blatantly and in such company showed they had 'no self-respect'—'they can't think much of themselves to do a thing like that'. Clearly such film shows could not form a common meeting ground for the community as a whole.

Dances too were invariably held in halls which had such close religious or political connection with one side or the other that these too were patronised predominantly or wholly by either Catholics or Protestants, seldom both. The exceptions were to be found only at the level of expensive formal dances in the County Town. There at the Hospital dance and the Golf Club dance Catholics and Protestants were to be found together—but of course since people came as firmly paired couples, or in organised little parties to such affairs, there was not the same opportunity for mixing as at the local hops. These took place either in the Catholic Parochial Hall or in the Church of Ireland Hall (not in the Presbyterian Hall since a clique in this church disapproved of dancing under any conditions), or in one or other of the Orange Halls—and again the Catholic dances often took place on a Sunday. The 'riff-raff' on either side might not be too particular about the place and time of the dances, but this involved only a tiny minority, for most youngsters were 'respectable' enough to keep to the rules about where and when they might dance. I think it will be obvious from all that has been said that most parents hoped devoutly that their children would restrict any thought of marriage to those of their 'own side', and since dances were specifically designed to bring about friendships with those of the opposite sex, parents sought by every means in their power to restrict their children's attendance to dances run by the 'right' religious group.

Even bazaars and sales of work that so often in the rest of the British Isles bring the whole of the community into contact with each other, failed to do so in Ballybeg. Fund raising was never undertaken for charities of a non-sectarian and non-political character. The only annual collection which might have been expected to have been an exception was Earl Haig's Poppy Day appeal—but although it was well recognised that there were large numbers of Catholic as well as Protestant ex-servicemen even in Northern Ireland, the association of the armed forces with Britain as a political unit meant that the organising of the appeal and donations to it were an entirely Protestant affair. For the rest, most of the appeals concerned local sectarian issues—fund-raising for the respective churches and for the various political organisations; for the bands and banners of Orange Lodges, for example. It was both interesting and significant of attitudes between the Catholics and Protestants that individuals could and did collect money and offerings for bazaars from neighbours of 'the other side' if the object were purely religious, but no-one could do this for a political purpose—it was good for all people to be supporters of religious causes, and neighbours, whatever their own faith, could worthily support each other here; for example, Mary Jamison (PD19) collected offerings in kind for the Presbyterian sale of work from her three nearest Catholic neighbours. To think of attending any bazaar, however, even though it was held for a religious cause, was quite a different matter. Occasionally someone might take a neighbour 'from the other side' to visit some particular stall for a brief period, but basically attendances at these functions were almost entirely confined to members of one side or the other.

It was, however, in the matter of schooling that sectarian influences exerted some of their strongest pressures on the pattern of social relationships. It was, in fact, only the children from the hill districts who came to know children of 'the other side' at school. Almost all schooling was sectarian, but in the days before school buses were thought of it was felt unreasonable for the Protestant children of the hill area to be expected to attend the Protestant school in Ballybeg since this would have entailed a walk of over four miles each way. These children therefore did attend the local Catholic primary school. It would be idle to pretend that the ensuing contacts between Catholic and Protestant children spread only sweetness and light—boys everywhere gang up and what more natural than that at this school the gangs should be recruited on a sectarian basis. Fred Richards (PD5) talking about Catholics said to me, 'I know what they're taught—I went to a Catholic school. Not that the teachers weren't more than nice to us, but we boys used to fight and then they used to call us, well, illegitimate [Fred was always very careful of his language when talking to me], because our parents hadn't been properly married because they hadn't been married in a Catholic Church.' Nevertheless, years in the same class and general school contacts undoubtedly gave the Protestant children involved an ease of relationship with the Catholics of their district, and sometimes long-standing friendships that were especially important in the case of girls, who as women would have so few occasions for coming into contact with each other. Yet it must be emphasised that it was only a very small proportion of children who came into close contact with any other than their co-religionists at school. Only the hill Protestant children went to the Catholic school. Children who lived nearer went, for the most part by foot, to the Protestant school in Ballybeg itself, even as in the case of the little 'infield' Jamisons, if this meant a walk of over six miles a day. With the increasing use of cars it was obvious that the tendency to separate schooling was going to increase rather than decrease.

In the great majority of cases, therefore, Catholic children went to Catholic schools and Protestant children went to Protestant schools, and out of school they had hardly any activities in common.

Because of the importance of overtly sectarian ties, many other contacts that people had tended to be also with members of 'the same side', even in contexts which were not felt really to require this. For example, the great majority of members of the local branches of the Farmers' Union, the Young Farmers' Club, the Poultry Society and the Women's Institute were Protestant, although this was certainly not in accordance with the wishes of the organisers of these groups—indeed the contrary was the case. It must be emphasised, of course, that even amongst the Protestants it was only a minority who belonged to these groups. Indeed local membership was so small that there were no Ballybeg branches of any of these organisations, and since their meetings were relatively difficult to attend for those without cars, this restricted their appeal. Nevertheless, it was significant that whilst there were, for example, about a dozen of the Protestant farmers I knew who were members of the Farmers' Union, only two of the Catholics in the same area had joined, a man called Owen McConnell and young Jo McKinley (CD26).

The reasons for Catholic failure to join these groups were manifold. The reason normally expressed was that they felt that the farming groups particularly were really meant for the more prosperous farmers and that when these talked about technical matters they could have little to say relevant to farmers without much money behind them. This was a reasonable argument and one that accounted also for the reluctance to join shown by the poorer Protestant farmers. In addition, however, there was almost certainly another unexpressed reason for inhibiting Catholic membership. All these groups had been founded by Protestants, who counted amongst their numbers most of the more progressive farmers and those women who were socially most sophisti- cated. It is a reasonable guess that since they must have first persuaded their kin and closest contacts to join, it was not long before the groups had a nucleus of members, all or most of whom were Protestants. Any Catholic coming to a meeting would then be instantly aware of this, and feel inevitably a little socially uneasy and out of place in the gathering, just as the Protestant felt out of place at a 'Gaelic' football match—it is a matter of common observation that in every context the average Ulsterman's first reaction on joining any collection of people is to assess their religious affiliations. The sight of close Protestant neighbours would certainly be of some assurance to such a Catholic visitor. But only where, as in Jo's case, with his friendship with Keith Baxter, there existed a really strong relationship with keen members was the Catholic likely to attach himself to the group. Thus without any wish to turn these organisations into Protestant movements, the normal pattern of making contacts with others through the pre-existing network of relationships inevitably led to the development of just this kind of situation.

When we come to examine those relationships which had some kind of economic element, as between farmers and those who offered them services from which they derived a monetary benefit, the situation appeared on the surface to be confused, but in reality it was relatively simple. The members of each religious group felt a definite moral responsibility to patronise members of their own group if other things were relatively equal, and if those offering the service were not felt by the very nature of their calling to be in some senses opponents. On the other hand, if those offering the service were thought to have interests inherently antagonistic to those of the local people, or if no-one of an individual's own group could offer a comparable service, then it was considered perfectly natural to patronise members of the other religious group.

It was of course natural that the farmers should have perceived the interests of cattle and sheep dealers to be somewhat opposed to their own, since inevitably the one wanted to pay as little as he could and the other to be paid as much as possible. It was, I think, therefore natural that I could discover no feeling that a farmer *ought* to patronise a dealer of his own group even if necessary at the expense of accepting lower prices for his animals. On the contrary, it was thought that a farmer would be a real fool not to get the best prices he could from whoever was prepared to pay them, no matter what the dealer's religious affiliation. In practice it was probable that a disproportionate number of deals took place between the members of the 'same side' either because, as we saw in the case of Paul's buying and selling of heifers, the kinship network was a significant factor in determining the pattern of local sales, or because there was a tendency for farmers to come into particular contact with those regular dealers who were particular friends of their closest contacts who tended to be those of the same side. Nevertheless, there was no feeling that there was any moral obligation on a Protestant farmer to sell to a Protestant dealer, or a Catholic to a Catholic, because it was a relationship in which few holds were barred.

The situation was noticeably different in the case of the relationships of farmers to the feed merchants, and the public generally to the shopkeepers. Here too it is difficult to disentangle completely the factor of the sense of loyalty to one's own side from the more general sense of obligation to support close connections who, simply *de facto*, were also members of one's own side. There was a marked tendency for shopkeepers to take on as 'apprentices' youngsters from local farming families. This was not said to be done in order to attract their connections as customers—the explanation usually given was that such youngsters were more reliable and hard-working than the 'riff-raff' from Ballybeg itself—nevertheless these links and the fact that the shopkeepers themselves had many kinship and organisational links to the surrounding areas brought them clients on this basis alone. For example, one small hardware shop which was Protestant and competing against a much larger Protestant shop of the same type relied heavily on customers from the rural district from which the owner had originally come, and of whose Orange Lodge he was the Master. It was, nevertheless, perfectly clear that, over and above such links, individuals felt that they ought to support shopkeepers of their own side rather than the other. Thus Mary Jamison (PD19) carefully distributed her grocery purchases between the two main Protestant grocers, Groves and McCulloughs, and Paul distributed his feed purchases between McCullough (who was both grocer and feed merchant) and Black, the main Protestant feed merchant. It was quite inconceivable to either that they should have patronised

Michael McCurdy, who was the big Catholic grocer and feed-merchant; and this was despite the fact that he was a brother of their Catholic neighbour, Patrick McCurdy (CB100), whom they held in highest esteem. Had Michael been a Protestant the link through their neighbour would certainly have made Paul and Mary his customers. No-one thought that for them not to patronise him was in any sense an act of personal unfriendliness—it was simply their obvious, bounden duty to go to the other shops.

There were two pubs, one Protestant and the other Catholic owned in Ballybeg, but the clientele of each was not rigidly segregated on a religious basis (they were segregated of course on the basis of sex, since no woman ever entered either of them to drink at the bar—public houses were strictly for males only). In general, groups of men composed of Catholics only went to the Catholic pub, and Protestant groups to the Protestant pub. Nevertheless it often happened on a Fair day especially that a group of buyers and sellers of mixed religious persuasion would go for a drink together. This was by no means uncommon.

Where no member of an individual's 'own side' offered a particular service no embarrassment was felt in seeking it from the other side. In Ballybeg the only newsagent was a Catholic and was patronised by everyone, and naturally took both Unionist and Nationalist papers. The only men's hairdresser was also Catholic and had both Protestant and Catholic customers. There was no Catholic-owned shop that sold furniture or the larger household goods, and the bigger Protestant hardware shops had many Catholic customers on this account.

There was an interesting situation in regard to chemist shops. There was a Protestant shop that sold patent medicines, but the owner was not a pharmacist. Many Protestants were getting into the habit therefore of going to the Catholic pharmacist for all their chemists' requirements. This was perhaps partly because the elderly couple who kept the Protestant chemist shop were, to say the least, idiosyncratic. They belonged to a small sect violently hostile to clergymen of any kind and they were on principle rude to even Protestant clerics, and tended to be uncivil to members of the Church of Ireland in general. Moreover, they had their own special method of accounting which led them to try, on each transaction, to separate the cost from the profit and to put the exact money into different drawers. As it was only after this that they would give their customers their change, shopping here was a lengthy process.

Nevertheless, despite all these drawbacks, some Protestants scrupulously bought their patent medicines from this couple and went to the Catholic pharmacist only to have prescriptions made up. Some Protestants, however, felt that this was not really satisfactory. Indeed, I heard one professional man telling friends that they ought themselves, and ought to persuade their friends, to take their prescriptions not to the Ballybeg pharmacist at all, but to a town five miles away where there was a struggling Protestant widow, a good pharmacist, who 'could do with all the help she could get'.

Religious differences were not the only factors behind this argument; the Catholic pharmacist was a newly-arrived stranger, the Protestant was a local person in difficult circumstances, but the appeal was primarily to the Protestants' sense of obligation to their own side.

The same kind of appeal was made by Catholics. The Protestant doctor's practice had suffered significantly from the inroads of the new Catholic doctor who had come to Ballybeg after the setting up of the Health Service. He had relied explicitly on Catholic loyalties to recruit many of the Protestant doctor's Catholic patients. For many years the Protestant doctor had been the only medical practitioner in Ballybeg. Undoubtedly a clever man, he had been to Ballybeg what Dr. Cameron was to Tannochbrae. With the new conditions, however, it seemed there might be room for two doctors in the district and the Catholic doctor, a complete stranger to the area, had arrived. There was certainly some persuasion by the Catholic clergy to get their parishioners to go to the new man; medical relationships might well involve matters of faith and morals and they must have felt that their attempts to persuade Catholics to switch doctors was perfectly justifiable. What was significant, however, was that so many had apparently done so against their better judgement. The Catholic doctor was scarcely a popular man, and he was youngish, not in itself a characteristic to recommend a new doctor to a country practice. Yet for the most part only those Catholics who felt particularly grateful to the Protestant doctor had failed to make the change. In Ballybeg itself one such was the family of a prosperous widow whose husband the older doctor had attended through a long illness. Of the families we examined in detail, the O'Hanlins (CD14) had not changed because they believed it was the older man's skill that had enabled Teresa to have a longed-for son after a series of miscarriages; and Mrs. Devine (cc9) had not changed either, because her younger daughter was delicate and she feared to change the treatment she was getting. It was significant, however, that she felt it necessary almost to apologise to me for not having changed her doctor. 'A lot of people,' she said, had gone to the new man, but didn't I think it was 'wiser to stick with the man you know's good?' Nevertheless, most Catholics had changed and one unlooked-for consequence was that now even when people waited in a doctor's surgery it was likely that all the other patients would be co-religionists.

The separation of Catholic and Protestant networks was, of course, most marked in the case of kinship. In any small rural community we expect a great deal of intermarriage and in Bally-beg there were certainly convoluted kinship ties. What was different when it was compared with similar districts in other parts of the British Isles was that there were here two rigidly separated sets of convolutions. There is of course, from time to time, a marriage between a Protestant and a Catholic, but the separation into two distinct systems is maintained by the almost universal refusal to recognise kinship across the division.

This fact has to be stressed because it was extremely important. Intermarriage bridged no gaps. It was rare, but in so far as it is possible to generalise about such an occurrence, the couple were usually married in the wife's church and the husband dropped most of his former contacts even when he did not actually change to his wife's denomination. He ceased any attendance at his church and membership of the associated organisations and political groups. Most important was the fact that tensions were set up between him and his kinsfolk, and especially between them and his wife, that put all normal kin-based contacts between them out of the question. We have already seen how marriage with a Catholic broke the ties between Andy and Nelly Stuart (pc100 and pc101) and their brother (pc102). I had personal experience of the kind of tension that could exist between such a wife and ordinary members of the husband's group—coming one day into Mary Jamison's (pd19) kitchen I found there a woman and a young boy who were strangers to me helping Mary with odd jobs. The woman was not introduced to me nor to Mary's in-laws when they came into the room—no-one except Mary seemed able even to see the woman, and the only conversation consisted of stilted remarks made by the in-laws to each other or to Mary. The woman spoke only to

Mary and only in whispers, and the whole atmosphere was extraordinarily frigid. When the woman had gone, Mary explained to me that the woman was a Catholic who had married a Protestant and whose child was a Catholic. The husband had never actually 'turned', but when he died she had acted as if he had become a Catholic and had had him buried away from his own people in the Catholic cemetery. Now the widow was in desperate financial difficulties and had turned to Mary for help because they had been at school together. Mary, basically a warm-hearted soul, had taken pity on her and although she had little enough spare cash had found jobs for her to do around the kitchen and the farmyard as an excuse for giving her and the boy meals and a little money. In fact Mary continued to do this for several weeks. Mary's in-laws, all her in-laws, who had never known the woman as a neighbour, for she came from Mary's home district, were outraged and affronted at her presence. They displayed no hostility towards the boy, but refused to speak to his mother, and she continued to exhibit timid, almost fearful self-effacement. It can, I think, be imagined that if this were the reaction of those not related to the husband his kin would have been even more antagonistic.

The lack of kin ties linking the two 'sides' was of enormous social significance because kinship was so important in the field of social relationships. We have seen that in some ways kinship had generally less significance than might have been anticipated, since kinship recognition extended over only a very limited distance. This was true amongst both Catholics and Protestants and in both the mountain and the infield. Nevertheless those kin who were recognised everywhere played an important part in people's lives; a fact made very clear by an examination of the role of kinship in moulding the social relationships of those households that have been examined in detail.

In the first place, as we have seen, kinship played an important part in determining who could and who could not be visited informally. So far as women were concerned this was a vitally important factor in the lives of all but the most sophisticated. Women like Mrs. Baxter (PC20) and Betty Laird (PD32) did have a few female friends on whom they could call informally, but such women were a tiny minority. For the most part women could only visit with ease those to whom they were fairly closely related—and this applied equally, for example, to both the infield and 'mountain' Jamisons, to Michael McKinley's mother (CC13) and to Jo

McKinley's mother (cb6). In the uplands, of course, women often had in their houses unrelated male visitors who called to see their menfolk—but the significance of such visits was limited by the fact that most of the conversation took place between the men on topics interesting to them alone. Women depended for their social contacts very much on their kin.

Kinship also played a part in determining the pattern of visiting for men, although here conversely it seemed to be most significant in some respects for the more sophisticated men. Hill farmers, such as Andy Stuart (pc100) and Michael McKinley (cd27), had a range of close neighbours on whom they could call very informally; with such men kinship links with local farmers, where they existed, were important but the mere fact that men were near neighbours could be almost equally as important. Here kinship became significant primarily in determining the pattern of visiting further afield, for this seemed often shaped by the kinship network of the individual or his wife. In the infield where the patterns of neighbourhood co-operation and sociability were different, especially for the yeomen, men like Albert Baxter (pb15) and Alec Laird (pc22) seldom spent an informal evening in a neighbour's house and were, like their wives, dependent for most of their visiting on relatives, whom they went to see normally in company with their wives. Patterns of co-operation in farm work were everywhere influenced by considerations of kinship. In the hills co-operation over work occurred mostly between those living close together, but other things being equal, kinship played a part in the selection of swopping partners. In the infield co-operation was of two types, the borrowing of machinery, which seemed based on contiguity, not kinship, and co-operation over work which typically involved kin, when it did occur.

It is also important to emphasise again that although explicitly recognised kinship was limited, circles of 'kith' extended beyond. It was naturally with and about kith and kin, and their kith and kin, that people gossiped, and with their doings and opinions that the individual was concerned. It mattered whether they prospered or not and how people treated them. It was in the possibilities and probabilities of their marriages and their inheritance prospects, their buying and selling of land, that real interest lay. Despite the fact that wide extensions of kinship were not recognised and that kin groups as such did not exist, it followed inevitably therefore that those totally excluded from this network remained essentially

L

strangers and outsiders however close contacts might be in some respects. By denying the possibility of kinship connections, therefore, Catholics and Protestants very seriously limited their ties with each other.

The very importance of kinship thus inhibited contacts between Protestants and Catholics who, by definition, could not be kin. Moreover, even when contacts did take place other factors restricted the development of real understanding.

It was in this crucial regard that when Catholic and Protestant did meet the greatest efforts were made to prevent any controversial topic from being discussed. The obvious aim was to prevent social relations being ruffled by disagreements over subjects on which it was accepted that there could be no consensus. It is perhaps worth saying that in Ulster, even at relatively sophisticated levels outside Ballybeg, comments on religious differences may reach extraordinarily crude levels. For example, I have heard the matter of the participation or non-participation of the congregation in the Communion cup explained in terms of wine bibbing: Catholics saying Protestants are only Protestants because they want the chance of a drink at Communion, and Protestants asserting that the priest excludes others from taking the wine because he wants it all himself! Clearly those whose repertoire of arguments in favour of their own faith consists of statements at this kind of level cannot enter into religious debate with their opponents without the immediate danger of a quarrel. If, to avoid that possibility, they remain silent on these issues they never learn what it is others believe. The less obvious aim was the desire to protect many areas of an individual's beliefs from being disturbed by the necessity of defending them rationally against non-believers; and, less importantly perhaps, the desire not to arouse the kind of hostility in members of the other side that would occur should they feel themselves to be getting the worst of an argument about things in which they passionately believed. Confrontations on the main issues were fraught with such social peril that they had to be avoided at all costs. The result, however, was that Protestant and Catholic lived inter-mixed and, as we have seen, in some cases and in some contexts had close and friendly contacts, and yet for the most part managed to remain in almost complete ignorance concerning each others' beliefs.

Political beliefs too were similarly tabooed subjects. To my knowledge no Unionist or Nationalist ever button-holed a friend from the opposite camp and asked him to explain quietly and seriously why he voted as he did—still less did anyone ever corner such a friend to try to put his own views earnestly across to him. This fact was brought home to me when Jo McKinley (CD26) saw in me a splendid opportunity to try to discover what his Protestant neighbours were thinking, and took me aside to try to get me to tell him about it. All Jo's friendly contacts with Keith Baxter (PD30) were not sufficient to enable them to discuss these problems themselves—as Jo said to me, it was simply a question that could never be mentioned between them.

What has to be stressed is that the topics which were avoided were not only clear-cut matters of religion and Ulster politics, for many apparently neutral topics could lead to, or imply attitudes towards, the main forbidden subjects. This was of course true of any item of world politics of which the people of Ballybeg became aware, whether the matter had to do with choosing a new American president, or an event concerning, say, Tito or Franco. It was immediately assumed that there were Catholic and Protestant viewpoints on these questions, which meant they could not be discussed fully in 'mixed' company. It was the same with many apparently unpolitical items of local gossip—in so far as they were bound to refer to those who were either Catholic or Protestant, gossip carried implications which meant that views expressed had to be watched if the company included people from both groups. Sport, of course, as we have seen, was highly symbolic politically, so that it was only racing and betting that were really neutral subjects. Cultural activities similarly carried their load of political or religious connotations. Such things as symphony orchestras were obviously not part of the Ballybeg scene and virtually no-one would have wanted to talk about them anyway. What did interest people were local choirs, local drama groups, local bands and local musical competitions; but all these groups were recruited from one side or the other, they performed music or plays which were often explicitly or implicitly connected with one side or the other; even the competitions that they entered were often linked with one side or the other—a competition for bands playing traditional Irish music, for example, had firm Nationalist connections. Talk about even these things, therefore, could not be neutral.

In view of all this it is not surprising that it is only with members of the same side that individuals could relax enough to talk freely, to say what they thought. It was assumed that in mixed religious company the individual had to be on his guard in a way that was not true even of strangers of the same side. For instance, I stayed with a Catholic family when I went first to Ballybeg and almost immediately, within a few days of my arrival, I was invited into the house of Protestant neighbours, whom I had not previously met—the wife saying to me, 'Do come in and have a cup of tea; the people you're staying with are very nice, but it's not like being with your own, is it?' The assumption was that I would be able to relax and feel at home only in a Protestant household. It was an assumption based on a lifetime's experience of the Ulster situation.

The natural outcome of this situation was an intense concern with knowing the religious affiliations of all those encountered. Outsiders visiting Ulster often put down to bigotry the fact that the Ulsterman's first question after encountering anyone for the first time always seems to be 'What is he?' In fact this question is not in itself an expression of religious prejudice but an obvious response to the necessities of social existence in this area. In practice this question does not have to be asked of every chance-met stranger for the simple reason that a high proportion of people proclaim their group membership by wearing the badges of one or other of the many organisations with clear religious affiliations. So important is it, however, to be able to determine the allegiances of strangers that many Ulster people seem to have developed an extreme sensitivity to signs other than explicit badges that denote the affiliations of those they meet. Each looks automatically for slight indications from another's name, physical appearance, expression and manner, style of dress and speech idiom to provide the clues that will enable the correct categorisation to be made. In situations like that of Ballybeg, of course, these signs are not normally of great significance since most people are known by sight and therefore their affiliations are not matters for speculation. It must be emphasised, however, that religious affiliation is the most important characteristic of any individual, normally out-weighing in significance even that of sex. People talked about 'the Jamisons' or 'the Devines' and immediately conveyed messages about Protestant or Catholic membership without the necessity of giving any further information about any individual member of either family. It was inconceivable that in Ballybeg there could have been any case of mistaken sexual identity—but the embarrassment such an event would have caused could scarcely have been greater, or even as great, as that caused by mistaken religious identity!

8 Religious prejudice: stereotyping

In all the circumstances described in the last chapter, of the lack of contact between Catholic and Protestant, and the lack of real communication between them when they did meet, it is not surprising that each used stereotypes in thinking and speaking about each other, for each remained basically a stranger to the other.

Part of the stereotypes Catholics and Protestants held about each other were simply due to slight over-generalisation from the facts. Most Protestants ascribed the characteristics of the poor, the labourers and the 'mountainy' to Catholics in general; for most Catholics the 'typical' Protestant was the prosperous infield farmer. This kind of equation was not surprising since it had a factual basis.

In the first place most 'mountainy' people were Catholic. Because I was dealing with only the fringes of the 'mountainy' area there were a fair number of Protestant households in this part of the study; but further into the hill district the proportions of Protestants declined steeply and there were many townlands wholly or almost wholly Catholic. Conversely in the infield, whilst there were considerable numbers of Catholics present, the farms were predominantly owned by Protestants.

The difference in the economic positions of the two groups can be seen also if the people living in the townlands I studied intensively are listed according to whether they were farmers or non-farmers; and if farmers, then according to the size of their holdings (see table overleaf).

Of these figures two categories deserve special comment. In the first place the extent to which labourers as a category were associated with membership of the Roman Catholic church can only be understood if the figures for Ballybeg town itself are taken into con-

sideration. There, of thirty-six unskilled labourers twenty-five were
Catholic and eleven were Protestant. The second category that
deserves particular mention is that of the 'yeomen', for all those
in the rural district were Protestants. Even if we include Ballybeg
itself the picture is only slightly altered. There, if we use the same
kind of criteria, and count as yeomen those who made considerable
use of rooms other than the kitchen and had particularly high
standards regarding food and clothing, there were in fact three
Catholic families who came into this category. Of these, two were

	Protestants	Catholics	Total
Wage-earners (unskilled, not necessarily agricultural)	7	10	17
Small farmers (incomes of under about £600)	7	20	27
Medium farmers (incomes between approx. £600 and £900)	13	13	26
Large farmers (incomes over approx. £900)	8	7	15
'Yeomen'	8	0	8

recent immigrants, the doctor and the pharmacist, and only one
was local, the family of a shopkeeper, whose daughters at any
rate tended to mix almost exclusively now with kinsfolk and the
two other Catholic 'yeomen' households. At the same time there
were seven Protestant households which came into the 'yeomen'
category.

It was therefore not surprising that when Catholics talked about
the 'bigger farmers' and 'the well off' they generally meant
Protestants. Indeed, Catholics discussing the district with me
generally used such euphemisms when they wanted to tell me
about Protestants. Often a Catholic would assume a Protestant
to be better off than he was himself unless the contrary were known
without a doubt. For example, soon after I first arrived in the area
I asked Mrs. Devine's brother, Bernard O'Hara (cc8), who farmed
in the infield, to tell me the kind of difference that existed between
his farm and that of Fred Richards (pd5). I had wanted to get his
opinion on environmental differences, and had deliberately asked
him to make a comparison with a mountain farm that I knew to
be relatively prosperous and roughly the same size as his own. Later

I realised that Bernard would have known relatively little about the farm of a Protestant outside his immediate neighbourhood; at the time, however, his answer surprised me. From his tone I realised at once that to him the significance of my question was a matter not of differences in environment but of differences in the religious affiliation of farmers. He said shortly, and with some acidity, 'There's no difference at all, except he'll have a tractor and I haven't.' Fred of course did not have a tractor, but those who could fulfil certain criteria could get a loan towards the purchase of a machine, as Paul did later. Bernard's answer, therefore, was both a statement about his belief in the relative prosperity of Protestants and something more, for it carried the implication that Protestants enjoyed unfair advantages in gaining help from the Ministry of Agriculture. This kind of assumption was widespread and, as has already been indicated, was in part related to the general belief amongst the poorer Catholics and Protestants that outside authorities made their decisions not in accordance with objective merit but on the basis of personal considerations.

Part of the Catholic stereotype about Protestants also pictured them as hard-working but money grabbing. Mountainy Catholic farmers who had encountered energetic, market-oriented Protestant farmers tended to say disparagingly that those 'better off farmers' (i.e. the Protestants) had no time for anything but work and that they were unfriendly, with little concern for their neighbours. In part this was a comment simply based on observed fact —most of the Protestant farmers did live in the infield where, as we have seen, there was less contact and co-operation between neighbours. Partly, however, the belief seemed to stem from the desire to find a justification for refuting these farmers' implicit claims to superiority. In terms of values that *really* counted they could be thought of as inferior to the speaker, for it was immoral to put money before social relationships.

In the statement there was, moreover, a further implied criticism that these rich farmers were intellectual Philistines, in contrast to Catholics. In this assumption there was again an element of straightforward observation. There was an intellectual content to Irish nationalism. Enthusiasm for the cause gave a keen interest in Irish history and literature. If at times this enthusiasm, because it was held by people without much formal education, seemed somewhat naïve it was even more remarkable that it should have existed at all because they had so few advantages; moreover, it was an interest that by extension gave them a genuine respect for certain kinds of cultural and academic pursuits that given the poverty of the background was surprising. Kevin Whitelock (CD18), for instance, thought it important to tell me, as no local Protestant would have done, how shocked he had been during the war to meet servicemen who had known nothing of Shakespeare. Certainly in Kevin himself, his cousin Margaret (CE3), the Devine youngsters (CD22, 23, 24) and Jo McKinley (CD26), I encountered a group of young people who were 'literate' in a way that I did not find matched amongst any comparable group of Protestants. Significantly Kevin and his friends themselves could scarcely believe that a local Protestant could have similarly 'educated' interests. When I mentioned to Kevin and Jo that Fred Richards (PD5) possessed a large number of books on such serious topics as world affairs, they were visibly surprised; indeed their glances at one another and their raised eyebrows seemed to show a disbelief they were too polite to express openly. Their views were in part based simply on what they had observed; in part they were bound up with their nationalist claims to the 'cultural' superiority of the 'Irish'.

Perhaps because there were so few Catholic 'yeomen' there seemed to be comparatively little variation in the attitudes towards Protestants between the different ends of the Catholic social scale, although there was some difference in emphasis. The more prosperous Catholics, like their poorer brethren, believed Protestant farmers to be unfairly favoured by officials, but I did not hear from them, as I did from Kevin and his friends, the accusation that even the vet who graded the cattle at the Ballybeg fair was influenced by political and religious bias. In particular, Kevin was sure the vet was acting unfairly in giving the cattle sent by Protestants a higher grade than those of the Catholic farmers.[1] Infield Catholic farmers (who sent their beasts in a better condition) were, however, prepared to accept that the vet was in fact unbiased. It was noticeable, moreover, that infield Catholic farmers like Liam McDermot (CC101) did not suggest that Protestants were too keen on work or too indifferent to those around them—on the contrary they were ready themselves to speak of the 'laziness' of the mountainy farmer, just as were the Protestant infield farmers.

---

[1] Kevin probably had statistics on his side—the more progressive the farmer the more likely he was to present an animal in an acceptable condition, and Protestants formed a majority of such farmers.

Amongst the Protestants, as might be expected, there appeared to be a greater divergence of opinion about Catholics simply because Protestants were more socially divided.

Just as the Catholics had used terms such as 'better off farmers' when they had wanted to talk to me about Protestants, so 'yeomen' Protestants especially used the terms 'lower class', 'labourers', and 'poor' or 'mountain' farmers as synonyms for Catholics. Sometimes this was done deliberately, all knowing perfectly well what was implied; sometimes the substitution was almost unconscious and if the speaker realised what he was doing he would correct himself for my benefit. To discover attitudes to status differences, for example, I sometimes asked 'yeomen' and other infield Protestants questions about 'poor' farmers and labourers, and often my informants would begin at once to discuss religious relationships until they suddenly realised I had not been using euphemisms.

Very often, of course, not merely were Catholics equated with the poorer sections of the population, but there was a derogatory element in the stereotype. Thus, for Mrs. Baxter (PC20), not only was the main characteristic of Catholics the fact that they were 'low class' people, but they were also 'rough'. For example, it was in the context of complaining of the 'rough' treatment Keith had when he was a patient in the local hospital that she said, 'of course the nurses were of the lowest class—well, not the lowest class perhaps, but there were a lot of Roman Catholics amongst them'. Similarly, Betty Laird (PD32), in some ways a much more 'liberal' person than Mrs. Baxter, associated Catholics with 'antagonistic' labourers. Almost in the same breath she told me first that 'all the labouring men are R.C.s—you'd hardly get a Protestant at all to labour' (the only exceptions she knew were Jim Thompson (PC103) and his son), and then she went on to say that there was a lot of class antagonism locally and that all the labouring men of the district would vote Labour if they had the chance—what stopped them was that they were all, irrationally, Irish nationalists; irrationally so because she thought they were bound to lose economically if they got their way and Northern Ireland ceased to exist as part of the United Kingdom.

Protestants from the infield and from Ballybeg also associated Catholics with 'mountainy' ways, and were slightly contemptuous of these characteristics. Thus an infield Church of Ireland farmer, Jack Maloney, told me, with a little scorn in his voice, 'No-one stays up all night at wakes now, except the Catholics,' although hill people generally kept this custom. Similarly he told me, as did others, that 'only Catholics ceildhi nowadays', a statement that again overlooked the behaviour of hill Protestants.

I was particularly interested to be told that 'only Catholics believe in cures and charms', i.e. that certain complaints could be healed if the sufferer would go to an individual possessing, usually by inheritance, the 'gift' of curing certain diseases, normally by the recitation of a charm. As it happened, one of the Catholic farmers in the area, Owen McConnell (CD101), did possess such a 'cure'; it had been passed on to him, he said, by his mother who had received it from her father, and so on back down the generations. To be handed on effectively, he said, it had always to be transmitted to someone of the opposite sex. The 'cure' was for any kind of issue of blood in humans or animals.[2] Two things about this case particularly interested me. The first was that the farmer concerned, far from being a poor, old-fashioned hill farmer, was one of the most prosperous and advanced of the Catholic farmers; he was, unusually, an enthusiastic supporter of the Farmers' Union and was one of the first men in the district to take advantage of the then new method of pig rearing which involved the regular feeding of antibiotics to protect piglets against disease. The other point was that this 'cure' enjoyed locally a very high reputation amongst many people, Protestants as well as Catholics, and since it was much cheaper than going to the vet it was a very popular method of treating cows suffering from 'redwater' disease. I was, therefore, in a position to point out to my informant who told me that 'cures' were only used by Catholics that I knew of a number of Protestants, including such highly thought of farmers as the infield John Jamison (PD25) who had gone to Catholic Owen McConnell to seek his help. Unperturbed, my informant assured me there was a difference—this particular 'cure' was known so positively to be effective, on such good local authority, and it was so cheap that of course local Protestants used it—but this did not

---

[2] One other point about this 'cure' is worth mentioning—the words were almost identical with a charm used for the same purpose and quoted by Reginald Scott in his *Discoverie of Witchcraft*, 1584. The Ballybeg charm was as follows: 'By the blood of Adam that always looses/by the blood of Christ that always gains/By that same blood I command thee to flow no more/for the sake of Jesus of Nazareth.' Scott's charm runs: 'In the blood of Adam death was taken/In the blood of Christ it was all too shaken/And by the same blood I do thee charge/That thou do run no longer at large' (Scott, p. 155).

mean they believed superstitiously in 'cures' in general—only Catholics did that![3]

This kind of generalised identification of poor and 'mountainy' ways with Catholicism was naturally not accepted by the hill Protestants without some modification, although they too accepted the identification of Catholics with labourers generally, and especially the 'layabouts' in Ballybeg. Like the infield Protestants, those in the hills thought it characteristic of these labourers, and indeed of Catholics generally, that they should try to 'diddle' the welfare services. That the more prosperous Catholics themselves despised such behaviour, though it was a known fact, was often ignored when general opinions were expressed. In both the hill district and the infield, Protestants told me stories of farmers who could get labourers (implicitly or explicitly Catholics) to work for them only provided the men were allowed Friday morning off to go to Ballybeg to collect their 'dole' for being unemployed. In so far as these incidents were true it of course implied that the farmers were themselves benefiting by not paying for the insurance stamps for these labourers, but the incidents were depicted as part of a deliberate Catholic plot to get something for nothing from the state. In both areas I was also told stories of labourers and other Catholic patients who, although perfectly fit, demanded certificates of sickness from their Protestant doctors, and who, on being refused, made this the excuse indignantly to change to Catholic doctors. This again was depicted as a kind of general Catholic plot.

Where hill Protestants did differ in their attitude to Catholics was, as might be expected, in the statements they made about the latter's readiness to keep up those customs which were generally thought old-fashioned, but were in fact the common practice of the hill district. They did not say that only Catholics 'swopped' or 'ceildhied', but they tended to say that Catholics were generally speaking more traditional than they were themselves.

[3] The attitude of prosperous infield Catholics was ambivalent. On the one hand they too regarded 'mountainy' ways with scorn; on the other—such patterns were 'Irish' and therefore to practise them was to validate the politically significant claim to 'Irish' descent.

9 Protestant prejudice: the influence of denominationalism

So far we have touched on only the fringes of the problem of religious and political prejudices in Ballybeg. Now we must explore the matter more deeply, and in particular we must examine Protestant anti-Catholic prejudice.

In part I must concentrate on this aspect of the problem for, despite the fact that in most ways my Catholic informants were extremely helpful and friendly, everything that they had ever learned made it difficult for them to speak with complete frankness to me, a Protestant, about Protestants. In any case, however, it would have been Protestant anti-Catholic prejudice that I would have wanted to explore because it seemed to present the bigger problem. Most outsiders to areas such as Ballybeg come away believing that Protestants are more prejudiced than Catholics. If any proof were wanted it exists in the fact that Catholics have no avowedly anti-Protestant organisation, whereas the Protestants have the Orange Order, whose explicit *raison d'être* is to encourage and express anti-Catholic bias. Because this is so we must consider from many points of view the significance of this movement, and the different degrees of support it receives from different sections of the Protestants.

One important, if obvious, point to make at the outset is that in so far as Protestants wanted to unite as Protestants, they needed a special organisation through which to manifest this unity—an organisation not tied to any particular denomination. This was because Protestants were divided into different denominations. Moreover, to a degree surprising to the outsider, the different denominations displayed mutual hostility.

The major Protestant denominations in the Ballybeg area were the Presbyterians and the Church of Ireland. In some ways these two groups were sociologically similar since they were both 'churches' rather than 'sects', expecting to claim as members all the children of members, and to recruit by birth rather than by the conversion of adults from other denominations. They were also similar in that both contained a wide socio-economic range of members, and a substantial proportion of the congregations of both churches, though especially that of the Church of Ireland, were from the poorer sections of the Protestant population. Interestingly, a majority of both Presbyterian and Episcopalian men who did attend services remained silent, joining neither in the hymn singing nor, in the Church of Ireland services, in any of the responses except the Creed. In this the behaviour of the men differed from that in the other two local Protestant denominations, the Methodists and the Baptists, both of which had, by comparison, only small congregations. The reason for this difference was almost certainly, in part, the result of the different social composition of the denominations. In general, the poorer the farming family, the more rigid the dichotomy between men's and women's behaviour —the greater the proportion of poorer members in the congregation, therefore, the more likely it was that a significant proportion of the members would define very active participation in religious activity as something to be eschewed by all proper men. The other factor which may have influenced the behaviour of Baptist and Methodist men was their sense of personal responsibility for the organisation of the services. Neither group had its own clergyman and each had to rely on visiting ministers and lay preachers, so that most of the organisation had to be done by members of the congregations; moreover, each had a tradition of recruiting adults as well as the children of members, and this perhaps had produced a situation in which men played an unusually active part, since for a man to change his denomination, even within the Protestant fold, was a considerable decision. Men who made such a change might be expected to show their commitment to their new church.

It was, perhaps, this traditional pattern of recruitment to the Baptist and Methodist churches that, at an institutional level, made the relationships of the members of these denominations, even with the Presbyterian Church, a little difficult, for to some extent they were seen as competitors. It may be difficult for the English to appreciate this since in England there is a very large pool of non-believers in which the different denominations can fish for converts without attempting to entice away the adherents of other churches. In much of Ulster, however, not merely are all individuals divided at birth into Catholics and Protestants, but Protestants are from birth attached quite firmly to particular denominations. Indeed so firm is this attachment normally that the size of a church membership is reckoned not in individuals but in 'families', that is in households.

The smaller Protestant denominations in Ballybeg were therefore regarded as having stolen their members from other churches. Sometimes they are accused of having deliberately set out to attract converts from other Protestant denominations: this was implied by one Presbyterian woman who said of the Salvation Army 'Self-denial Week' campaign, 'I always support them when they come round to the door, but they opened a meeting in Enniskillen and their people are all former members of other congregations.' Sometimes the accusation was not that they had actively poached, but merely that they had provided a welcoming refuge for people who for one reason or another had quarrelled with their clergymen, or with other members of the congregation, but who would have returned to the fold had another church not been there to admit them. Indeed it was usually assumed that those who had joined the smaller denominations had done so as the result of such quarrels rather than because they had considered deeply the dogmatic differences between the denominations. For example, I was given two accounts of why certain families had joined the Methodist church in the early years of this century. I was told that a number of very respectable Church of Ireland people had changed because they had become irritated at the behaviour of their then Rector, especially at his alleged habit of getting drunk in company with the local doctor and throwing bottles out of the Rectory windows at passing members of his congregation. It was also explained that a number of Presbyterians had joined because at about the same time they quarrelled with their Minister because he had failed to denounce from the pulpit a locally notorious 'Home Ruler' (i.e. an advocate of Home Rule for the whole of Ireland) when he had visited their church one Sunday.

Indeed, paradoxical as it might seem, it appeared that despite the strong feelings of denominational loyalty felt by most people, secession was not uncommon. An individual or a family might leave a particular church because a disgruntled member could thus punish the whole congregation, since they all felt diminished by the defection. Consequently secession, or threats to secede, might occur over matters that had no doctrinal significance. During my stay, for example, one Presbyterian threatened to leave that church because the wife of the caretaker was rude to friends of his when, as an amateur theatrical group, they were rehearsing in the church hall.

Under such circumstances jealousy between even the non-conformist denominations was perhaps inevitable. To understand the relations between the Church of Ireland and the Presbyterian Church, it is first of all necessary as so often in Ireland, to know something about their historical relationships.

It is widely known that to Catholics Protestantism is the religion of those they regard as their traditional political oppressors: it is less widely realised that historically the Presbyterians regarded the Established Church in the same light. There were few Presbyterians who did not know tales of persecutions they suffered from the agents of the Anglican Church in the seventeenth century. Significantly there is a common phrase 'black-mouthed Presbyterians' that members of other churches often assumed to be somehow a reference to Presbyterian dourness, but Presbyterians themselves said it arose from the times when their Scottish Covenanting forefathers were harried into the hills and their mouths were stained black by the juice of the berries that were their only food, all because they refused to accept the Prayer Book. Politically, until the beginning of the nineteenth century and the repeal of the Test Acts, the position of the Presbyterians was, like that of other nonconformist churches, in many ways similar to that of Roman Catholics. It was, of course, no worse than that of non-conformists in England, but there were few areas in England where a nonconformist denomination was as economically powerful as was the Presbyterian Church in many respects in Ulster, and consequently few areas where the political disadvantages of nonconformity were so deeply resented. Significantly in the great rebellion of 1798 the Presbyterians in Ulster joined forces with the Catholics and rose against the English landlords and the Episcopalian church. There is therefore an old-standing antagonism between the Church of Ireland and the Presbyterian Church in Ulster.

In the Ballybeg district there were occasions when the two main Protestant denominations held united services. In the first place, a joint service took place each year on the Sunday preceding the Twelfth of July. It was held alternately in the Presbyterian and Episcopal churches, and involved a parade of all the local Orange

Lodges (it should be noted that it was an 'Orange' festival that united the denominations). A second annual joint service was also in a sense politically inspired. This was the Armistice Day service that was similarly shared between the Presbyterian and Episcopalian churches. Finally it was customary for the evening Harvest Festival service of each of the Protestant churches to be attended by large numbers of visitors from other churches and denominations and, indeed, the Presbyterian church cancelled its own evening service, usually very poorly attended in any case, on the occasion of the Harvest Festival in the Episcopal Church.

These joint services were neither free from friction, nor really a sign that much of an ecumenical spirit filled the participants. The most marked example of actual friction, during my visit, occurred when the Cadet Force failed to turn up to the Armistice Day parade service at the Episcopal church. This was because the Commanding Officer of the force had quarrelled with the Church of Ireland authorities. They had decided that all the money collected should go to the Church of Ireland's War Orphan Society; but the C.O., a Presbyterian, objected and on principle thought that half the money should go to the Earl Haig Fund. Even when no quarrel marred these occasions, relations between the leaders of the churches were difficult. The Rector would not attend services in the Presbyterian Church at all. The Presbyterian Minister did attend special services in the Parish Church, but necessarily in a private capacity as he was neither specially invited nor allocated a particular seat.

To some extent, perhaps, the relationships between the two main Protestant churches were made peculiarly difficult by the particular characters of the individuals who led them. The Presbyterian Minister was young, idealistic and egalitarian. He was losing the inevitable naïvety with which he had come to his first church, but he was still being repeatedly surprised at the way in which local people expected him to be able to manipulate the world of officialdom beyond the confines of Ballybeg—he had neither the desire nor, he felt, the ability to take on such a role and failed to understand why people should expect this of him when his task, as he saw it, was to preach the gospel and act as a spiritual shepherd of his sheep. The Rector, on the other hand, fully appreciated the local expectation that he should help people in their relationships with the somewhat mysterious outside world of bureaucracy. An elderly man, it sometimes seemed that he would have fitted happily into one of Trollope's novels. He was conscious of his own social and intellectual superiority but willing to put this at the disposal of anyone who would recognise it. He enjoyed particularly good relations with the Roman Catholic population, some of whom preferred to seek his help rather than that of their own priest when they found themselves in financial trouble or wanted to make useful outside contacts. It was noteworthy too that when, sometime after I had left the area, Jo McKinley (CD26) was arrested on suspicion of I.R.A. activities, it was the Rector who immediately stepped in to secure his release. His attitude, however, aroused all the latent anti-authoritarianism and anti-clericalism of the Presbyterians, who asserted he preferred Catholics just because they were more inclined to touch their caps to him. Obviously there was little in the character or outlook of the Episcopalian and Presbyterian clergymen to lead to the kind of warm personal regard between them that might have bridged the institutionalised differences between their churches.

Even between individual members of the different congregations there was a certain amount of veiled hostility arising out of denominational differences. Indeed it is significant that strict rules had grown up relating to inter-denominational marriage amongst Protestants. It occurred quite frequently but it seemed as if the potential tension between the households concerned was only checked by the strict rule that a woman should attend her husband's church and bring up his children in his denomination.

Betty Laird's (PD32) refusal to comply with this custom was very indicative of the subordinate position accorded the in-marrying husband. Her awareness that in the eyes of many she had done the wrong thing in not changing her allegiance from the Presbyterian Church to the Church of Ireland may perhaps have made her particularly antagonistic to the Episcopalians. For instance, in one of our very early conversations she showed her resentment at what she thought of as their claims to social superiority, recalling an incident which had happened years previously when her younger brother, then attending the local school, had apparently answered a question put to him by the visiting Rector with insufficient respect, and the teacher had bawled, 'Can't you address the Rector as "Sir", you ill-mannered Presbyterian brat?'

Betty Laird was, however, far from being the only woman to express denominational prejudice. Mary Jamison (PD19), when she was a nurse, had often had to attend the Church of Ireland with her patients, but as she admitted, she had deliberately shut her ears to what was said, and had managed to remain, like the staunch Presbyterian that she was, totally ignorant of the form of the Prayer Book service.

Mrs. Baxter (pc20), on the other hand, took up a fairly common Church of Ireland attitude, when she spoke contemptuously of the 'goody-goody Presbyterians'. She also implied they were socially inferior, a common assumption of 'yeomen' Episcopalians—but jibes about the relative social standing of the different denominations were made from both sides; it was a common Presbyterian accusation that Church of Ireland members who were not well off were too servile, and people pointed to Jim Thompson (pc103) as proof of the fact that poor Episcopalians were content with the kind of status no decent, egalitarian Presbyterian would have accepted for a moment.

A lot of this talk was only semi-serious; indeed in part it was banter used when members of the different denominations teased each other about their allegiances; but like all joking relationships this tendency to tease arose from the existence of certain genuine tensions between the various Protestant churches. Contrary to what might at first be supposed, despite the existence of strong ties binding Protestants in their common opposition to Catholicism the inter-denominational conflict between the Protestant denominations was much stronger than in modern England.

Denominationalism was certainly one reason why the Orange Order was so important, for it brought Protestants of all denominations together. Almost every Protestant in the area was a member of the Orange Order. In the area I studied in detail there were only four exceptions to the rule that all Protestant men joined the order. One was Albert Baxter (pb15) whose wife, we saw, had persuaded him to let his membership lapse because she thought there were too many roughs among the members; and the second was her son, Keith, whom she had persuaded not to join. The third was Campbell Wright (pc5). He told me that he had, as a young man, been going to join but the members of what was to have been 'his' lodge had got so drunk that Twelfth that in disgust he withdrew his application for membership. Many, like Bill Jamison's sons (pe5 and 6) and young Dick Richards (pe3), were taken along to the local Lodge while they were still mere boys, to become members of the band, an important subsidiary group in most Lodges. Membership of the Lodge itself, however, was sought usually only when the boy was seventeen or eighteen; only then, when he had been proposed and initiated, could he attend the real meetings of the Lodge.

The members of the Orange Order met, usually monthly, in the hall of the particular Lodge to which they belonged. In the Ballybeg district there were three: one in Ballybeg itself, and two in the rural areas outside. The primary basis of recruitment to a Lodge was proximity, although the picture was made a little complex by the fact that men normally remained attached to the Lodge they had joined in youth no matter where they subsequently moved. In consequence the boundaries of membership of a particular Lodge could not be drawn very exactly. Thus one farmer, Jack Maloney, still belonged to a group on the other side of Ballybeg where he had been brought up and not to his local Lodge. Even more strikingly, John Turner, a man who had come to farm in the area from a different county, had never changed his old membership and still travelled back twice a year to his old home to attend important Lodge meetings there, and still joined with this Lodge to march on July 12th. Sometimes men even perpetuated this pattern by taking their sons to join these more distant Lodges. Paul Jamison (PD10), for instance, belonged to the central Ballybeg Lodge and not his nearest one because his father, Old James (PB8), when he quarrelled as a young man with his family, had left the group to which his brothers and old neighbours belonged and had changed to the Ballybeg Lodge. Later, perhaps because the quarrel had never really been healed, he had taken Paul and his other sons along there too. Usually, however, sons joined the nearest Lodge.

The fact that young recruits normally joined the neighbouring Lodge was, of course, significant because to a considerable extent Lodge ties cut across denominational cleavages. The boys in the band of the Lodge in the area I studied included Baptists, Presbyterians and members of the Church of Ireland. These ties were the more important just because men developed a strong attachment to their own lodge and a sense of loyalty to its members. The Parade on July 12th was not only an expression of Protestant opposition to Catholics, although this was its most obvious function. Internally there was intense competition between the different Lodges to see who could muster the best turn-out. Those members and their wives who expended time and money freely on the Lodge's regalia and band instruments were, in this respect, hoping as much to score points off fellow Protestants, and especially nearby

Lodges, as to overawe the Nationalists. Obviously the more intense the feeling for the Lodge, the greater its significance in binding together men of different Protestant denominations.

Many of the older and more respectable Protestants of the area were also linked together because they belonged to the 'Royal Black Preceptory', in effect a senior branch of the Orange Order, which met centrally every second month in the Orange Hall in Ballybeg. Men like old William Jamison (PB9) and Jack Maloney and John Turner belonged, though neither Paul nor Bill Jamison had joined. The only actual qualification for membership was prior attachment to the Orange Order, but in practice it was believed that the members tried to exclude those whom they thought potentially unreliable, either because they were too young or prone to become unruly if they drank. Significantly perhaps, of Mary Jamison's two brothers, the somewhat unsteady Jack (PD20) was not a member, but the older, more sober Harry Christie (PD17) had joined; and it was indicative of the attitudes of members that at one combined Orange and Black Parade when Jack got involved in a drunken fight (with another Protestant), Harry refused to go to his help because he was wearing his 'Black' regalia and would not bring it into disrepute. The effect of this pattern of recruitment was to bring together over an even wider area than the Orange Lodge, the more sober Protestants of all denominations.

It may seem irresponsible to suggest that anything good can come out of antagonism and bigotry, but it would be a mistake to overlook certain aspects of the Orange Order which made a positive contribution to life in the society.

The demonstration every Twelfth of July by the Orange Lodges may, for example, seem to outsiders anxious for good community relations to be primarily provocative in effect. It is an annual occasion for public reminiscing about Protestant and Catholic clashes over the last three hundred years, and for bigoted speeches. Yet there is another side, and an important one, to these annual festivities. To the site chosen for a Twelfth procession there came, from all over the county, Lodge bands and Lodge members and supporters. Each group of players was as resplendent as local funds could make it, and the instruments of each band were competitively expensive. At the head of each band floated a banner, huge and gorgeous like a multicoloured sail, borne aloft by a couple of stalwart (and, hopefully, sober) Orangemen who held the poles, and were accompanied by a train of little boys tugging at ropes.

The banner proudly identified the Lodge and displayed some symbolic scene—such as King William resplendent on his white horse. Then came the band, either in some multicoloured Scottish tartan and playing bag-pipes; or in some blue or scarlet bandsmen's uniform, blowing on brass or silver instruments. The noise was literally indescribable, for apart from assigning each Lodge its place in the processional march the organisers attempted no further interference with these highly independent groups. Each of perhaps forty bands, during the mile or so of its march between the town centre and the 'field' where the speeches are made, lustily played its own repertoire quite regardless of the efforts of its next-door neighbours. 'The Lord is my Shepherd' on brass marched bravely and simultaneously next to 'The Sash my Father Wore' played on bag-pipes (by pipers totally unconcerned by the fact that the tune demands semi-tones that bag-pipes do not possess). Such a demonstration was a mixture of colour, gold and purple and scarlet, and a unique cacophony that trumpeted forth not only hostility to foes, but local pride in this climax to long, hard work, and the release of jubilant, bacchanalian carnival.

No observer could forget the dark side of all this, the intra-community tensions that are its *raison d'être*, but to ignore this other aspect is to ignore something very important in the life of the people.

IO Protestant prejudice:
the influence of income and area

In saying that denominationalism played a significant part in making the Orange Order important I have still left a great many things unexplained. We may grant, if only for the sake of argument, that it is reasonable to expect that some kind of 'pan-Protestant' organisation should have devloped. This fact, however, scarcely explains the intensity of the movement's hostility to Roman Catholicism.

The extent of this hostility was revealed in the very rules of the Order, at least as I was taught them in Ballybeg. They went as follows:

An Orangeman is devoted to, and humbly and reverently serves God the Father to whom he has access by His Son, Jesus Christ, who is the only Mediator between God and man;

An Orangeman promises diligently to read the Holy Scriptures and to attend religious services;

He promises to bring up his offspring faithfully in the Protestant religion;

An Orangeman is gentle and courteous, not acting with hostility towards his Roman Catholic neighbours, but seeking by his example and conversation to spread the Protestant faith;

An Orangeman must avoid the company of wild characters;

He promises not to take the name of God in vain, and to abstain from cursing and swearing;

He promises to uphold the laws and not to belong to any organisation or to swear to any oaths which has as their purpose the breaking of the law;

He swears loyalty to the Sovereign and her heirs being Protestant, and to the Constitution of 1688 and the Protestant succession;

An Orangeman is not, never has been, and never will become a Roman Catholic;

An Orangeman is not married to, and never will marry a Roman Catholic;

An Orangeman seeks by all lawful means to withstand the spread of Roman Catholicism.

An even more explicit, if less pious, indication of the attitude of Orangemen was to be found in the traditional 'Orangeman's toast', which I was also taught, as something of a joke. This ran:

'To the pious, glorious and immortal memory of William, Prince of Orange who came from Holland to save us from Popery, brass money, and wooden shoes, and gave to us our freedom and an open Bible; and he who will not drink this toast may he be damned, rammed, crammed into the great gun of Athlone, and shot from there into Hell, into the hottest part of Hell, with the door locked behind him and the key in an Orangeman's pocket!'

The other point that needs explanation is that anti-Catholic antagonism was expressed more strongly by the poor Protestants (including in this term the hill Protestants) than by any others. This was, and is, regarded as a very common phenomenon in Northern Ireland. In some districts this seems to be shown by the very pattern of membership of the Orange Order itself. This was not the case in the border areas where membership was almost total, but in areas such as north Antrim it was accepted that most Orangemen were working-class Protestants. Even in Ballybeg, however, it was assumed that it was the poorer Protestants who were the most enthusiastic Orangemen and the most bigoted anti-Catholics. One of the few non-members of the Order, a sophisticated farmer, said to me 'some of those mountainy Orangemen, they're as wicked as cats' (meaning that they were fierce and spiteful in their relations with Catholics). It was a belief that was in varying ways repeatedly expressed, especially by the 'yeomen' Protestants, and seemed borne out by the suspicion of the hill Protestants themselves that some of the yeomen were insufficiently enthusiastic Orangemen.

It is of course a pattern which has received some recognition by those discussing the recent troubles in Northern Ireland. Journalistic comment has tended to suggest that explanations of anti-Catholicism in general, and the bias of the poorest Protestants in particular, can be explained in simple economic terms. Protestants, it is argued, have gained for themselves social and economic privileges to which they seek to cling. When Catholics seek to gain a fairer share of the economic pie this naturally arouses antagonism. It is understandable that it should be the poorer and less privileged Protestants who show the greatest overt antagonism, for the same kind of reaction can be seen amongst poor whites living with a coloured population. Poor whites are very anxious to keep the coloured population subordinate just because they themselves are so poverty-stricken and have such a low status. It is vital to them to keep the coloured population down because if they could no longer be regarded as inferior then the poor whites would lose the last vestiges of their self-respect; and job advantages that colour prejudice gives the whites are specially vital to the economic position of the uneducated. Certain aspects of the situation in Ballybeg might seem to fit in with this pattern—but at the very least an examination of the facts suggests that any explanation in such terms grossly over-simplifies the problem.

In the first place the amount of economic competition between the relatively poor Protestants and Catholics was limited. It will become clear in the later analysis that there was a certain antagonism generated between farmers of different faiths over land; but this antagonism was far from being directly economic in its origin. Such competition as there was over land was more often directed to its symbolic worth than its monetary value. Ownership of a farm meant the symbolic occupation of an area. The transfer of a farm from a Protestant to a Catholic or vice versa was an issue that was emotionally more important if the townland in which the farm was situated had previously been owned entirely by the members of one faith; in such a case the transfer of the farm was much more of a blow to the losing side than it was if the townland ownership had previously been mixed. Moreover, the renting of particular fields on short leases to the members of the other side was quite acceptable. Again it would seem reasonable to postulate a direct economic motive had it been the case, for instance, that Protestant hill farmers appeared to nurture any hope of obtaining infield farms for themselves; it would then perhaps have been reasonable to assume that they would violently discourage the sale of land to Catholics, hoping that they themselves might buy farms from infield Protestants at under the free market price. In fact, however, such hopes of infield farms seemed not to enter their minds. Moreover, it would be quite unrealistic to consider the question of apparent competition for land without recognising that in practice although there was still regular demand for land locally, that demand was in fact declining and declining particularly in the hill region of marginal farming. Competition for land, as an economic asset, was therefore distinctly limited.

Between the poorer Protestants and Catholics competition was also limited in another direction. Housing was not then an issue that I ever heard raised when the question of sectarian relations was discussed. This was not surprising since at that time there was very little housing organised by the local council—which in any case had a Nationalist majority. Even employment seemed not to be a serious issue. Local employers were all small and their employment policy seemed not to give rise to much contention. It was accepted that shopkeepers took 'apprentices' of their own faith, but so far as their other employees were concerned they took whomever they could get and were thankful if they could get reasonably good workmen, whatever their faith. In so far as local Protestants sought to avoid labouring jobs, competition between them and Catholics was in any case avoided. Moreover, most people were perfectly well aware of the realities of the situation. Those without education or special skills knew that if they wanted decent jobs they would in all probability have to seek them in Scotland or England where no attention whatever was paid to the religion of a potential employee. Those with some educational background might, for example, have a personal interest in hoping that the government and others employing white-collar workers would discriminate in favour of Protestants; the unskilled who could not hope to be able to compete seriously with the urban worker in Belfast in any case had very little personal advantage to hope for from any such discrimination.

It was, moreover, apparent that in pursuing their everyday activities the ordinary farmers were not in competition with each other to any noticeable extent. Those who manifestly competed with each other in such a way as to raise clearly the question of sectarian loyalties were the shopkeepers and the professional people in Ballybeg. In their case they clearly were economic rivals because of the way in which their 'market' was divided up on religious lines. Where the market had been divided for some time, this economic rivalry was almost masked by everyone's acceptance of the fact. It was, for example, so much a matter of course that Protestant grocers had Protestant clients, and Catholic grocers had Catholic clients, that the division of the customers on religious grounds was taken for granted. Grocers for the most part thought of other shopkeepers amongst their co-religionists as being their main competitors.

When a new situation developed, as it had for example over

the Health Service, then the element of Catholic/Protestant competition came to the forefront. Prior to the introduction of the
Health Service the doctors in this and neighbouring areas had been
almost entirely Protestants. This was understandable since the
majority of the more affluent inhabitants were Protestant. It was
on these people that a medical man had to rely for his living—
indeed to a fair extent the fees they paid subsidised the service he
provided for the poorer people, including of course many Roman
Catholics. When the Health Service was introduced for the first
time, a doctor was paid as much for treating the poor as the better
off, and it became economically possible for a doctor to run a
practice that did not include the latter among its patients. This
for the first time gave an opening to Catholic doctors which they
very naturally took. It as inevitable that on entering an area
like Ballybeg they recruited patients along religious lines. It was
equally inevitable that the already established Protestant doctors
should resent as unethical this manipulation of religious loyalties
to 'steal' their patients—I suspect that many of the stories of
Catholic patients switching doctors to get time off that their health
did not warrant stemmed from the fact that patients wanting to
make a change of doctor were embarrassed and waited for an acceptable occasion that could excuse a breach with their former doctor.
On 'objective' economic grounds it ought to have been the professional men and the shopkeepers who manifested the strongest
religious bias.

That no simple economic explanation could account for anti-
Catholic bias was illustrated nicely by the clearest case I myself
witnessed of an attempt to discriminate economically against
Catholics. At the committee meeting of Protestants concerned with
the organisation of the sports meeting and fête to mark the
Coronation, one man suggested that no Roman Catholics should
be allowed onto the grounds to sell things like sweets and ice-
cream. He justified his viewpoint by saying, as was true, that only
Protestants had contributed to the funds raised for the occasion
and therefore it was unreasonable that Catholics should benefit
from it, especially when they professed themselves uninterested
in the occasion. Immediately, however, another man got up to say
that any ban like this would be quite wrong—that Catholics should
be allowed to sell goods like anyone else. Now it was true that the
first man was a rather struggling shopkeeper, whilst the second
was an affluent one; but contrary to what the cynical might

suppose, the first was an ironmonger with nothing either to gain or lose from the matter, whilst the advocate of Catholic participation was a grocer who sold confectionery.

Attitudes about social status and especially about intermarriage also could scarcely be interpreted in 'racialist' terms. It is perfectly true that some Protestants assumed that Catholics normally had a social status lower than their own, but these were the infield Protestants. I mixed a great deal with the poorer hill Protestants and they never gave me directly or indirectly the impression that they thought of their Catholic farmer neighbours as anything but their social equals, and I could never detect anything but complete social equality in their personal relationships with their Catholic neighbours. True they looked with disfavour on intermarriage and on too friendly relations of Protestant adolescents with Catholic youngsters, but even here the attitudes were scarcely typical of a white/coloured situation. Very little anxiety was shown about Protestant girls in relation to Catholic boys. I observed many times that if a Catholic boy started to flirt with a Protestant girl nobody frowned on it and the girl was expected to flirt good-naturedly back. She was not expected to cut the boy short or act disdainfully towards him—that would have been very bad manners. The point was that the people had confidence in the girl's training in chastity and religious loyalty—a girl was unlikely to let a Catholic boy 'get her into trouble', and it was unthinkable that she would otherwise change her religion just in order to marry one. What aroused anxiety was the behaviour of a Protestant boy who started to get too friendly with Catholic girls. They were far less sure of a boy's morals, and what is significant for this argument, it was accepted that if he made a Catholic girl pregnant he was under much the same obligation to marry her as he would have been had she been a Protestant—indeed this situation was said to be the start of most mixed marriages. This was scarcely a poor white/coloured situation. Yet the poor manifested most prejudice, at least verbally.

In order to analyse just what was behind the expression of anti-Catholic attitudes, especially by the poorer Protestants, and their enthusiasm for the Orange Order, I want to begin by looking at some of their anti-Catholic views. In particular I want to examine the views of Mary Jamison (PD19). She spoke to me more frankly than anything else partly because she was a woman talking to a woman, partly because she was not so sophisticated that she was self-conscious when she expressed biased opinions, and partly because I knew her very well.

Mary assured me that she was not against Catholics themselves, only on guard against Catholicism. But Nationalism, whether it manifested itself in Republican symbols, or in antagonism to symbols of Ulster's independence, swiftly aroused her anger. She boasted of Jack (PD20), her brother, in the 'B' Specials: 'He stopped a car one night when he was on the border patrol. They (the Catholic passengers) were coming home from a dance and the girls in the back cheeked him. They laughed at him because he couldn't search them as there wasn't a lady policeman present. So he got them out of the car and made them take off their shoes and walk about in their stockinged feet. That soon made them nervous!' On other occasions, she told me about, an incident the previous year when 'some Fenians' on St. Patrick's Day had put up a Tricolour on the top of a tall pole, and had tarred it to stop the 'B' men from climbing up to get it down—she snapped angrily: 'Doesn't that show the ingrained wickedness of them?'

It was also apparent that even when she might not approve of a particular Protestant's action in relation to a particular Catholic, if it came to a confrontation it was immediately seen in 'us'/'them' terms. For instance, when I asked her if she had ever heard of 'B' men firing unnecessarily she told me: 'Thompson, the leader of the "B" men at Ballyduff (her home district), had got into trouble for that—there was one time when he was summonsed but he and McSweeney, the man he fired at, were both acting out of spite. Thompson owns a pub in Ballyduff and McSweeney used to drink in another (R.C.) pub there and stay in it till all hours of the morning, playing cards. Well, Thompson didn't think that was right, so one night when he was on duty he met McSweeney on his way home and ordered him to stop. Well, right enough, Thompson didn't give him the correct signal, but McSweeney knew he ought to stop well enough; but he didn't, so Thompson fired (into the air). Well, they brought Thompson up for trial at Belfast, but he got off, and when he came home all the "B" men went down to the station and carried him back shoulder high.' It was an action of which, by her tone, Mary thoroughly approved.

Significantly Mary knew many stories of violent or mean acts by Catholics against Protestants, both in general and out of her own or her family's experience. Most dramatically she told me that 'Fenians' in Belfast had damaged a number of Protestant churches during the war. In fact in the bombing of Belfast it happened that several Protestant churches were hit whilst Catholic churches escaped. The reason seems to have been simple—the main target area was the old Dockside district which happened to have no Catholic churches, perhaps because it had been built up at a time when they were not officially permitted to exist. In Belfast itself I had heard popular explanations attributing the facts, according to religious persuasion, either to the Lord defending his own or to Satan attacking the godly. Mary, however, had a simpler explanation—she was quite sure that 'Fenians' had taken advantage of the bombing to go round blowing up Protestant churches.

Talking of an incident nearer home, she told me: 'You can never trust the R.C.s. I had a cousin, Angus; I can just remember it. He was nearly home one night when he met a party of nineteen men. He thought they were "B" men, so he stopped the cart, but they were Fenians. They couldn't stand Angus because he was a staunch Orangeman and a "B" man, so they set on him and knocked him unconscious with the butt of a rifle, and put him into the house of one of the local Catholics. Well, when he didn't come home his friends went out to look for him and they couldn't find him anywhere; so the "B" men rounded the Fenians up and put them against a wall, and the man in charge threatened to shoot them if they didn't say where Angus was. So they told and they got him, but he died later of a brain tumour. Wasn't that an awful treacherous thing for neighbours to do?'

Even when not violent, Catholic neighbours could be mean. Mary quoted the example of what had happened to her brother Jack (PD20) when he went to an auction of land near his home. The fields were in a townland that was all owned by Catholics and he had not expected to be able to buy them. (As I have said, it is a matter of considerable pride for people to be able to say that their townland is 'all Catholic' or 'all Protestant', and each side has its own auctioneers who know all the bidders and are expected to declare, should the highest bid come from the wrong side, that the land has not reached its reserve—privately this is regarded as standard and acceptable practice.) By an oversight Jack's bid was accepted. In consequence 'The R.C.s were terrible annoyed. Then the farm between it and our home farm went for sale. My father could have bought it before the auction but he didn't because he thought that Conway (a Catholic neighbour) wanted it. Well, Conway bought it and he hadn't hardly got into it when he closed the right of way to my brother and ordered him off the land. Then Conway summonsed him and Jack lost an awful lot of money. They swore a whole pack of lies—that the lane was ditched (i.e. had not been useable by carts) and all kinds of things, and they won. Harry said afterwards that they'd only got the decision by lying, and they made him apologise in two papers. There was another man who went with my brother in the case, but he was an R.C. so Conway said he didn't mind him using the way. But Conway met my other brother, Harry (PD17), one night and walked home with him to his farm and teased him and tried every way to get Harry to strike him, but Harry is less hot-tempered than Jack and just laughed at him. Jack would have struck him, never mind the consequences. He followed Harry right on to our land. I'd have hit him then for he'd no right to be there.'

Apart from such particular incidents that Mary quoted she showed some of the general Protestant opinions we have already discussed. She was sure Catholics had no scruples about trying to abuse the Health Service and, indeed, that they felt politically virtuous in doing so—'There's not a Roman Catholic in the country,' she said, 'that hasn't two pairs of spectacles and false teeth.' Catholic doctors, she thought, were always ready to say a Catholic was sick even when he was healthy, if only it would get him government money. 'Catholics have their own people in the Civil Service in Belfast and they tell them how to get money they don't deserve.' This particular remark led Mary to make the only direct statement advocating economic discrimination that I have ever heard from her, for she went directly on immediately to say that 'It's wrong to give Catholics important jobs like that when they only abuse their position.'

What made Mary particularly indignant at what she conceived to be Catholic determination to milch the welfare state was the fact that their actions might lose its benefits not only to themselves but for everyone else as well. Although they were ready to grab with both hands all and more than they were entitled to in Northern Ireland, they were seeking to get political union with the Republic and this would land themselves and everyone else in poverty—'They'd eat grass to get living in the State.'

Mary was convinced that the poor, the Catholic poor as well as the Protestant poor, were worse off in the Republic than ever they were in Ulster. But it was not only an economic loss she feared if the Nationalists ever gained a United Ireland, but rule by the Church of Rome.

Mary herself had a deep-seated fear of the Roman Catholic Church as an institution, and a particular antipathy to and fear of the priests. When I asked her directly what it was she most feared about living in a politically united Ireland she said, 'It would be the same as living under Rome, with the priests dominating everything.' She was convinced that priests deliberately set out to keep their flock in ignorance, and she told me, seemingly half believing it, that she had heard that the reason priests were careful to administer extreme unction only when they were really convinced someone was dying was that they then confessed that Roman Catholicism was wrong and that the priests had been deceiving the individual all his life. She felt convinced that the priests kept their people poor by grabbing from them any spare cash they had. To convince me she told me of the time she had spent some weeks nursing a Catholic neighbour. The woman had been very ill and the doctor 'not knowing how poor they were' had said she should have a nurse in the house. This the family was quite unable to afford, so knowing that Mary had some training they came and begged for her assistance, which meant that for weeks Mary was almost continually in the house. Mary, who had been used all her life to the regular visiting of the Presbyterian minister which took place unaccompanied by payments, was apparently shocked when in the first week of her work in her neighbour's house the parish priest had called and had been given ten shillings, and then, separately, two curates had called and been given five shillings each, and her neighbour had burst out in apparent desperation, 'I don't know what I'll do if any more come, I've no money I can give them.' The incident had confirmed Mary's worst fears. Ultimately it was her belief that the priests wielded great power over the political behaviour of their flock that made them most obnoxious to her—nothing would convince her that a priest might ever act as a moderating political influence—in the last resort Catholics 'do what the priest says' and she said 'they'll vote as he tells them'.

Most of Mary's remarks could at least to some extent be paralleled in the remarks of other people both from her own district and from other areas as well. I have already commented on the widespread assumption that Catholics set out to scrounge from the welfare services and there is no need for further discussion on the point here. Her belief that the Catholics, by following their Nationalist policies, would also be prepared to lead the Province blindly into poverty for all was equally widespread; the very phrase she used: 'they'd eat grass to get living in the State' was one that I heard again and again when local Protestants discussed this subject.

Mary's distrust of priests was equally widespread. Perhaps the most extreme instance I came across was that of a woman in Ballybeg who, being almost totally confined to her house by ill-health, passed her time in watching through the window the comings and goings of her neighbours and weaving fantasies about them. One of her stories was that a Catholic neighbour, ill with cancer, had died in agony because the priests had persuaded the man that by refusing pain-killing drugs in this life he would be spared some of the pangs of purgatory. Much more reliable inform-ants, however, had their own stories about priests. Mrs. Scott (PC4), Campbell Wright's sister, like Mary emphasised the extent of the local Catholic's awe of the priest. She told me that she had had a Catholic child in her house, a school friend of her daughter, who had told her seriously that 'The priest could raise the dead, only God wouldn't like it.'

Many, like Mary, thought of the priest as *the* political extremist. Betty Laird (PD32), for example, was full of tales about the local clergy's actions against a Scottish (non-Nationalist) Catholic family who had lived in Ballybeg for a while at the end of the war. She said that the family had dared to fly a Union Jack to celebrate the end of the war, but it was seized and taken down and burnt by some Catholic lads—and Betty assured me it was done on the Curate's orders. The daughter of the family had wanted to go to a dance in the Orange Hall, held to celebrate the victory, but Betty said the girl had told her that the Parish Priest had sternly for-bidden her to go and Betty was sure his main motive was political bitterness. In defiance the girl had painted her sandals red, white and blue and had gone to the dance, but the family had found it advisable to leave the district very soon afterwards.

Even the Rector himself, thought of as being very sympathetic with the ordinary Catholic, seemed to have little room for priests in general. He told me that he had been on very good terms with a parish priest who had been in the district some years previously, a man from a local family. When this man had to leave the district he had come to the Rector and had asked him to keep a helpful eye on his kinfolk. The Rector was apparently somewhat startled at this suggestion and foresaw the possibility of embarrassing situations, and so he had asked his friend whether his successor might not object. The man had answered (and to the Rector this had seemed most significant), 'I don't know who he'll be, but I don't trust him whoever he is!' And it was on the priest's control over his people that the Rector too blamed what he regarded as the political intransigence of the Catholics, saying in exasperation: 'They'll plough for you, they'll harrow for you, but they'll not vote for you!'

In so far as Mary focused her antagonism to Catholicism and Nationalism on the power of priests and on what she believed to be the economic disadvantages that would inevitably accompany the emergence of a United Ireland dominated by the Catholic hierarchy, she was expressing widely held views. Moreover, it must be stressed that such views were held not merely in Ballybeg and similar areas but very widely indeed throughout the Province. Indeed if the rules of the Orange Order and the 'Orangeman's toast' are examined carefully it will be seen that such fears are implicit even there; they indicate quite clearly those real or imagined aspects of Roman Catholicism to which the Ulster Protestants generally were most antagonistic. Whilst Ulster Catholics tended to ascribe their acknowledged poverty to the machinations of the Protestants, the latter believed it the inevitable consequence of the Catholics' adherence to a church that imposed heavy financial burdens on its members, prevented them from limiting their families sensibly, and sought to keep them docile through ignorance. 'Popery, brass money and wooden shoes' seemed inextricably connected. The 'open Bible' of the toast had become for the Protestants a symbol of their right to think for themselves without asking the permission of any higher authority, just as the book censorship imposed by the Republican government had become a symbol of 'Catholic authoritarianism'. Even the first sentence of the rules of the Orange Order, a sentence which might, to the outsider, appear to be merely a theological statement, was in fact understood to be a frontal attack on the authoritarianism of the Roman Catholic church. This was thought to rest on the claims of the priesthood to mediate in a crucial way between God and man, and on the priests' manipulation of this key spiritual role for political ends especially, it was believed, through the sinister manipulation of knowledge gained in the Confessional.

N

In fact a general anti-authoritarianism and anti-clericalism under-lay much anti-Catholicism.

Some of Mary's remarks could be acounted for by the fact that she was a woman, for women tended to express more prejudiced viewpoints than did men. In part this may have been because in talking to me they were talking to a woman and were therefore expressing themselves more freely than the men. I think, however, that there was more to it than this. In the first place it would be understandable if women dealt more in stereotypes than did the men because usually a woman knew fewer members of the 'other side', or knew them less well, than did her menfolk. It was the men, of course, who periodically exchanged blows, but the women who were more likely to express suspicion. A woman, just because she confined most of her visiting to her kin, was seldom on very intimate terms with those not her co-religionists. To some extent they remained strangers to her always, and it was that much easier to believe sinister things about them. There was also another point, however, for it was primarily a woman's task to produce her children as properly socialised beings, and in this context that meant convinced little Catholics or Protestants—it was, I think, not only religious instruction but also religious prejudice that was learned, and in a sense had to be taught at the mother's knee.

Sometimes it seemed that Mary took great exception to Catholic behaviour that a man would have viewed more lightheartedly. As we saw earlier, some Protestant young men were regarded as mischievous enough to be capable not merely of putting up the Union Jack on St. Patrick's Day, but of themselves secretly hoisting the Tricolour on July 12th, just to watch the fun. Again, one day visiting the Maloneys, a prosperous Church of Ireland family of infield farmers, I mentioned that I had heard a rumour that an attempt was to be made to fly the Republican flag on the coming Easter Monday. Instantly one of the young sons said indignantly, 'I'd scrag any boy I found flying the Tricolour'; but his father had laughed and said 'Aye, maybe you'd scrag him, and maybe I'd scrag him, and maybe they'll find a way of flying it none the less.' The father, Jack Maloney, certainly accepted that physical force was a perfectly proper reaction to such a symbolic challenge, but his relaxed chuckle at the thought was very different from the heated indignation shown by Mary. I found similar, apparently sex-based, differences of attitudes over other issues. For example, in the instance I have already quoted, in which Mary said that Catholics ought not to be given good civil service jobs because they would abuse their positions, she was at once answered by a man sitting next to her in the kitchen who said that Catholics had to have a share of the good jobs 'to be fair'.

In part, however, Mary's attitude seemed clearly to reflect the view of the poor, 'mountainy' Protestants as opposed to the more sophisticated infielders. This was particularly so with regard to her attitudes to violence. The incident, which she recounted with approval, when her brother Jack lost his temper with the Catholic girls in the car was 'pure ignorance' to the more sophisticated Protestant. The case of the indignant publican who fired irresponsibly was also deplored by them. In part these differences in attitude reflected merely some differences in attitude to violence generally in the two areas. Blows and fights between men, even co-religionists, were more common in the hill areas than in the infield. It is perhaps worth pointing out too that Mary, who was only mildly disapproving of the publican's action, would have been horrified had he instead informed the ordinary police that his Catholic rival was allowing drinking after hours. That to Mary would have been a thoroughly mean act, far worse than shooting off a gun.

It did seem, however, that Mary's attitudes and her recital of incidents involving threats and violence reflected another kind of difference between the hill and valley Protestants. In the hills there was a greater sense of the existence of a direct threat from certain Catholics, a greater emphasis on the need for self-defence, and a much stronger feeling that even apparently good neighbours amongst the Catholics could be 'treacherous'.

It seemed significant that Fred Richards (PD5) told me, as if it had been yesterday, of the struggle his grandfather had had when he had first come to their farm in the 1880's. He had been very poor and was glad to get permission to build a house on a dry knoll rising out of semi-bog, and to make a farm at the cost of draining some of the land. Local Catholic families, however, claimed that they had had turf-cutting rights in the area and tumbled the walls of the house as fast as they were put up. Fred said his grandfather could never have succeeded had the men of the Lodge not rallied to him; they had helped him to build the house, 'and guarded it for six months after'.

In a similar vein, Elizabeth Jamison (PC10) vividly recalled the Land League days. The 'Land League' had various aims and activities designed to benefit tenant farmers. Locally, however, its main activity was thought to be the running of a 'raffle' in which tickets were issued in return for money to be spent on terrorist activities—the prizes in the raffle being Protestant farms (to be freely acquired). The purchase of tickets even by Catholics was often scarcely spontaneous, and Elizabeth remembered the night long ago when Land Leaguers had called on her father. To the terror of her mother and herself they had forced her father to contribute to their funds with the threat that otherwise 'the family's coffins would be ordered for the morning'. By contrast, the one tale I was told by a valley farmer of personal involvement with the Land Leaguers was told with the memory of irritated amusement rather than fear. The man said that one day when he was a boy, their ploughman, an old Catholic labourer who had been with the family many years, came in at breakfast and with naïve pleasure told them they had nothing to worry about from the Land League—he had won their farm when the raffle tickets had been drawn the previous night and he would see they kept it!

Betty Laird (PD32) an 'infielder', told me which Catholics she believed to be members of the I.R.A., but none of them was her immediate neighbour—they were young 'layabouts' either in Ballybeg itself or in the hill district, where she did not even know the Protestants very well. She complained of how bitter Catholics got at election times, but the substance of her complaint was merely that they would, for a while, refuse to speak to Protestants.

The stories I was told in the hill district seemed more immediate even when they had happened a good while previously. Elizabeth Jamison, speaking of the troubles of the 1920's, assured me that in her district the pressure on Protestant families had been so strong that 'They'd have had to have left the area if the "B" men hadn't been formed. They were thinking of doing so—but the R.C.s are frightened of the "B" men because they know they'll shoot.' She told me that the Wrights, their neighbours, had been visiting a friendly Catholic family, the Rooneys, when suddenly the whole farmyard seemed to fill up with men they knew to be 'Fenians'. They had come apparently to punish the Rooneys for being friendly with Protestants, and the Wrights had slipped out another way and called out the 'B' men, who rounded some of the 'Fenians' up, and discouraged further acts of intimidation.

Elizabeth's attitude to the 'B' men was typical of the 'mountainy' Protestants, when she spoke of them as if the existence of this organisation was vital to the continued existence of Protestants in her area. Even in the infield the existence of the 'B' force was regarded as important, of course, and young Protestants felt they had an obligation to serve in the 'Specials' even at inconvenience to themselves—Keith Baxter (PD30), for instance, joined shortly after I left the district, although with his farming responsibilities his periodic night patrol duties were a considerable nuisance. It was only in the 'mountainy' areas, however, that I found the feeling that ultimately the 'B' men were the one group on which local Protestants could rely for their defence, and the one group on whose existence the continued presence of Protestants in the area until that time had depended. All the stories I was told from the past were never recounted with the idea of telling me dead and gone history—on the contrary, they were repeated with the clear intention of making me realise the kind of problem the people felt themselves to be facing in their everyday lives.

There was one further respect in which there seemed to be a fairly clear cut differentiation between the attitudes of infield farmers and the attitudes of the 'mountainy' Protestants: time and again I heard the latter suggest that Catholics were treacherous, although this was an accusation I seldom heard from infield Protestants. I have quoted the occasion when Mary, commenting on the attack of her cousin, Angus, burst out: 'Wasn't that an awful treacherous thing for neighbours to do?' More often, however, the accusation was implicit. Thus Elizabeth Jamison (PC10) told me that years previously she had come home from market with the wife of a Catholic neighbour, known as 'Dirty Johnny'. The woman was drunk and had turned to her, when they were nearly home, and said 'When I'm greatest with you I could stick a knife in you to the haft!' On another occasion a visitor to the Jamisons' farm, describing one of the local Catholics, said: 'All the time he's smiling at me I can feel the knife slowly turning.' Again, Willy Richards (PC9) remarked: 'Catholics are great neighbours, till one day they could do you a bad turn, and then they'll do it.' He was echoed on another occasion by Fred Richards, who said of Catholics in general: 'Catholics are great neighbours—they'd carry you on their backs at midnight.' This was said with apparent sincerity, but then he reflected and went on 'even if they might stick a knife in you after—some of them would, some of them wouldn't'.

Further evidence of the same sort of attitude was to be found in the use of the word 'sweet', to describe a person nice to your face but ready to do you a bad turn should occasion arise. It could be used perfectly well for a co-religionist—for example Mary Jamison told me one of the Protestant women I visited was 'sweet', because her brother had once courted Mary, who had written him affectionate letters, and the woman whom Mary had thought to be her friend had shown them to Paul when he was courting Mary. It seemed, however, to be only in the 'mountainy' district that the term 'sweet' was used to distinguish certain Catholic neighbours who were particularly distrusted, despite their apparent friendliness. Of the Jamisons' closest Catholic neighbours the McCurdys were regarded as absolutely trustworthy, but McIlhaggar was definitely 'a sweet wee man' despite his many acts of neighbourliness. To Andy and Nelly Stuart (PC100) and (PC101), the McKinleys (CD27) seemed utterly reliable, and the Brooks (CD9) were all right; Kevin Whitelock (CD18) was not sweet because he was so openly hostile to Protestants, but they suspected the McFaddens (CD7) of being 'sweet'.

The use of the term 'sweet' by Protestants in the hill district to separate the true from the false amongst the outwardly friendly was significant for two reasons. Obviously it gave expression to the latent sense of distrust that could exist between neighbours, but it was also evidence that these Protestants, however biased they might seem, did not view Catholics as an undifferentiated hostile group; rather they picked out and put in a special category from amongst their Catholic neighbours those of whom they were paticularly suspicious.

We must consider, however, not only verbal attitudes, but recall also actual behaviour. If this is examined we see that paradoxically hill Protestants, and indeed some other poor Protestants, had greater contacts and more friendly contacts with their Catholic neighbours than had the infield Protestants, or the more affluent Protestants of Ballybeg itself.

Mrs. Baxter (PC20), the 'yeowoman', added to her condemnation of the 'ignorant' poorer Protestants the fact that they were bigoted against Catholics, but because of the status difference between herself and her Catholic neighbours she was not on informal visiting terms with any of them, and even with the 'yeomen' Catholic families in Ballybeg her contacts were minimal—indeed she was interested in them primarily in a political context. For instance she asked me how many children one of the women had, and when I started off by telling her the name of the eldest son who had moved to the Republic, she said sharply, 'Oh, I don't count him, I'm not interested in him, he's not on the voting strength.'

Betty Laird stressed to me that she was not anti-Catholic and in our first long conversation told me literally that 'some of my best friends are Catholics'. When I probed a little, however, I found that her only close Catholic friend had been the temporarily resident Scottish Catholic girl whose pro-British attitude had caused her such difficulties with local Catholics. After this girl had left the district Betty ceased to have any intimate contacts with Catholics.

It seemed equally significant that the family of one Methodist farmer, who explicitly condemned the bigotry of Orangemen and refused to join a Lodge for that reason, actually had very little to do with Catholics. On my first visit to his farm, when I was collecting preliminary information from several houses in the neighbourhood, I asked his daughter a few very simple questions about the family in the next farm up the road. She answered, as if it were a matter of course, that she could not tell me all I wanted to know because her family saw very little of them as they were Catholics. The questions I had asked were all of the kind that in the hill area I had come to expect one family to be able to tell me about their neighbours no matter what their religion.

There were friendly contacts, of course, between Catholic and Protestant farmers in the infield. I have, for example, commented on the amount of co-operation that took place between Keith Baxter (PD30) and Jo McKinley (CD26)—but they saw very little of each other in their homes, and could not mix in this context on an informal basis. Owen McConnell (CD101), the owner of the 'cure' and the sophisticated farmer, who was also a slightly footloose bachelor, was the one Catholic who had really easy relationships with Protestant farmers—he visited a nearby Protestant household quite often, and also went off on various occasions with Harold Heath (PD102), the neighbouring Protestant bachelor farmer; but Owen was something of an exception.

In Ballybeg itself there was little contact between the more affluent Catholic and Protestant households. It is true that the one family with whom the Protestant police sergeant permitted himself to be on friendly terms was a sophisticated Catholic household—nobody would accuse him of favouring them should they get into trouble, an accusation that would certainly have been levelled at him had a similar relationship existed between him and a Protestant family; but this link also was exceptional.

Between the Protestant professionals and shopkeepers on the one hand and the Catholic professionals and shopkeepers on the other, there was, however, very little contact. Indeed because these people had no need to co-operate with each other as the farmers had, and were not so isolated that they could not in emergencies seek the help of kinsfolk or co-religionists, there was in general very little contact across the religious boundaries. Perhaps it was significant that in Ballybeg itself the clearest case of Catholic/ Protestant co-operation involved two sets of brothers regarded as 'spivs' by the respectable. Both were enterprising—one pair had converted an old hearse into a motorised shop which they took round the countryside, to the annoyance of established shop-keepers, both Catholic and Protestant; the other pair had started earning money for themselves as young lads during the war. Their father had been an eccentric saddler who, convinced that horse hair was going to disappear from the market, tried to corner all that was going and sent his sons to seek it out. The boys found, however, that it was easier to sell the old man some of the hair he had already accumulated in his store and were said to have done this regularly. These brothers had now joined up into a most successful smuggling group whose exploits, the bane of the sergeant's life, were delightedly recounted by most of the rest of Ballybeg's inhabitants. Apart from this heartening example of Catholic/Protestant economic co-operation, however, there were few joint enterprises and little social mixing here.

By contrast in the hills there was a considerable amount of co-operation and contact. There were not only exceptional cases of very close co-operation such as that between Andy Stuart (PC100) and Michael McKinley (CD27)—even people whose main work contacts were with their co-religionists recognised real obligations to their neighbours of 'the other side' at weddings and funerals, and their relationships in all contexts were egalitarian. A most striking example of this friendliness seemed to be provided by Mary Jamison (PD19) herself whose opinions I have quoted because they seemed so prejudiced. It was, after all, Mary who a short time previously had spent several weeks nursing, quite without pay-ment, her sick Catholic neighbour. It was also Mary who went out of her way to help the Catholic widow, her former schoolmate, who had committed almost the worst crime possible in the local code, not only by marrying a Protestant but burying him as a Catholic.

The problem is to reconcile the existence in the hills of relationships between Catholics and Protestants that were in some ways better than those in the infield with the verbal expression by hill Protestants of greater prejudice and hostility, and the belief of the infield Protestants that the hill Protestants were much more bitter than they were themselves. Indeed infield Protestants were so convinced of this that they sometimes said to me with some indignation of the Protestant hill farmers, 'those men wouldn't leave the Catholics any way of living at all'.

One obvious reason for the hill Protestant attitude was the existence of an element of greater anxiety that arose just because they did form a small minority in a largely Catholic milieu. When in the past trouble had broken out they had been more vulnerable, both because of their fewness in numbers and because they were more distant from the kind of help that the ordinary police force could give. It was not altogether surprising that it was the hill Protestants who particularly valued the 'B' Specials.

It seemed, however, that there was also an important psychological factor in their attitudes that was at least in part independent of any objective risks they had run. Those whom the hill Protestants had to fear were some of those with whom they had the closest of neighbourly and apparently friendly contacts. Here, I think, a clue is provided by the use of the term 'sweet'.

Despite the considerable degree of separation of the social networks of Catholics and Protestants, even in the hills, it is obvious that there, in general, contacts between them through school and through neighbourhood ties were much stronger than in the lowlands. In many ways, I have argued, hill Protestants enjoyed much closer and better relations with their Catholic neighbours than they did with the more prosperous of the Protestant infielders. Quite clearly, therefore, there were some psychological factors involved in Protestant/Catholic relations in the 'mountainy' areas that were absent elsewhere. Those who were potentially hostile were, it is true, always in a sense outsiders because of the extent of social separation of the two groups. Nevertheless, they were outsiders with whom there were many close and friendly contacts. They were 'neighbours' in an area where neighbourliness was very important. There was therefore, I think, an element of deep ambivalence in the feelings that Protestants and Catholics had for each other. This emerged in the very different statements which the same individual could make quite sincerely in different contexts. Fred Richards (PD5) was the staunchest of Orangemen and 'B' men. When someone mentioned the rumour that the Nazis had planned to invade Ireland and organise it centrally, he said, 'Sure Hitler might have conquered England,' looking at me with withering scorn, 'but if he'd come to Ireland and tried to rule the North from Dublin he'd have had it!' This was said, of course, in the context of thinking about the overall political future of Ulster and the consequences for it of union with the South. Yet when this same man's thoughts were turned to the local situation, in the context of his relations with his neighbours, his response was much less militant. In this context he remarked to me about Catholics, 'Sure what's the difference between us anyway, excepting we go out and demonstrate and get drunk on different dates.' The Protestant was both ambivalent himself and aware of the ambivalence of his Catholic neighbours. An attack, symbolic or actual, by local Catholics was an attack by friends. 'Treachery' was therefore inevitably a constant psychological threat to the hill Protestant in a way that it could not possibly be to the more socially remote, infield Protestant. The accusation seems to have been the result of the fact that a man's foes were (almost) those of his own house.

II Protestant prejudice:
the influence of the 'class' structure

Whilst the attitudes of the hill Protestant may in part be explained by his own very special psychological problems and by the greater objective threat that he faced, this is not the whole story. To understand the attitude of the poorer Protestants generally, and especially the strength of their attachment to the Orange Order, we must look more carefully than we have done so far at their attitudes to other Protestants of higher status than themselves.

We have already seen that, compared with the Catholic population, the Protestants were more evenly spread through the different status categories in Ballybeg. The inevitable corollary was, of course, that the Protestants were socially more deeply divided than the Catholics, just as they were religiously divided. The social divisions of the Protestants were the greater just because within their group were most of the 'yeomen', towards whom, as we have seen, others felt particularly antagonistic. The divisions present in Ballybeg were not, however, the only ones that had to be taken into account. Ballybeg was not isolated from the rest of the Province. What went on in the rest of Northen Ireland and especially in Belfast was also important in influencing local behaviour and attitudes. To understand the reactions of the poorer, less sophisticated Protestants of Ballybeg, it is important to realise that these attitudes were partly determined by their reactions to the socially superior Protestant establishment of Ulster. There was much about this to which the poorer Ballybeg Protestant was profoundly antagonistic. The basic political problem of the poorer Protestant was that to secure his independence from the Irish Republic he had to support politically those whom he neither liked nor trusted. This seemed to be true very generally, and to reflect back on social relationships in Ballybeg.

In the first place, he had to vote for incorporation in the United Kingdom although he felt considerable dislike for the English. Experience amongst ordinary Ulster Protestants, before ever I went to Ballybeg, had taught me that their stereotype of the Englishman reflected in almost every detail the Englishman's wartime stereotype of the Prussian. The Englishman was efficient but ruthless, subservient to rules and regulations to a comical extent, pompous, humourless, and often cruel. An additional English characteristic was to be a godless heathen. In Ballybeg itself I heard anti-English stories and jokes from Protestants at all levels. Sometimes these stories were lighthearted: a chuckle at the remembrance of the expression on the face of the stuffy, class-conscious English soldier when he found the doctor who had examined him in the morning selling him a railway ticket in the afternoon (because the doctor was lending a hand for a few minutes to the station-master who was running the station like a one-man band); the pompous English visitor at the hotel, ordering a 'simple' little dinner, who was ultimately deflated by the patient proprietor telling the girl who was serving, 'Mary, just give him bacon and eggs like the rest', was also the cause of amusement. There were, however, less amusing stories. It would perhaps be salutary for the English to realise that even the hill Protestants I knew, so strong in their support for the Orange Order and the 'B' Specials, still remembered with a sense of outrage the activities of the British security forces, the Black and Tans, who were in the area from 1916. What these Protestants found outrageous was the way in which the Black and Tans had treated all Catholics with hostility. For example, a bridge on the main road near James Jamison's (PB8) house was blown up in an attempt to destroy a lorry load of police (Kevin Whitelock's (CD18) father was believed to have had a hand in it—'wasn't that a treacherous thing to do?'). What shocked the Jamisons was that the next day the Black and Tans had arrived and had forced all the local Catholics, without distinction, to take a hand in in the rebuilding of the bridge. They had taken the McCurdys, although the local Protestants could have told them they were innocent, and they had even press-ganged Old James Jamison himself because they had found him in the McCurdys' yard helping Patrick to doctor a horse, and they knew so little about the situation that they couldn't believe he was a Protestant—it had taken him a little while to establish his identity. Fred Richards (PD5) had emphasised to me how badly the Black and Tans had treated the Catholics.

Before these forces had come, Fred asserted, hardly any of the Catholics had wanted independence; but afterwards 90 per cent of them had done so. In effect Fred was expressing the local Protestants' sense of indignation at the way their neighbours had been treated by outsiders, and at the same time he was telling me that the Nationalist movement was really the fault of the English, not of Ulster Protestants. Fred was the type of Protestant who, had he known of it, would have been very angered by the fact that Jo McKinley proudly hung, in his subsidised house, a picture of the 1916 Dublin rising. But Fred was himself furiously indignant that those captured after the rising should have been executed by the English as traitors—that he thought had been shocking, 'I wouldn't do that to my enemies!'

It was fortunate that before I went to Ballybeg I knew something of the general Ulster attitude to the English; that I knew that I not only had to accept a kind of personal responsibility for Oliver Cromwell, the Potato Famine and the Black and Tans, but that I had also to be careful to do absolutely nothing to justify any aspect of the stereotype. When Jo McKinley's mother told me that 'No-one would ever think you were English', I knew she was not only paying me the biggest compliment of which she was capable, but that had I done nothing to earn it my relations would have been difficult not only with Catholics but with Protestants also. Obviously, even strong Unionists found certain aspects of Unionism not wholly to their liking.

It was also the case that the poorer, less sophisticated Protestant had to vote for Unionist leaders for whom he felt, in many cases, a profound distrust. Some he distrusted because they were 'almost Englishmen'. Basically, if a man spoke like an Englishman he was thought of as being English, no matter how long his family might have owned property in Ulster; a point of view made understandable by the fact that everyone in Ballybeg, without exception, had some kind of an Ulster accent. The possession of an English accent implied that the speaker had been educated in England and still had his social ear turned in that direction. This fact meant that it was assumed automatically, for example, that however much such a man might publicly declare his devotion to Protestantism, this was no more than the mouthing of catch phrases, designed to win political support. Such piety was regarded very cynically. Even many of the 'genuine' Ulstermen amongst the Belfast politicians were suspect in Ballybeg. Time and again it was made clear to me

that Belfast Unionist politicians were suspected of being potentially ready to sacrifice the welfare of areas distant from the capital,
and especially those on the border, for the sake of areas nearer
Belfast where most Unionist supporters lived, and on whom, therefore, most Unionist politicians depended. Economically they were
not thought to have local interests at heart. Moreover, it must be
remembered that many of those who voted Unionist would have
liked a much more socialist type government; only the Labour
Party's traditional backing of the Nationalist cause prevented this
latent support coming into the open. Mary and Paul Jamison, for
example, said they would certainly have voted Labour had they
lived in England—they did not find the Unionist politicians'
espousal of Conservative type policies endearing. Moreover, it was
quite widely believed that the 'Belfast men' might as a last resort
hand some of the border areas, including Ballybeg, over to the
Republic to get rid of a large number of Nationalist supporters.
This suggestion was repeatedly denied by the Unionist leaders.
This, however, did little to stop the suspicion of at least the less
sophisticated people. Not appreciating the economic and other
difficulties involved in any such idea, they believed that, as they
saw it, they might be the victims to be thrown to the lions to
preserve the rest of the Province.

Finally it was apparent that the 'leaders' of the local Protestants,
the professionals and the yeomen, whose manifestations of social
distinctions assured them some unpopularity in any case, were also
regarded with some measure of the distrust felt for the Belfast
men.[1]

The attitudes to them were naturally ambivalent. As might be
expected, such people were voted on to committees and asked to
take all kinds of prominent positions. They were useful in such
roles for several reasons. They could most easily meet sophisticated
outsiders on equal terms, and even manipulate them, and were,
therefore, chosen to act as delegates to outside gatherings. I have
also suggested elsewhere that they were called on to act as explicit
leaders partly because for an individual to do this in an open
gathering was almost necessarily not 'modest'; it almost seemed that
it was only those whose professional status allowed them to act as
a leader as part of their role, or those who were relatively unconcerned with the opinion of their neighbours, who were prepared to stand up in an open meeting to express their opinions.

[1] Harris (1961).

Yeomen and professionals voted into positions of prominence were useful just because they could carry the burden of immodesty. Their selection did not necessarily mean that they were liked and trusted. Mary Jamison (PD19) remarked suspiciously to me: 'Doctors and those sort of people don't make much difference (between Protestantism and Catholicism) in their religion, do they!'

These attitudes manifested themselves in the immediate antagonism felt for any local leader who advocated religious toleration in the abstract, or who showed the slightest expression of political unorthodoxy. The Presbyterian minister told me, with half-humorous resignation, that he had learned never, in the hearing of the local people, to say a word of criticism of any kind about any of the Unionist politicians. He found that if he said anything against any of them, even a man whom he knew to be the subject of a good deal of cynical comment amongst his congregation, his listeners immediately rose indignantly to their defence. He said he had learned to keep his mouth firmly shut on such topics since he aroused only resentment and did no good. I saw for myself that when he took the opportunity of the Orange July service to preach on the text: 'If a man love not his brother whom he hath seen, how can he love God whom he hath not seen', he aroused a flurry of indignant comment, even from those whom I knew to have, in some contexts, very good relations indeed with their Roman Catholic neighbours.

People were antagonistic largely because in the context in which he spoke they understood his meaning to be that he was critical of the Orange Order. This renewed their fears about his political reliability (had he not been a student in Dublin?) that had first been roused by his original refusal to join the Orange Order when he came to the area. It had been expected that he would join the order to act as Chaplain of one of the Lodges in the Ballybeg district, as his predecessor had done. When he adamantly declined he had caused consternation and resentment both amongst his own congregation and amongst the Protestants generally. Those who were not members of his church could do little to express their displeasure. Amongst the Presbyterians, however, there had been a substantial boycott of his church services. Some of the usually consistent attenders amongst the men had become erratic in their church-going, whilst sporadic attenders like Paul Jamison (PD10) did not go at all. Even some of the women from the staunchest

Orange families had, like Mary Jamison, suddenly become irregular and had stayed at home on a number of Sundays. The boycott only lasted a few months. Talk by some families of secession from the church came to nothing; and in view of the fact that the Orangeman's induction oath bound him, at least in theory, to support the church, it was difficult to make the boycott an overt policy of the Lodge. The Presbyterian congregation had, therefore, drifted back, but many still nourished a sense of discontent at the Minister's refusal to join the Order.

This brings us once again to a consideration of the significance of the Orange Order. Differences in attitudes to it were extremely important indications of other underlying differences in attitudes, an understanding of which is crucial to our analysis. It will be helpful, therefore, to go through the objections raised to the Orange Order and see who it was who raised objections, for the nature of the objections made by some reveal the nature of the attractions the Order exercised over others.

This fact is clearly shown by the objection of many of the yeomen and the women that the Orange Order encouraged drunkenness. Even the Rector, who had become a Lodge chaplain and who thought on the whole that the Lodge was a good thing because it 'gave an opportunity for like-minded people to come together', admitted regretfully that the meetings were sometimes an excuse for excessive drinking. The cynical said that even those Lodges (there was none in the Ballybeg area) that firmly labelled themselves as 'Temperance' Lodges, merely meant that they did not store drink on Lodge premises, not that the members were teetotallers. The accusation of drunkenness was one on which the members themselves felt particularly vulnerable since they accepted, in other contexts, the norm that drunkenness was a bad thing. Thus, when Campbell Wright (PC5) gave the drunkenness of Lodge members as his reason for not joining the Order he was picking on the one point on which they felt they had no answer to him—his excuse for opting out was based on values the members themselves acknowledged. It is impossible to doubt, however, that one of the reasons for the popularity of Lodges was that they provided drinking clubs at which attendance could be represented as a moral duty.

The women voiced another objection to the Orange Order which might at first sight appear paradoxical—they complained that the movement, so overtly concerned with Protestantism, turned the minds of the men away from their religious duty. Mrs. Baxter (PC20) openly voiced her disapproval of the movement and told Willy Richards (PC9) and his wife, who tried to extract a contribution for a Lodge banner from her, that it would be better if people gave less time to the Orange Order and more time to their churches. Often Mrs. Baxter was in a minority in her attitudes, but in this respect a lot of the women would have supported her; I heard the same opinion from many of them. Indeed, although some women did become involved in raising funds for their husbands' Lodges, by and large women were not particularly enthusiastic about the movement. Significantly an attempt had been made some years previously to organise a women's Orange meeting in Ballybeg, but it had failed for lack of support (and the only one in the region was that attached to Kildrum Lodge to which Fred Richards' wife belonged). To Mary Jamison the idea of a women's Orange Order was rather an absurdity, because she, like many other women, saw participation in the Order as an essentially masculine activity.

It seemed quite true, and it was accepted even by the men, that the more enthusiastic a man was in attending his Lodge the less likely he was to be a regular worshipper in his church. It was, indeed, a common piece of folklore that a clergyman a few miles away had wished the Orangemen, at their July parade service, a 'Happy Christmas' because he knew he would not be seeing many of them again before the next July. There was nothing very mysterious about this tendency, for the Orange Order provided an alternative channel through which an individual could express his loyalty to his Protestant neighbours. He could prove he was a 'good' Protestant by attending Lodge meetings.

The significance of this was shown by the way in which people would heave a sigh of relief if an unruly youth bowed to public opinion and joined his local Lodge. One of the Ballybeg Protestant boys was causing his relatives some anxiety both because he was, they thought, overfond of Catholic company, especially that of Catholic girls, and because he was generally undisciplined. His family responded not by trying to make him go to church, but by putting all their efforts into getting him to join his father's Lodge. (Indeed in another area, similar to Ballybeg, a young man pointed out to me, as evidence of his reformed character, the fact that he had recently joined his Lodge!) In general men never criticised the 'Protestantism' of a man provided he himself attended

o

his Lodge and his children attended church. It is important to stress here, moreover, the significance of the dichotomy between the sexes of attitudes to church and Lodge. To a marked extent in those families like the Jamisons, where there was a very strong division between the spheres of the sexes, there was the assumption that the Lodge was to the man what the church was to the woman. This again was a positive attraction to unregenerate males. Lodge meetings got them out of what would otherwise have been virtually compulsory church attendance.

Bearing in mind the fact that the very things that were voiced by some as objections to the Lodge constituted a part of the Lodge's attraction to the majority, we can consider now the accusations that the Orange Order was too egalitarian and that it encourages bigotry.

It was because Ballybeg's Presbyterian minister explicitly thought that the Orange Order, in its overt hostility to Catholics, was a bigoted, unchristian organisation that he had refused to join it; indeed he had wanted no contacts with it. We have seen already that Mrs. Baxter would let neither her son nor her husband be members of the Lodge, partly because of its bigotry. The Methodist non-member snapped 'Some of those Orangemen, they're as wicked (spiteful) as cats'. The other side of Mrs. Baxter's (PD20) objection to the Orange Order was that it was too egalitarian—she did not think it right for farmers and their labourers to sit down together in Lodge meetings. In this complaint she was, of course, exaggerating—it was rare for farmers and labourers to sit there together just because so few Protestants were labourers; but certainly Protestants of very different social status did regularly 'sit down together' in the Orange Hall. Moreover, they did this, it is important to note, in a context in which it was strongly asserted that 'All Brethren are Equal'. It was to this overt egalitarianism that Mrs. Baxter was really objecting. Although no-one else expressed quite such explicit objection to this as she did, it was clear that those who normally enjoyed high status in the community sometimes spoke somewhat ruefully about this aspect of Lodge meetings. The Minister of Kildrum, for instance, complained to me about the way in which the members of his congregation, once he became a member of the Orange Order, had tried to apply the rule about the 'equality of Brethren'. He said he had joined the Lodge hoping to exercise some influence within it, but he had found himself sadly disabused—his members used the meetings to put their views with more than usual force to him, explicitly justifying their attitude by referring to the 'equality' rule.

Undoubtedly this rule was one of the very things that made the Lodge so attractive to the less influential Protestants and made them so anxious that professionals and yeomen should join the Orange Order. It was felt that such people could be spoken to more plainly at Lodge meetings than anywhere else. This undoubtedly had been a very strong element behind the anxiety to force the Ballybeg minister to join the movement; there were those, and not only the Presbyterians, who wanted to place the new clergyman in a situation in which all, even chaplains, met on a (relatively) equal footing.

The role of the Lodge in providing an arena in which views could be freely expressed by those of lower status to those of higher status has a significance which makes it worthwhile examining the point more fully.

It can, I think, be argued that one advantage of the Lodge from the point of view of those of lower status was that they could there speak out without being considered lacking in 'modesty'. In this respect the behaviour of Fred Richards (PD5), a member of Kildrum Presbyterian Church and of Kildrum Lodge, was instructive. Fred's attachment to his Lodge was something that he explained himself in terms of his thankfulness to fellow Lodge members for their support of his family in the past. In practice, however, it seemed equally important that it gave him an opportunity to carry on amicable warfare with the Minister for Fred had, in the context of Lodge affairs, become one of the Minister's chief opponents. Nevertheless it seemed that in the context of church meetings Fred took no very active part in the proceedings, and usually left any discussion that there was to the Elders. It was primarily in the Lodge meeting that he felt free to speak. One reason at least for this seemed to be that whereas in situations where the ordinary hierarchies of status applied, the ordinary man who spoke forcefully tended to arouse such resentment that he preferred to sit silent at almost all costs, this was not the case in the Lodge. There, just because it was asserted that all were 'equal', the ordinary man could make his voice heard without it appearing that he was trying to claim a particularly high status for himself. He could, therefore, speak without arousing the antagonism of his fellows. Part of the anxiety to get local key men into the Lodge arose not only because it placed them in a situation in which their inherent superiority was denied, but because it was a situation in which the man in the street could tell them publicly what he thought and yet not lose his reputation for 'modesty'.

This may have been one reason why people like the yeomen thought the Orangemen were such bigots; just because it was at the Lodge meetings that the ordinary Protestant could tell them what they really thought. Yet I do not think that this was the full answer. We have seen that, especially when actual behaviour is taken into account, there was comparatively little objective evidence for the greater 'bigotry' of the poorer Protestants. What I suspect is that an important factor influencing the views expressed was the antagonism felt by the poorer for the more prosperous Protestants themselves, an antagonism compounded partly of distrust and partly, of course, of jealousy. Because of the distrust felt we have seen that such people were the last from whom the ordinary man could really accept a call to religious toleration, even when the poor Protestant, for the greater part of his relationships with Catholics, was himself extremely tolerant. There seemed, however, to be another factor also—the charge of insufficient loyalty to the Protestant cause may have provided a basis from which to attack those who otherwise seemed out of reach of the ordinary man who wanted in some way to express the resentments he felt. It was difficult for the poorer Protestant to find values in terms of which he could place himself on a par with those who seemed to him clever, prosperous and sophisticated. Most of the moral weapons had, in a sense, been appropriated by the Nationalists, with whom it was impossible to appear to make common cause. If the ordinary Protestant wanted to denigrate his social superiors he had to do it in terms which left no doubt in anyone's mind that they were still, nevertheless, on the same political side. This is virtually an impossible matter to prove, but I suspect that it was the charge of faltering anti-Catholicism that had come to supply this need. If loyal Protestantism were the real ultimate value, then the ordinary man knew that ultimately he was a more worthwhile person than 'the doctors and people of that sort' who 'don't make much difference in their religion'. It was, moreover, on issues such as this that the ordinary man could safely enjoy himself in attacking verbally his social superiors. If I am right, it is small wonder that the latter threw the charge of bigotry at Orangemen in general.

To sum up, the 'mountainy' Protestant and the poorer less sophisticated Protestants in general had certain very definite anxieties about neighbouring Catholics, about the Roman Catholic Church, and about the consequences that might follow from the formation of a United Ireland. The foundation of these fears was multifarious and those who think they can be explained simply in terms of 'racialism' are guilty of over-simplification and distortion. The consequences of the existence of these anxieties were made more complex by the fact that the Protestants as a group were split by various cleavages, both denominationally, and almost more important in terms of social status. There was considerable distrust felt by those Protestants who were less prosperous and influential for those at the top, and this attitude was reinforced by particularly marked misunderstandings of the workings of the outside, bureaucratic world. Poorer Protestants believed that while they would suffer all sorts of disadvantages in a United Ireland the leaders would probably be able to take care of themselves, to come out on top, to see that they personally did not suffer from any political change. The distrust felt for the political leaders and the local establishment meant that they were those from whom the ordinary Protestants could least accept demands for religious toleration. Those who in personal relationships were for the most part very tolerant, in practice reacted with antagonism to calls for toleration from their leaders. The one institution in which the uninfluential and the unsophisticated could deal with their leaders as equals without acting improperly was the Orange Lodge. Here leaders could be safely criticised; here some attempt could be made to expose them to the force of public opinion. Often because of all the factors discussed, the opinions expressed to the leaders tended to be more extreme than the opinions usually expressed outside amongst the ordinary members; hence in part the reputation of the Lodge for bigotry and the tendency for the most sophisticated of the leaders not to join the Orange Order, thus depriving the ordinary Protestant of the one situation in which he could easily express his opinions to his local leaders. The only outcome, unless other things changed, was inevitably greater frustration.

12   Ballybeg and Northern Ireland

Because there is today such tension and anxiety in the relationships between Catholic and Protestant it might be assumed that
there are no redeeming features to the Ulster situation, but I hope
it will have become clear that to some extent at least the cleavage
between the two main religious groups, much as it is to be deplored,
does carry with it certain compensations since it results in a general
intensification of social life.

In the first place it is important to remember that for the
majority of the time relationships between Catholics and Protestants are peaceful as we have seen. In most years though people
may be aware of the possibility of violence, in fact violence does
not occur. Moreover, from some points of view just because the
cleavage exists individuals who might perhaps be isolated are
on the contrary drawn into close relationships with other people.

The very binary opposition between the two religious groups
gives the individual an unusual degree of importance. Just because
in Ballybeg the maintenance or alteration of the local political
situation was dependent on relative numbers, and because in
Ballybeg those numbers were almost even, every member of each
group was important to his fellow members. People not only
counted up the numbers of their opponents, as Mrs. Baxter did,
they also counted up their supporters. For this reason even
strangers found there was a warm welcome from long-established
residents—of course in certain contexts they remained outsiders
but nevertheless each newcomer was someone's welcome adherent.
It seemed undoubtedly the case that ties between the members of
one group were stronger than they would have been had no
cleavage existed. Individuals were seldom isolated; almost everyone attended church and/or was a member of some political group,

and they participated in many semi-social gatherings that had as
their object the promotion of some religious or political cause.

It seemed that even the adults' attitudes to children and adolescents were made more friendly by the strength of the recognition
that it was on them that adults had to count for the fulfilment of
their political hopes, and for this reason if for no other everyone
was anxious to involve the young in community life. The relationships between the generations in Ballybeg were very much more
relaxed than those depicted by Arensberg in their pre-war study
of County Clare. There relationships, especially between fathers
and sons, were marked by restraint and formality;[1] by contrast in
Ballybeg fathers and sons, the old and young in general, joined
together in amusements such as card-playing and drinking at the
pubs without a feeling of restraint. Of course the senior generation
was busily engaged in passing on its prejudices to the next; that is
not a fact that can be overlooked. But in so far as this involved a
father, say, in taking his son along to play in the band of his Orange
Lodge bridges were built between the generations, and adolescents
were given a valuable sense of importance they might otherwise
have lacked.

I have stressed already that relationships between Protestants
and Catholics were for the most part peaceful. It is also worth
pointing out that paradoxically, just because of the cleavage
between the religious groups relationships between individuals
belonging to different groups might be particularly 'neighbourly'.
An individual could afford, if he wished, to be brusque and awkward towards members of his own group who asked a favour. The
same man towards members of 'the other side' would be much
more amiable for fear that any refusal to help might be put down
to religious prejudice on his part. It is perhaps not surprising that
I met Protestants who seemed genuinely to think that under
normal conditions Catholics made the best neighbours, and
Catholics who were as convinced of the same thing about Protestants—such people were speaking out of their own experiences.
Perhaps it was partly just because it was the very best of neighbours
who might turn hostile that the adjective 'treacherous' seemed so
appropriate.

It is also important to note just how careful the people were to
try, in normal circumstances, to avoid any behaviour likely to
cause hostility, in other words to keep the latent hostility latent.

[1] Arensberg (1959), pp. 121-6.

The display of pictures in every house, which told the chance visitor quite clearly to which side the inhabitants belonged, and the wearing of badges of one kind or another, which often revealed the allegiances of chance-met individuals, were useful not merely because they symbolised in-group unity. Just because they made loyalties clear they made it possible to use the appropriate behaviour patterns that made peaceful relationships possible.

Indeed it must be reiterated that along with all the prejudiced attitudes went much toleration. Not only was it accepted that it was a right and proper thing for parents, even one's opponents, to bring up their children as loyal members of their own side; right and proper for them to see that they married 'endogamously'; right and proper for adults to observe the correct behaviour for their own group—it was also accepted that, within limits, even religious 'discrimination' in commercial transactions was right and proper. There were no large employers in Ballybeg whose employment policy might have given rise to bitterness. The most important employers were the quarry owner and the Northern Irish Transport Board, both of whom employed both Protestants and Catholics, though Catholics thought the best jobs were reserved for Protestants. After them came the shopkeepers who certainly sought their co-religionists as assistants, but this was accepted as so normal that it gave rise to no more comment than did the fact that customers patronised the shops of co-religionists. This tolerance of prejudice even extended to those letting or especially selling land, when they tried to see that that too went to co-religionists. Mary's brother Jack (PD20) went to the auction not seriously expecting to be allowed to buy the farm he wanted because it was Catholic owned, and he would not have resented it had he been prevented from doing so; what irritated him on this occasion was that having bought it he felt it was not within the rules of the situation that he should be denied access to it by having a right-of-way closed to him.

This acceptance within limits of prejudiced behaviour was undoubtedly an important factor in inter-group relationships. Faced with the politico-religious cleavage in their midst the people, for the most part, sought to promote quiet friendly ties across this division. In their attempts their main problem was perhaps that despite their best intentions links between Protestants and Catholics remained so limited.

It is very significant, however, that in so far as good relationships between the religious groups were dependent on a kind of tolerant acceptance of prejudice they were necessarily also dependent on the recognition that the community was fundamentally dichotomised. This fact of the dichotomised local community leads to a consideration of the nature of the link between the social patterns existing in Ballybeg and the pattern of Protestant and Catholic relationships in Ulster generally. We are here dealing with two linked questions. What is the relationship between social experience in the community and perception of the wider society? And what is the connection between categorical relationships in the wider society and interpersonal relationships in the local community?

In order to handle these wider issues it is necessary to look at some of the recent literature on the kind of connection existing between sub-groups and the wider society. This literature is for the most part more concerned with the structure and the organisation of racial minorities and ethnic groups in themselves rather than with the relationships between their members and the 'majority' in the local and the wider society. Nevertheless if not directly then indirectly it is possible to extract from this literature ideas relevant to the theme under discussion here.

In his recent book on race relations[2] Rex is explicitly concerned to extend the term so far beyond the area to which it is normally restricted that what he says can be considered as potentially relevant to the Ulster situation. He is really concerned with certain kinds of inter-group relationships where the groups are not necessarily in any way regarded as genetically determined, but where he regards one of the groups as oppressed. He wants, he says, to help oppressed minorities and feels that to attach the term 'racism' or 'racialism' to the ideas of the 'oppressors' will help the downtrodden since it is agreed that 'racial' concepts are 'not respectable'.[3] Without going into the question of whether good intentions should pave the road to terminological inexactitude we may, for the sake of following his argument, follow his usage in this instance.

According to Rex:

Race relations situations and problems have the following characteristics: they refer to situations in which two or more groups with distinct identities and recognisable characteristics are forced by economic or political circumstances to live together in a society. Within this they refer to situations in which there is a high degree of conflict

---

[2] Rex (1970). [3] Ibid., p. 161.

between the groups and in which ascriptive criteria are used to mark out the members of each group . . . Finally within this group of situations true race-relations situations may be said to exist when the practices of ascriptive allocation of roles and rights referred to are justified in terms of some kind of determinist theory, whether that theory be of a scientific, religious, cultural, historical, ideological or sociological kind . . .[4]

By 'deterministic' he means a belief that members of one group necessarily have qualities of an unpleasant or disvalued kind.

Clearly this kind of situation may be held to exist in Ulster and it is therefore worth while examining the kind of relationships that by implication he believes exists between local experience and group identity and between group identity and the situation within the society as a whole.

It seems that Rex visualises a fairly straightforward relationship between interaction between individuals and a sense of group identity, and between the development of 'racial' sub-groups and the nature of society. The crucial ascriptive criteria are developed to mark out one group from another in order that the members of one group may pursue hostile policies against members of the other; and primarily it is the actions of the dominant that bring the 'racial' groups into existence. These interaction situations are linked, however, to a general policy persued by the majority in the society at large, for the interaction situations arise where the latter seeks to curtail effectively the rights of the subordinate group, the minority, and to do this they practise 'discrimination' defined as choice based on visual criteria relating to group membership.[5] This denial of rights is by implication more extensive than anything that could be imposed at the local level were the actions not backed up by some kind of determination to curtail rights in the wider society. Rex does not explore the pattern of inter-relationships between individual members of subordinate and dominant groups in contexts where the question of the curtailment of rights does not arise. Nor is he explicitly concerned with the general problem of identification and self-identification of group membership, although this would seem to be important where, in the absence of clear genetically determined group distinctions, group boundaries may lack clear visual distinctiveness.

On the question of the relationship between the existence of 'racial' groups and society at large the main factors that by implica-

[4] Rex (1970), p. 160.　　　　[5] Ibid., p. 121.

tion Rex considers relevant are: the size of the sub-group; its readiness to identify with other similar groups in other areas; its determination to get and its definition of parity of status. These ideas are implicit in Rex's prognostications about the future of race-relations, in the strict sense, in England. These, he says, will depend on the numbers of the coloured population and the influence on them of Black Power ideology, with which he thinks they will inevitably become imbued. Once this occurs, if their numbers remain small they will probably take up a position of 'militant self-defence', but if their numbers increase significantly then a situation will develop like that in the United States where, Rex believes, the most likely alternatives are either that the coloured population will shoot their way into 'status positions equal with whites' or there will be continuing rioting.[6]

Extrapolating from Rex's ideas about 'race-relations' in the literal sense it would appear that he would postulate a fairly simple relationship between Catholic/Protestant interaction in the local community and the society at large. 'Society' denies certain rights to the Catholics; at the local level this is manifested in a hostile interaction situation, thus producing the concept of Catholic group identity, which is fostered by a Catholic and 'Irish' ideology; the sub-group being large and self-conscious is attempting to shoot its way into status positions equal with Protestants.

Another recent major contributor to the analysis of deeply divided social situations is M. G. Smith, through his work on 'plural' societies. Primarily he is concerned with classification, with analysing the conditions under which a 'plural society' may be said to exist, and in doing this he considers the characteristics which he believes distinguish the sub-groups in such a society. They are identifiable by what he calls 'institutional' differentiation. This is a concept that has been criticised for a certain vagueness, but he says: 'We have simply to ask (in the case of say kinship or religious institutions) whether the paternal or the maternal, the judicial, or the priestly status and role have the same definition and institutional contexts among different groups. If they have the groups share a common institutional system, if not then the society is 'plural'.[7]

Were we to take this aspect of Smith's definition at its face value then it would have to be said that Ulster is not a 'plural society', and therefore that what Smith has to say must be irrelevant. If

[6] Ibid., pp. 112–4.   [7] Smith (1965), p. 84.

Ulster is a 'plural' society it must be because of distinctions between the Protestants and Catholics, yet clearly we cannot differentiate between them on this kind of institutional basis or the commonness of their culture has been shown. True, for example, the role of 'priest' of the Roman Catholic church, and the role of 'minister' in the Presbyterian church differ in their definitions and institutional contexts, but so do the roles of 'minister' and that of 'priests' of the Church of Ireland; yet were the only religious division in the Province that between the two latter churches I doubt if anyone would think of calling Ulster a 'plural' society. On the other hand the 'paternal' and the 'maternal' roles have precisely similar definitions and institutional contexts amongst, say, small farmers, whatever their religious faith. Sub-group differentiation on the basis of these kinds of institutional similarities and dissimilarities would seem not to be particularly relevant.

Smith has, however, given what seems a much more significant (at least from the Ulster viewpoint) definition of the 'plural society' when he says that a society has a plural *culture* in so far as its constituent sub-groups differ culturally in matters that are basically of private concern, but that a true plural *society* exists when sub-groups differ culturally on matters of *public* concern, for example in their educational systems; and a society is *structurally* plural in so far as the sub-groups are incorporated explicitly or *de facto* differentially in the political sphere,[8] i.e. when one group, as a group, has fewer political rights than another. Since undoubtedly Catholics and Protestants differ in their attachment to organisations that are of public concern, and most certainly in their educational systems, and since Catholics certainly believe they have fewer political rights than Protestants, Ulster would seem to come quite obviously within the scope of Smith's analysis. We may therefore examine it in somewhat more detail.

True *structural* pluralism exists, according to Smith, when there is total disenfranchisement and citizenship is withheld, or alternatively when the scope of the 'substantive differentiations' between the groups are 'sufficiently rigorous and pervasive to establish an effective order of corporate inequalities and subordination by the different sub-cultures, and the type of government possible within economic, social and other opportunities that these permit and enjoin'.[9]

In other words, it seems that by implication Smith assumes that

[8] Smith (1969), p. 430.   [9] Ibid.

sub-groups are made significant when those with power in a state withhold from sub-group members various kinds of rights, and that economic, social and 'other' opportunities are all dependent on the possession, in a real sense, of the franchise. He has little to say about the perception of group membership and the problems of self identification. He does, however, see a significant connection between the existence of sub-groups with markedly different sub-cultures, and the type of government possible within the society. In a plural situation, he argues there is a 'medley of sectional value systems which rules out value consensus'. Therefore, 'Given the fundamental differences of belief, value and organisation that connote pluralism, the monopoly of power by one cultural section is the essential precondition for the maintenance of the total society in its current form'.[10]

It would appear, in summary, therefore that in Smith's view the existence of sub-groups of a kind that enable us to speak of a 'plural society' are dependent on the existence of a system that denies the members of certain groups political and civil rights equal to others, and that in turn where such sub-groups exist there is such a lack of any basic consensus in the society that the only possible form of government is the political domination of the minority by the majority. This view too might seem, at least at first sight, to suggest the kind of relationship many people believe actually to exist between minority and majority in Ulster. But we must at once make this proviso, that any lack of consensus there may be cannot be related back simply to some general lack of cultural consensus.

Banton in his recent book[11] on race relations is specifically concerned with analysing those situations in which genetically determined visual differences exist, or are believed to exist, between sub-groups in a population, and it might, therefore, appear that what he says is not easily applicable to the Ulster situation. He does, however, in the course of his attempts to classify the variations in patterns of race relations that may occur, discuss one situation that seems very relevant to Northern Ireland. In his description of the type of situation he describes as 'domination' he argues that one of the defining characteristics is that racial qualities are given fundamental significance as role-signs. Domination leads to a harsh dichotomy between dominant and subordinate groups: whatever their personal qualities, individuals are ascribed to one or other

[10] Ibid., p. 83. [11] Banton (1967).

category, and those in the lower are prevented from claiming the privileges of those in the upper category. As racial distinctions are drawn in a wide variety of situations, race is a sign of a basic role, like sex or age.[12] Whatever differences exist between racial groups and Ulster's religious groups in Ulster the religious role is certainly 'basic' in precisely this sense. Ulster's religious groups have therefore something important in common with Banton's racial groups in this situation of 'domination'.

Significantly, Banton's 'domination' seems to be identical with Smith's situation of 'structural pluralism'. Banton does indeed use the term 'pluralism' for a different type of race-relations situation, but this appears to be the same as Smith's mere 'cultural pluralism'. Banton's 'pluralism' exists where equality in political and civil rights has been achieved without dissolution of the boundaries of the minority group;[13] it is, on the contrary, the very absence of civil and political equality that determines, he thinks, the existence of a situation of 'domination'. It is at this point that Banton's discussion becomes of real interest to our present theme, for he here examines the interrelation between the social situation in the wider society and the emergence of race as a basic role sign in interaction in the local environment. He stresses that in the local situation relationships between members of the different groups may, at an individual level, be good but, nevertheless, he says the racial role is crucial in their interaction. This is because due to the structure of society at a higher level, the race-role becomes 'pervasive' because a member of the subordinate racial group can be forced to pay deference to a superior group member whenever they interact because the inferior lacks civil rights.[14]

In summary therefore he argues that the denial of civil rights leads to dichotomised local communities because no interaction of those with and those without these rights can escape definition in categorical terms.

Wagley and Harris in their book on minorities[15] without any question are concerned with the kind of situation existing in Northern Ireland, for they define the scope of their interests as encompassing sub-groups that emerge as the result of historical processes which have undoubtedly occurred in Ulster. For them 'minorities' result from one of three situations: as the result of

---

[12] Banton (1967), p. 71.
[14] Ibid., p. 71.

[13] Ibid., p. 74.
[15] Wagley and Harris (1958).

slavery in the past; as the result of the immigration of poor people; and as the result of the formation of a conquest state, in which case the 'minority' has developed out of the vanquished enemy. This last condition undoubtedly applies to Ulster given the events of the seventeenth century.

In many ways the approach of Wagley and Harris to the question of the development of minorities is more sensitive, in the sense of being more aware of a wide variety of possibilities, than any of the authors previously considered. So far we have seen writers concerned very largely with the way in which sub-groups, however defined, emerge as the result of the actions of those outside the group who wield power and authority. This aspect, of course, necessarily concerns Wagley and Harris also, but in addition they are also very much aware of the significance of self-identification of the members of the sub-group, and of their perception and definition of their situation. A 'minority' for them is by definition 'ethnocentric', believing its own customs, language, religion and physical characteristics, are better or more 'natural' than those of others.[16] This ethnocentrism is vital even if only because it leads to an insistence on endogamy on which the future of the 'minority' may well depend. Moreover, a minority exists because it *perceives* itself to be in conflict with other groups[17] and there is overt hostility between it and the majority.

In accordance with this broader approach to the subject of sub-groups within a society Wagley and Harris also believe that the question of minority emergence is linked to wider factors than the mere denial of civil or political rights. They see conflict as generated by competition between the minority and the majority for the resources and limited valuables existing within the larger society, and it is this competition that determines the relationships existing between the minority and the majority. Two types of factors influence the nature of this competition. In the first place there is the question of the type of valuables for which competition exists: these may be merely prestige symbols, such as membership of clubs and the acquisition of honorific titles, or competition may relate to educational opportunity, job opportunities, rights to acquire land and political power. (Clearly at this latter level they are discussing in terms of process the same situation that Smith describes, in terms of structure, as 'structural pluralism'.) Secondly there is the factor that they describe as the 'terms' of the

[16] Ibid., p. 258.   [17] Ibid., p. 260.

competition (something to which Rex seems to be referring when he discusses the relative size of racial groups). Relationships with the majority are influenced, Wagley and Harris think, by these 'terms', that is by 'whether or not the minority has the instruments and the opportunity to compete with the majority in the same arena . . . a minority well organised and vested with some legal rights is able to compete aggressively and conflict between the groups will be intense and overt'.[18]

The third factor recognised by Wagley and Harris as influencing the type of competition between the minority and the majority is something they take from an older analysis by Wirth. Wirth argued that minorities should be classified according to whether their political aims are 'pluralistic', the minority trying to preserve its own identity and culture upon a basis of tolerance of differences and equality of opportunity; assimilative, the minority seeking 'to merge with dominant group'; secessionist, the minority seeking to achieve political separation from the dominant group; or 'militant', the minority having as its goal 'political domination over the majority'.[19] In summary therefore competition between groups has to be considered to relate to the objects of the competition, the terms under which the minority competes and the political aims of the minority.

Turning to the consideration of the influence of the wider society on minority formation Wagley and Harris clearly recognise and stress the importance of discrimination against a group. Nevertheless they argue also that here too perception as well as actual discrimination is important. A group need not suffer actual discrimination to be a 'minority' in their sense. Speaking of the French Canadians, Wagley and Harris acknowledge that the extent to which they suffer real discrimination is doubtful. Indeed in some areas of Canada they hold authority and wield power and in these areas it is the English-speaking Canadians who make allegations of discrimination. Nevertheless, according to Wagley and Harris the important fact is that historically the French Canadians were conquered, not the conquering group, the dominated, not the dominating and, crucially, they *believe* themselves to suffer discrimination.[20]

This emphasis on the significance of self-identification is also made by Barth in the recent book on ethnic groups and

[18] Wagley and Harris (1958), p. 264.
[19] Ibid., p. 285, quoting Wirth, 1945, p. 361.   [20] Ibid., pp. 188–200.

boundaries.[21] In discussing ethnicity he is discussing something that again must have much in common with racial group membership, or Ulster religious group membership, since he says that an ethnic role 'classifies a person in terms of his basic, most general identity, presumptively determined by his background and origin'.[22] Indeed he goes further, for he also says 'regarded as a status, ethnic identity is similar to sex and rank in that it constrains the incumbent in all his activities, not only in some defined social situations. One might thus also say that it is *imperative*, in that it cannot be disregarded and temporarily set aside by other definitions of the situation'.[23] Yet the central problem that interests Barth in ethnicity is one that necessarily implies that the 'ethnic group', if group it be, may develop and persist in contexts in which an ethnic identity is not forced on members by the action of the majority.

The foundation for this statement is that Barth, in his introduction to the book, begins by rejecting morphological definitions of 'ethnic groups' as being at best irrelevant, and at worst as masking the central problem of ethnicity. Barth argues that in dealing with ethnic groups we are dealing with situations in which visible differences between categories of people are not immediately apparent, and therefore the fundamental problem is to understand why people maintain their allegiance to a particular group. It is therefore simply avoiding this issue to define an ethnic group in terms of its biological self-perpetuation, its shared and distinguishing cultural values, its constitution of a field of communication and interaction and its membership distinguished as a category from others. All this may certainly describe a central core of people distinguished from others by their 'ethnicity'. Nevertheless if the members of such an 'ethnic group' are not visibly distinct from others, and interact frequently with others, they will in fact in many ways be culturally similar to others. The real problem is, therefore, why some members of this ethnic category remain distinct and do not assimilate. What fascinates him is the situation in which inter-group boundaries are sharply demarcated even while the nature of cultural differences between the groups alter and individuals have a certain freedom to cross group boundaries.[24]

If the significance of group membership were entirely negative

[21] Barth (1969).
[22] Ibid., p. 13.
[23] Ibid., p. 17.
[24] Ibid., pp. 10–11.

P

there is no reason to suppose that individuals would adhere to an identification from which they could escape. For the individual to maintain his ethnic membership there must be 'pull' factors as well as 'push' factors, in other words. This kind of minority can exist only while its members identify themselves as members, and he suggests that a major factor in self-identification must be some kind of self-advantage. Like Wagley and Harris, in their discussion of minorities, Barth suggests that the precipitating factor leading to the development of an ethnic group is that of competition between it and the majority: indeed he suggests that a useful typology of ethnic groups could be made on the basis of the kind of competition that they experience, although this is not an idea he explores in any depth. He does assume, however, that ethnic self-identification may give the individual a certain kind of competitive advantage *vis-à-vis* others in his community.

Whilst Barth does not suggest any particular relation between patterns of interaction between individuals and the initial development of a sense of group identity, he does suggest that only certain patterns of interaction are compatible with the persistence of ethnic groups as he defines them. He argues that: 'Stable inter-ethnic relations pre-suppose . . . a structuring of interaction; a set of prescriptions governing situations of contact and allowing for articulation in some sectors or domains of activity, and a set of proscriptions on social situations, preventing inter-ethnic interaction in other sectors, and thus insulating part of the cultures from confrontation and modification'.[25]

In summary of what all these authors say, explicitly or implicitly, it can be said that whatever the name given to the groups under discussion the role of group member is seen to be a basic role, like sex or age or rank, and it seems useful, therefore, to call such units 'basic' sub-groups. An assumption of Rex and Smith and Wagley and Harris is that this kind of sub-group is brought into existence primarily by the majority discriminating against it, though Wagley and Harris are prepared to accept that under certain circumstances what is important is simply that the members of the sub-group believe they are the subject of adverse discrimination. Barth and Wagley and Harris believe that the fundamental causal factor in the development of 'basic' sub-groups is the existence of some form of competition between the sub-group members and others in the society. Barth suggests that this type of sub-group may

[25] Barth (1969), p. 16.

persist, if not develop, because its members derive certain advantages from identification as a minority. Rex, Banton and Barth explicitly or implicitly link the existence of these 'basic' subgroups with certain patterns of interaction between individuals: Rex and Banton see the essential nature of this interaction as deriving from attempts to express patterns of domination and subordination; Barth on the contrary stresses the importance, for the persistence of basic sub-groups, of patterns of signalling and receiving messages about sub-group identity in the context of everyday interaction. On the subject of the connection between the existence of basic sub-groups and the wider society only Wagley and Harris are interested in the complexities of the relation. They postulate a number of significant variables, especially the 'aims' of the minority and the 'terms' of the competition in which it is engaged. Smith suggests a relationship between a lack of general consensus and the pattern of government, whilst Rex postulates a relation between the size of the sub-group, its aims and the possible development of violence within the society.

It does not seem a particularly useful exercise to attempt to define the Ulster situation and the religious sub-groups morphologically. In the first place it seems more interesting to seek for correlations than to attempt an exercise in pigeon-holing. Further there are inherent difficulties implicit in seeking to apply the terminology of any of these authors to the religious sub-groups in Ballybeg. This study of Ballybeg has of course dealt with Catholics as well as Protestants, but neither the Ballybeg situation nor that of Ulster generally is to be explained by concentration on the Catholics to the exclusion of the Protestants; yet for the most part the terminology used can be applied only to the former. In other words, in defining the situation in the terms offered to us we would inevitably end by asking whether the Catholics as a group fitted one description rather than another; and in so doing our perception of the situation would itself be slanted. Or we should end by arguing for example that while the Catholics form some kind of 'minority' in the sense used by Wagley and Harris, the Protestants of Ballybeg form a kind of Barthian 'ethnic group'? Such arguments could perhaps be supported, but it seems infinitely preferable to search not just for accurate categorisation or for new refinements of definitions but to proceed instead, on rather different lines, to try to answer with the help of suggestions found in the works discussed the questions posed at the beginning of this section: what is the relation between the experience of sub-group membership and the perception of the wider society?; what is the relation between the structure of this wider society and the pattern of identification and self-identification with particular sub-groups?

The answers to these questions have a double interest. If they can be answered they should illuminate the Ulster situation. Further they should have a certain general theoretical interest. The point is that Ulster's religious sub-groups share characteristics of both Barth's ethnic groups and racial groups in the strict sense. Sub-group membership is not immediately visually apparent; on the contrary it has to be signalled, as Barth suggests, and hence the many badges worn voluntarily. Yet at the same time it is clear from all that has been said about the ties of sub-group membership in Ballybeg that psychologically and sociologically a change of group membership, at least while the individual remains within Ulster, is very difficult. In times of overt strife 'ethnic' boundaries in Ulster may be maintained by the murder of those who attempt to cross them, witness the assassination by the I.R.A. of Catholic members of the Ulster Defence Force; but even in more normal times the rupture of social ties presupposed by changed loyalties must put great strain on most individuals. In consequence these religious sub-groups have considerable theoretical interest since what applies to them probably applies also to a wide range of 'basic' sub-groups.

In discussing the nature of the relationship between the 'basic' sub-groups and the organisation of the wider society the causal factor most commonly postulated has been that the 'minority' are denied their civil or their political rights, or both. Our first task must be therefore to see whether this relationship holds in Northern Ireland.

The question of whether or not Catholics in Ulster are denied their rights is of course hotly disputed. The present disturbances in the Province were sparked off by an explicitly labelled 'Civil Rights' movement that certainly claimed that these rights were denied both at the political and the economic level. The most dispassionate survey of the position of Catholics made in recent years came, however, to the conclusion that the matter was not wholly clear cut.[26]

A survey by Barritt and Carter concluded that Catholics enjoyed equal rights with Protestants regarding parliamentary franchise,

[26] Barritt and Carter (1962).

both in respect to elections for the Westminster Parliament and the elections for Stormont.[27] On the other hand, Catholics suffered serious disadvantages *de facto* though not *de jure* in a number of local government constituencies. This was because in local elections certain property qualifications for the local government vote, of the type until recently widespread in the United Kingdom, had never been altered in Northern Ireland. In consequence Catholics as the poorer section of the community were adversely affected.[28]

It was in the field of employment that these authors found it most difficult to answer questions about the extent of religious discrimination. Employers seldom admitted discrimination, and usually there was no evidence that applicants for jobs were asked their religious affiliations, but discriminations did not depend on such direct information even when there was no personal knowledge of the candidate; Catholics are almost invariably educated at Catholic schools so that legitimate questions about educational background necessarily revealed religious adherence. The authors believed that discrimination was practised in local government employment, some preference being given by whatever party was in power in the Council to applicants who were assumed to be its adherents. Further, the fact that Catholics were kept out of the higher levels of the Civil Service was virtually admitted since the excuse was made to the authors that there were problems in appointing to important administrative and executive posts those likely to want to do away with Northern Ireland as a political unit.

In private employment the very small employer, whether Catholic or Protestant, displayed an open prejudice for 'his own'. A few larger firms were believed by the authors to be similarly motivated. Elsewhere they were much less sure of the evidence.

Barritt and Carter recognised that most Catholics believed that religious discrimination in employment was widespread and that the statistics proved this and that there were clear political reasons for Protestant managements to be discriminatory. Just because Catholics share equally in the parliamentary franchise relative numbers of Catholics in the Province are of vital importance. Because of different attitudes to birth control the Catholic population increases more rapidly than does the Protestant, and were it not for the fact that a higher proportion of Catholics emigrate there would now be a Catholic majority in Ulster. Catholics emigrate because they find it more difficult than Protestants to

[27] Ibid., p. 43. [28] Ibid., pp. 120–5.

get jobs. To the Catholic the situation of blatant discrimination seems very clear.

Statistics, however, can seldom be taken at their face value. During the last fifty years there has been a serious decline in Ulster in work for the unskilled and the agricultural labourer (a trend apparent even in Ballybeg) as the result of economic forces which have been far too widespread for the Northern Irish government to hope to be able to control; indeed much the same pattern of events has influenced the Republic of Ireland as well. When the Unionist government came to power they inherited a situation in which Catholics formed a majority of the unskilled labour force. Even in the total absence of discrimination it is certain that a higher proportion of Catholics than Protestants would have emigrated.

There are other statistics that suggest that Catholics are particularly discriminated against when they seek for better jobs, especially at managerial level, for it is clear that Protestants are over-represented and Catholics under-represented in this field. Here again the statistics by themselves do not give as clear an indication of the situation as might be imagined. This is because the educational attainments of Catholics tend to be lower than that of Protestants. Roman Catholic schools have a bigger proportion than do other schools of pupils with a working class background. Moreover Protestant secondary schools provide a better training for the Ulster examination system than do Catholic schools, which tend to be staffed to a significant degree by teachers from religious seminaries including in their number a high proportion from seminaries in the Republic whose trainees have not had contact with the Northern Irish teachers' training colleges.[29] One objective result was that Catholic schools were demonstrably weak in science teaching.[30] Were the Catholic population excluded by the Protestants from their own schools, then it would be wholly reasonable to explain the overall disadvantage suffered by Catholics seeking employment in terms of discrimination beginning with educational discrimination. Since, however, the right to the separation of their schools and the right to decide the content of the teaching courses are jealously guarded by the Catholic community it becomes less easy to state clearly that Catholic lack of success in seeking employment must be due to discrimination; too often managements have objective grounds for preferring Protestants.[31]

[29] Barritt and Carter (1962), p. 89.   [30] Ibid., p. 90.
[31] Ibid., pp. 93–107.

It would, of course, be naïve to believe that the desire, so politically advantageous, to give jobs to fellow Protestants has not had some influence on Protestant managements choosing employees. It would, nevertheless, be equally naïve to believe that Catholics disappointed in their search for jobs have not tended to assume that their failures have been due to discrimination when it may have been due rather to some educational advantage possessed by their Protestant rivals. Ballybeg provided examples of the parallel case of the readiness of Catholic farmers to ascribe to discrimination any failure on their part to obtain subsidies or other advantages even when other explanations seemed objectively more likely.

I am not here concerned to try to go beyond the work that Carter and Barritt were able to do and to assess more carefully the precise degree of discrimination or lack of discrimination operating in the field of employment in Northern Ireland. I am concerned to make the point that perception of the situation as well as objective reality are vitally important in the judgements made about the social situation. In Northern Ireland it is probably true that every Catholic believes he has personal knowledge of discrimination in economic matters if not against himself then against those well known to him, and it is in the light of this knowledge that he interprets such things as the emigration figures. His initial interpretation of these local level experiences which provide his objective evidence for discrimination itself, however, rests on a prior assumption that actions relating to economic affairs are designed to benefit government supporters and are not decided on an objective basis. In other words, the initial interpretation rests on the assumption of the over-riding importance of the rigorous dichotomisation of the society into two competing groups.

Granted this assumption, then much that is at first sight puzzling about the Ulster political situation becomes much more understandable. In the rest of the United Kingdom the prize for which politicians compete is the right to determine public policy for the country for five-year periods. The parties seek to gain the right to do this primarily by winning the adherence, for the time being, of the floating voter, the individual not finally committed to any party. Ousted politicians hope that by the next election their party's poor performance will have been forgotten, or at least that their rivals' failures will be more to the forefront of the public mind. Thus they can hope by winning back the support of the floating voter to be once again elected back into office. In Ulster, however, because of past history there was for many years virtually no floating vote; voting behaviour was to a considerable extent decided from birth by religious adherence. Moreover, the main question at issue was not simply the right to determine general public policy but, since the primary policy of the parties supported by Catholics was unity with the rest of Ireland, the issue has been the continued existence of Northern Ireland as a separate entity. Whilst this remained the issue the Unionist party had only one election to lose, for if it lost one it would not be able to fight another. It is at this point perhaps that Smith's idea of the significance of a lack of consensus in a society becomes significant. In the field of general values there is much consensus between Protestants and Catholics. What is significant is the extent to which there has been a total absence of consensus on this fundamental political issue. While this issue has dominated politics Ulster elections have been won or lost not on the basis of shifts of opinion about particular politicians but on the basis of the relative numbers of Catholics and Protestants within a given area. Hence the political importance assigned to the employment and emigration situation. Hence also another aspect of the political scene that is somewhat less obvious, the lack of concern with the 'floating' vote.

In the rest of the United Kingdom in the absence of a fundamental political cleavage there is, in effect, some disenfranchisement of the right- and left-wing extremists. To get into power politicians have for years competed for the middle-of-the-road floating vote; they do not have to worry about their more extreme supporters since their backing can, by definition, be assumed, and so party policies have been framed to win those in the centre to their opinions. In Ulster, on the other hand, the assumption of the dichotomised society meant for many years that the Unionist party felt that the chances of winning over any significant proportion of the Catholic vote was so remote that there was little point in designing policies specifically to woo Catholics; rather Unionist policies, in so far as they were independent of United Kingdom policies, were designed for obvious reasons to appeal primarily to Unionist voters, to forstall the growth of splinter parties.

The effect of this general political situation has been to exclude the Nationalist/Catholic from power: where the issue is the existence or non-existence of the state, gentlemanly moves in and out of power by the competing parties are scarcely possible. In addition the Catholic feels he has been denied any significant influence on policymaking—he is not the object of the wooing of the politicians in power except in so far as it has been necessary for them to pay attention to a large and well-organised minority that has always constituted a potential physical threat. The Catholic has the vote and there is little evidence that parliamentary elections have been gerrymandered. Nevertheless because the Catholic has been kept out of power by the majority and denied much influence on policy-making he has felt disenfranchised.

At an abstract level it is relatively easy to summarise the Ulster situation using the idiom suggested by Wagley and Harris describing the 'arenas' of competition between Catholics and Protestants, the 'terms' of their competition, and the 'aims' of the minority as competitors. It seems convenient to describe three arenas, that of national politics, local politics and the economic arena. We may also pay attention to the question of perception as well as objective fact.

In the national political arena the aim of the Catholic minority is 'militant' in so far as it is Nationalist, in that Nationalists by definition are seeking not equality of political opportunity for Catholics but the incorporation of Northern Ireland into the Republic, in which arena the Protestants would form a small minority. The assumption of most Protestants is that the aim of all Catholics is thus 'militant'; statements to the contrary are thought to be the result of duplicity, and apparent evidence to the contrary is to be treated with considerable reserve. In this arena the 'terms' of the competition between Protestant and Catholic are jurally equal and *de facto* equal, except in so far as a higher Catholic emigration rate from the Province nullifies the political advantage the Catholics would otherwise derive from their higher birth-rate.

In the local government arena, prior to recent reforms, the situation was somewhat different. At this level the aim of the Catholic groups may be said to be simply equality. Jurally there was no discrimination relating to the franchise between the two religious groups. *De facto* because of the retention of rules about property qualification Catholics in some areas were at a considerable disadvantage.

In the arena of economic competition the situation was very complex. Once again the aim of the Catholic groups at this level may be said to be simply equality. Jurally there was no discrimination in employment on the grounds of religious affiliation; in practice some employers did discriminate, at least to a limited extent, and because more managements were Protestant than Catholic, Catholics suffered somewhat more from this kind of disadvantage. Catholics were also seriously disadvantaged in competition for the kind of jobs available in Northern Ireland by the high proportion seeking for the relatively scarce unskilled or semi-skilled employment and by educational handicaps partly self-imposed, partly increased by the high proportion of Catholics coming from large working-class families. Employment failures by Catholics were interpreted by Catholics as the result of gross religious discrimination practised for the purpose of increasing Catholic emigration and thus maintaining Protestant political domination in the arena of national politics. In practice therefore the interconnection between the political and economic arenas was perceived to be very close.

In this summary it is clear that perception as well as objective fact plays an important part in the Ulster situation. Indeed this would seem to be generally true in any context where minority/majority relationships are important. In particular there is a very complex and subtle relation between acts of discrimination and the experience of discrimination, for these are not necessarily the same things, since the experience of discrimination depends on the actor's definition of events. In general the more clearly the members of a minority perceive the universe to be dichotomised the more likely they are to perceive themselves to be the target of adverse discrimination; further, the more they believe themselves to be the target of discrimination the firmer will be their conviction that they live in a dichotomised world. Discrimination may take place that is unperceived and thus not experienced as such. This happens when some category of people are treated 'unfairly' by others, but where those subject to this treatment believe it to be the result of some objective assessment of their qualities or capabilities as when women acquiesce in the disabilities they suffer, or an outcast group, believing in their own uncleanness, efface themselves in the presence of their superiors because they themselves believe that outcast presence contaminates. Conversely if in a society sharply divided into 'Xs' and 'Ys' a firm owned by Xs employing, say, lamplighters stipulates on the grounds of efficiency that it will employ only men who are over six feet tall, the plea of efficiency will not save it from the charge of discrimination if it does not take on Y applicants who are under that height. This will be particularly true if Ys in general are shorter than Xs. Indeed in general if there is strong competition between a majority and a minority group in a society, then any failure by the minority in any arena is likely to be ascribed to adverse discrimination, no matter what are the actual reasons for the minority competing in that field on unfavourable terms.

Once a society is thought of as dichotomised this structures all social perceptions. Given an X/Y cleavage, then any failure of Ys in any competitive field, for whatever reason, provides evidence to them that they experience adverse discrimination. Moreover, once such a social dichotomy exists, it is very difficult to counteract it since even the total elimination of discriminatory acts by Xs against Ys would not eliminate the perception of discrimination by Ys if for other reasons they remain at a competitive disadvantage in any arena; their failure here would continue to be perceived as due to discrimination. The importance of such dichotomisation was discussed years ago by Gluckman[32] when he argued that in a society with a single dominant cleavage, rooted 'in the fundamental conflict of the system', this cleavage tends to run through all social relationships in the system and influences their subjective interpretation of it. In the extreme case of South Africa conflict had reached the pitch where even those acts of the whites designed to raise African living standards could only be interpreted by the Zulu as direct attempts to bring about their downfall.[33] In less extreme situations suspicions of the dominant may not go quite so far but it certainly provides a ready explanation of misfortune suffered by a minority.

This brings us to an understanding of the curious fact that although the authors discussed referred variously to 'ethnic' groups, 'racial' groups and 'minorities' and these units were to some extent substantively diverse, yet in all these cases group roles, despite any such differences, were assumed to be 'basic', like the roles of sex or age. The reason I suggest is that all such groups have in common the fact that to a greater or lesser extent they live in a perceived dichotomous environment; they differ merely in the degree to which they see the world as divided into two.

In the case of the 'ethnic' group in Barth's use of the term the dichotomised area may be largely limited to the local community

[32] Gluckman (1958).   [33] Ibid., p. 65.

and it is only here that the ethnic role is basic. For a 'minority' the dichotomised area includes the wider political unit, so that the minority role is perceived to be significant in the encapsulating society as well as in the local community. For a 'racial' group the racial role may be held to be significant on a world-wide scale. Thus a remote Norwegian parish, for example, may be clearly dichotomised socially into Lapps and Norwegians, but this distinction is relatively so unimportant for the inhabitants of Oslo that Lapp identity is not there of particular significance. A Catholic role, however, is seen as 'basic' in Belfast just as much as it is in Ballybeg. For the Negro his racial role may well appear 'basic' beyond the confines of his own country.

If it is accepted that the main difference between the different types of 'basic' groups really relates to the area over which their membership confers 'basic' roles and the extent to which their members perceive society to be dichotomised, certain things follow. A dichotomisation of society at whatever level depends logically, as Barth shows, on the perception of a boundary that can be kept conceptually distinct. Further it must be possible to allocate, or to interpret differential allocations of wealth, status and power in terms of this boundary. This is the significance of any criterion, be it religion, ethnic origin, or physical characteristics, that can be used to make a clear distinction between members and non-members. Where there is no such clear-cut criterion differences, for example in the franchise dependent on property qualification, do not make a 'plural' society in any meaningful sense; lower the property qualification and the thirty-nine-shilling freeholder no longer continues to view the world as divided into 'forty-shilling freeholders' with the vote, and others. Conversely, given the religious dichotomy in Ulster and the fact that a majority of those with lower incomes are Catholic any property qualification at all in the local government franchise continues to be seen by all Catholics, whatever their incomes, as an anti-Catholic measure. In practice it seems that perhaps the most potent factor leading the members of a sub-group to dichotomise their environment is the belief that the criterion by which it itself is defined is a significant basis for the making of unfair allocations of wealth, status and power.

Two things are implied in saying that the environment is perceived to be dichotomised. Not only are external events interpreted in terms of the dichotomy but the events so interpreted are thought relevant to local intergroup relations. One difference between ethnic groups and racial groups involves the extent of this dichotomy. Ethnic-group membership may have only local relevance and then national events will not be seen in terms of ethnic gains or losses, nor will these events influence local relations. Conversely where the racial role is interpreted as having world-wide significance many external events are interpreted in racial terms and are fed back to influence local race-relations, so stimulating further racial interpretations of local events. In Ulster the religious group lies midway between the racial and ethnic group. Religious differences are held to be of universal significance, but it is primarily in Ireland that religion is perceived to determine the allocation of wealth, status and power. Thus from Ireland generally and Ulster in particular information about events comes to places like Ballybeg as a stream of messages about religious group membership that inevitably influences local relationships between Catholics and Protestants.

The literature on minority/majority relations often reads as if only the majority were 'prejudiced', and indeed this study has concentrated on Protestant prejudice. But in the literal sense of prejudging issues and of allowing these pre-judgements to influence behaviour, minority and majority are equally prejudiced in so far as they interpret events in dichotomous terms. Levi-Strauss argues that it is a fundamental characteristic of the human mind to conceptualise in terms of binary oppositions; he of course has in view the fundamental processes of thought and the use of successive oppositions to make increasingly fine distinctions in terms of which the social environment is classified.[34] It seems all too true, however, that people tend to perceive their social environment in terms of a single set of binary oppositions, and all too easy for a single pair of social oppositions to be given wide explanatory significance.

To reiterate; this perceived dichotomy is at the heart of the problem of 'minority' relationships with the dominant group and the reason why there is a very clear parallel between the relationships between Catholics and Protestants in Northern Ireland and a race-relations situation. The situations are similar in so far as a minority, however defined, perceives *Society* to be dichotomised on the basis of the very criterion that is used to delineate the boundaries of the minority itself. The differences between the Catholic minority in Ulster and a racial minority is that the latter

[34] Levi-Strauss (1966).

Q

can perceive a dichotomy based on colour to have universal significance, whilst the more sober Ulsterman has to recognise that society outside Ireland is not simply divided into opposed groups of Catholics and Protestants.

When we consider the connection between the situation in Ballybeg and Catholic and Protestant relationships in Ulster as a whole we do not, I think, need to concern ourselves with the niceties of the degree of 'institutional' variation between the groups. What matters at the local level is the dichotomisation of the spheres of social interaction and the fact that there exist, in broad terms, a Protestant social sphere and a Catholic social sphere, the separation between the two being manifested in the fields of kinship, education, organisational membership and thus in many informal situations also. In other words, the actor in Ballybeg lives within a dichotomised social environment. This recognition of dichotomisation based on real social experience is extended beyond the borders of Ballybeg by the relevance, actual and perceived (and perceptions are to some extent formed by local experience), of the religious dichotomy at the level of Northern Ireland as a whole. We can express this tendency to dichotomise in a different way by saying that the actor who identifies himself as being on a particular side in the local situation identifies himself always with the same side in disputes and events that occur at the centre. Events there are evaluated in terms of gains or losses for one or other side at the local level.

This brings us to a consideration of the mechanism whereby the division in the wider society becomes significant for the pattern of interaction between individual actors in the local community. Obviously the primary significance of the religious role is that it allocates individuals to one or other of the interaction spheres. But it is important to note that even in situations in which Catholics and Protestants do interact the religious role is crucial. We have seen that Banton has argued that racial identification becomes manifest through patterned interaction between individuals, and that the race role becomes 'pervasive' since this pattern is manifest in every situation where members of the different racial groups meet.[35] Banton, as we saw, has in mind patterns of domination and subordination expressed in etiquette. In Ballybeg there was a very different situation since Catholics and Protestants of the same social standing interacted as equals. Interaction between

[35] Banton, ibid., p. 71.

them was nevertheless patterned so that even in those contexts where they did meet the consciousness of the religious role was made 'pervasive', however friendly their relationships, by the existence of this recognised pattern. Moreover, this pattern depended on the existence of a dichotomised perception of events happening outside as well as inside Ballybeg. In Ballybeg the religious role was made pervasive partly by the fact that people believed, whatever the objective reality, that the religious dichotomy was relevant to almost every topic of conversation. It did not matter whether the topics were local grants for tractors or house improvements, prices gained from the 'grader' in Ballybeg Fair, or 'Stormont' policy about education and farm prices; sometimes dichotomisation even went so far that the activities of foreign, even atheistic, politicians were felt to be relevant. In Ballybeg in mixed religious company all such topics were either avoided or discussed in a manner that showed intense awareness of the supposed susceptibilities of members of 'the other side'. In other words, where Protestant and Catholic met the religious role was made 'pervasive' not from a desire to assert domination or to be able to discriminate effectively but most commonly from a concern with good manners and the desire for the continuation of good personal relationships with members of the 'other side' (the very use of which term in contrast to 'your own' expresses with great clarity the profound depth of the perceived dichotomy).

The significance of any such pattern, no matter what the good intentions that determine it, has however been discussed by Barth when in the passage already quoted he argues that 'Stable inter-ethnic relations pre-suppose . . . a structuring of interaction; a set of prescriptions governing situations of contact and allowing for articulation in some sectors or domains of activity, and a set of proscriptions on social situations, preventing inter-ethnic interaction in other sectors, and thus insulating part of the cultures from confrontation and modification.' In fact it was an important aspect of the interrelationships of Catholics and Protestants in Ballybeg that all serious discussion of political and religious questions between them was socially forbidden. The result was their, at times startling, ignorance of each other's beliefs and practices revealed to me most clearly when I was used by Catholics as a source of information about the attitudes and beliefs of their Protestant neighbours with whom they were in regular and friendly contact. Confrontation was avoided but at the same time so was the possibility of testing prejudices against reality. At the same time also the social dichotomy was reiterated.

The influence for interrelationships at the local level of opposed political aims is obviously crucial in all this. Were it not that such large issues divided them it is doubtful if the relationships of Catholic and Protestants with each other would need to be hedged with the taboos that make pervasive the awareness of religious identity. Separate education and even endogamy would not necessarily produce a belief in a dichotomised state. Without the awareness of major dichotomies of interest local social divisions would not be so strong. But given these political differences the social differences at the local level provide the ideal basis for strengthening the perception of a dichotomised society. Certainly if there exists at a high-level differentiation between 'groups' in terms of their political and civil rights this will be a major factor predisposing people to perceive their society as divided—but it is effective only where some sort of inter-group boundary already exists in other contexts and in terms of which differences in civil rights can be interpreted.

So we come to a full, and vicious, circle. There is local level social dichotomy which forms the best of bases for the perception of the wider social environment in terms of the dichotomy, and this perception of opposed interests at a multiplicity of different levels intensifies in every context of interaction the perception of religious group identity at the local level.

In the early 1960's Ulster's political outlook suddenly seemed brighter. The evidence, borne out by electoral results, suggested that sophisticated Catholics were becoming more interested in improving their lot within Northern Ireland than with dismantling it as a political unit, and sophisticated Protestants seemed able to contemplate with equanimity closer ties with Eire. The social dichotomy at the grass-roots level as described in this book nevertheless remained as one major factor to thwart the hopes of that time. The more interested Catholics became in their future in Northern Ireland the more concerned they naturally became with social reforms, but however much some Unionists appreciated this many rank and file Protestants remained so sceptical of the ultimate political aims of the rank and file Catholics (with whom on this subject they could not communicate) and so distrustful of their own leaders that any Unionist politician who was too reformist courted political suicide. The unsatisfied desires for reform provided one of the foundations of the early Civil-Rights movement, some of whose leaders had little knowledge of Ulster. These viewing the Catholics as the downtrodden 'working class' and aware of some of the internal 'class' type dissension amongst Unionists were quite sure that religion no longer mattered in Northern Ireland, the important political programme was that of uniting the poor against their exploiters. Had they known more about the social relationships underpinning the religious-group membership of the ordinary people these reformers might have been more careful to avoid a new polarisation of Catholic and Protestant. Ulster indeed provides an illustration of the fact that a real understanding of a socially divided society, however its groups be defined, depends not only on the analysis of the political and economic structure at the top but also on an examination of the society at the grass-roots level.

Bibliography

Arensberg, Conrad M. (1959) *The Irish Countryman* (originally published 1937). Gloucester, Mass., Peter Smith.

Banton, Michael (1967) *Race Relations*. London, Tavistock Publications.

Barritt, Denis P., and Carter, Charles F. (1962) *The Northern Ireland Problem: a Study in Group Relations*. London, Oxford University Press.

Barth, Frederick (1969) *Ethnic Groups and Boundaries: the Social Organization of Cultural Difference*. London, George Allen and Unwin.

Gluckman, Max (1958) *The Analysis of a Social Situation in Modern Zululand*, Rhodes-Livingstone Paper No. 28 (originally published 1940–42). Manchester University Press for Rhodes-Livingstone Institute (now Institute for African Studies, University of Zambia).

Harris, R. (1961) 'The Selection of Leaders in Ballybeg, Northern Ireland', *Sociological Review*, Vol. 9, no. 2, July, pp. 137–49.

Levi-Strauss, Claude (1966) *The Savage Mind*. London, Weidenfeld and Nicolson.

Littlejohn, James (1964) *Westrigg: the Sociology of a Cheviott Parish*. London, Routledge and Kegan Paul.

Rex, John (1970) *Race Relations in Sociological Theory*. London, Weidenfeld and Nicolson.

Scot, Reginald (1930) *The Discoverie of Witchcraft* (originally published 1584). Ed. Montague Sommers. London, John Rodker.

Smith, M. G. (1965) *The Plural Society in the British West Indies*. Berkeley, University of California Press (1969), 'Some Developments in the analytic framework of Pluralism', pp.

415–48 in *Pluralism in Africa*. Kuper, Leo and Smith, M. G. (eds.). Berkeley, University of California Press.

Tusser, Thomas (1812) *Five Hundred Points of Good Husbandry* (originally published 1557). Ed. H. Mayor, London, Lackington, Allen and Co.

Wagley, Charles, and Harris, Marvin (1958) *Minorities in the New World: Six Case Studies*. New York, Columbia University Press.

Wirth, Louis (1945) 'The Problem of Minority Groups', pp. 347–72 in *The Science of Man in the World Crisis,* Ralph Linton (ed.). New York, Columbia U.P.

Index

Household Index